What readers are saying about *Rails Test Prescriptions*

This a must-have book for those new to testing on a team that thinks, "We don't have time for testing," and for experienced developers looking to round out their testing skills. If you want to write better code, deploy with confidence, and accelerate your team's velocity, you should read this book!

► **John McCaffrey**
Rails Developer/Project Manager,
Railsperformance.blogspot.com

Rails Test Prescriptions presents a nuanced and unbiased overview of the tools and techniques professionals use to test their Rails apps every day. A must-read for any Rails developer, whether you've never written a single test or you've written thousands.

► **David Chelimsky**
Senior Software Engineer, DRW Trading

Rails Test Prescriptions is a great resource for anyone interested in getting better at testing Rails applications. New readers will find many helpful guides, and experienced readers will discover many lesser-known tips and tricks.

► **Nick Gauthier**
Developer, SmartLogic Solutions

If you are comfortable working with Rails, yet have no experience writing tests for it, this book is an excellent resource for getting up to speed on the most successful tools used to test drive your development.

► **Adam Williams**
(@aiwilliams)

Noel has dispensed a fantastic collection of prescriptions for all kind of testing maladies. Whether you are a budding intern, or a highly specialized surgeon, this book will provide you with the information you need to improve your testing health.

▶ **Christopher Redinger**
  Principal, Relevance, Inc.

Testing is a given in the Rails world, but the varied options can be daunting if you are just starting to learn the framework. Noel provides a solid tour of the options and techniques for testing a Rails application that will help guide you past some of the initial dark corners. If you are entering the world of Ruby on Rails, I'd recommend keeping a copy of *Rails Test Prescriptions* at hand.

▶ **Corey Haines**
  Software Journeyman

Rails Test Prescriptions

Keeping Your Application Healthy

Rails Test Prescriptions

Keeping Your Application Healthy

Noel Rappin

The Pragmatic Bookshelf

Raleigh, North Carolina   Dallas, Texas

Our Pragmatic courses, workshops, and other products can help you and your team create better software and have more fun. For more information, as well as the latest Pragmatic titles, please visit us at http://www.pragprog.com.

The team that produced this book includes:

Editor:	Colleen Toporek
Indexing:	Potomac Indexing, LLC
Copy edit:	Kim Wimpsett
Production:	Janet Furlow
Customer support:	Ellie Callahan
International:	Juliet Benda

ISBN-10: 1-934356-64-6

ISBN-13: 978-1-934356-64-7

Printed on acid-free paper.

P1.0 printing, February 2011

Version: 2011-1-31

Contents

Part I

Getting Started with Testing in Rails

Chapter 1

The Goals of Automated Developer Testing

1.1 A Testing Fable

Imagine two programmers working on the same task. Both are equally skilled, charming, and delightful people, motivated to do a high-quality job as quickly as possible. The task is not trivial but not wildly complex either; for the sake of discussion, we'll say it's behavior based on a new user registering for a website and entering pertinent information.

The first developer, who we'll call Ernie,[1] says, "This is pretty easy, and I've done it before. I don't need to write tests." And in five minutes Ernie has a working method ready to verify.

Our second developer is, of course, named Bert. Bert says, "I need to write some tests."[2] Bert starts writing a test, and in five minutes, he has a solid test of the new feature. Five minutes more, Bert also has a working method ready to verify. Because this is a fable, we are going to assume that Ernie is allergic to automated testing, while Bert is similarly averse to manually running against the app in the browser.

At this point, you no doubt expect me to say that even though it has taken Bert more time to write the method, Bert has written code that is more likely to be correct, robust, and easy to maintain. That's true.

---

1. Because that's his name.
2. Actually, if Bert is really into Agile, he probably asks, "Who am I going to pair with?" but that's an issue for another day.

But I'm also going to say that there's a good chance Bert will be done before Ernie.

Observe our programmers a bit further. Ernie has a five-minute lead, but both people need to verify their work. Ernie needs to test in a browser; we said the task requires a user to log in. Let's say it takes Ernie one minute to set up the task and run the action in his development environment. Bert verifies by running the test—that takes about ten seconds. (Remember, Bert has to run only one test, not the entire suite.)

Let's say it takes each developer three tries to get it right. Since running the test is faster than verifying in the browser, Bert gains a little bit each try. After verifying the code three times, Bert is only two and half minutes behind Ernie.[3]

At this point, with the task complete, both break for lunch (a burrito for Bert, an egg salad sandwich for Ernie, thanks for asking). After lunch, they start on the next task, which is a special case of the first task. Bert has most of his test setup in place, so writing the test only takes him two minutes. Still, it's not looking good for Bert, even after another three rounds trying to get the code right. He's still a solid two minutes behind Ernie.

Bear with me one more step, and we'll get to the punch line. Ernie and Bert are both conscientious programmers, and they want to clean their code up with a little refactoring. Now Ernie is in trouble. Each time he tries the refactoring, he has to spend two minutes verifying both tasks, but Bert's test suite still takes only about ten seconds. After three more tries to get the refactoring right, Bert finishes the whole thing and checks it in three and a half minutes ahead of Ernie.[4]

My story is obviously simplified, but let's talk a moment about what I didn't assume. I didn't assume that the actual time Bert spent on task was smaller, and I didn't assume that the tests would help Bert find errors more easily—although I think that would be true.[5] The main

---

3. In a slight nod to reality, let's assume that both of them need to verify one last time in the browser once they think they are done. Since they both need to do this, it's not an advantage for either one.

4. Bert then catches his train home and has a pleasant evening. Ernie just misses his train, gets caught in a sudden rainstorm, and generally has a miserable evening. If only he had run his tests....

5. Of course, I didn't assume that Bert would have to track down a broken test in some other part of the application, either.

point here is that it's frequently faster to run multiple verifications of your code as an automated test than to always check manually. And that advantage is only going to increase as the code gets more complex.

There are many beneficial side effects of having accurate tests. You'll have better-designed code in which you'll have more confidence. But the most important benefit is that if you do testing well, you'll notice that your work goes faster. You may not see it at first, but at some point in a well-run test-driven project, you'll notice fewer bugs and that the bugs that do exist are easier to find. You'll notice that it's easier to add new features and easier to modify existing ones. As far as I'm concerned, the only code-quality metric that has any validity is how easy it is over time to find bugs and add new behavior.

Of course, it doesn't always work out that way. The tests might have bugs. Environmental issues may mean things that work in a test environment won't work in a development environment. Code changes will break tests. Adding tests to already existing code is a pain. Like any other programming tool, there are a lot of ways to cause yourself pain with testing.

1.2 Who Are You?

The goal of this book is to show you how to apply a test-driven process as you build your Rails application. I'll show you what's available and try to give you some idea of what kind of tools are best used in what circumstances. Still, tools come and tools go, so what I'm really hoping is that you come away from this book committed to the idea of writing better code through the small steps of a TDD or BDD process.

There are some things I'm assuming about you.

I'm assuming that you are already comfortable with Ruby and Rails and that you don't need this book to explain how to get started creating a Rails application in and of itself.

I am not assuming you have any particular familiarity with testing frameworks or testing tools used within Rails. If you do have familiarity, you may find some of the early chapters redundant. However, if you have tried to use test frameworks but got frustrated and didn't think they were effective, I recommend Chapter 3, *Writing Your First Tests*, on page 33 and Chapter 4, *TDD, Rails Style*, on page 53, since they walk through the TDD process for a small piece of Rails functionality.

Over the course of this book, we'll go through the tools that are available for writing tests, and we'll talk about them with an eye toward making them useful in building your application. This is Rails, so naturally I have my own opinions, but all the tools have the same goal: to help you to write great applications that do great things and still catch the train home.

1.3 The Power of Testing First

The way to succeed with Test-Driven Development (TDD) is to trust the process. The classic process goes like this:

1. Create a test. The test should be short and test for one thing in your code. The result of the test should be deterministic.

2. Make sure the test fails. Verifying the test failure before you write code helps ensure that the test really does what you expect.

3. Write the simplest code that could possibly make the test pass. Don't worry about good code yet. Don't look ahead. Sometimes, just write enough code to clear the current error.

4. Refactor. After the test passes. Clean up duplication. Optimize. This is where design happens, so don't skip this. Remember to run the tests at the end to make sure you haven't changed any behavior.

Repeat until done. This will, on paper at least, ensure that your code is always as simple as possible and always is completely covered by tests. We'll spend most of the rest of this book talking about the details of step 1 and how to use Rails tools to write useful tests.

If you use this process, you will find that it changes the structure of the code you write. The simple fact that you are continually aligning your code to the tests results in code that is made up of small methods, each of which does one thing. These methods tend to be loosely coupled and have minimal side effects.

As it happens, the hallmark of well-designed code is small methods that do one thing, are loosely coupled, and have minimal side effects. I used to think that was kind of a lucky coincidence, but now I think it's a direct side effect of building the code in tandem with the tests. In effect, the tests act as a universal client for the entire code base, guiding all the code to have clean interactions between parts because

> **A Historical Parallel**
>
> What's a Rails book without a good Franklin Roosevelt anecdote, right?
>
> There's a widely told and probably apocryphal story about FDR meeting with a group of activists pushing a reform agenda—exactly what the group wanted seems to have been lost to history.
>
> Anyway, when they were done with the meeting, FDR is supposed to have said to them, "I agree with you. I want to do it; now go make me do it."
>
> Ignore for the moment the question of whether this statement makes sense as politics; it makes perfect sense as a test-driven development motto. Your requirements determine what your applications *want* to do. Your tests *make* the application do it.

the tests, acting as a third-party interloper, have to get in between all the parts of the code in order to work.

This theory explains why writing the code first causes so much pain when writing tests even if you just wait a little bit to get to the tests. When the tests are written first, or in very close intertwined proximity to the code, then the tests drive the code's structure and enable the code to have the good high-cohesion/low-coupling structure. When the tests come later, they have to conform to the existing code, and it's amazing how easily and quickly code written without tests will move toward low-cohesion and high-coupling forms that are much harder to cover with tests. If your only experience with writing unit tests comes only long after the initial code was written, the experience was likely quite painful. Don't let that turn you away from a TDD approach; the tests and code you will write with TDD are much different.

1.4 What Is TDD Good For?

The primary purpose of this style of testing where the developer is writing tests for her own benefit is to improve the structure of the code. That is, TDD is a software development technique rather than a complete testing program. (Don't believe me, ask Kent Beck, who is most responsible for TDD as a concept and who said, "Correctness is a side effect" on a recent podcast.)[6]

Automated developer tests are a wonderful way of showing that the program does what the developer thinks it does, but they are a lousy way of showing that what the developer thinks is what the program actually should do. "But the tests pass!" is not likely to be comforting to a customer when the developer's assumptions are just flat-out wrong.[7]

Automated developer testing is not a substitute for *acceptance testing* with users or customers (which can itself be partially automated via something like Cucumber) or some kind of QA phase where users or testers pound away at the actual program trying to break something.

This goal can be taken too far, however. You sometimes see an argument against Test-Driven Development that runs something like this: "The purpose of testing is to verify that my program is correct. I can never prove this with 100 percent certainty. Therefore, testing has no value." (RSpec and Behavior-Driven Development were created, in part, to combat this attitude.) Ultimately, though, testing has a lot of positive benefits for coding, even beyond verification.

Preventing regression is often presented as one of the paramount benefits of a test-driven development process. And if you are expecting me to disagree out of spite, you're out of luck. Being able to squash regressions before anybody outside of your laptop sees them is one of the key ways in which strict testing will speed up your development over time. To make this work best, of course, you need good tests.

Another common benefit you may have heard in connection with automated tests is that they provide an alternate method of documenting your program. The tests, in essence, provide a detailed, functional specification of the behavior of the program.

That's the theory. My experience with tests acting as documentation is mixed, to say the least. Still, it's useful to keep this in mind as a goal, and most of the things that make tests work better as documentation will also make the tests work better, period.

To make your tests effective as documentation, focus on giving your tests descriptive names, keeping tests short, and refactoring out com-

---

6. http://twit.tv/floss87. Good interview, recommended.
7. He says, speaking from painful experience....

mon setup and assertion parts. The documentation advantage of refactoring is removing clutter from the test itself—when a test has a lot of raggedy setup and assertions, it can be hard for a reader to focus on the important functional part. Also, with common features factored out, it's easier to focus on what's different in each individual test.

In a testing environment, blank-page problems are almost completely nonexistent. I can always think of *something* that the program needs to do, so I write a test for that. When you're working test-first, the actual order in which pieces are written is not so important. Once a test is written, the path to the next one is usually clear, and so on, and so on.

1.5 When TDD Needs Some Help

Test-Driven Development is very helpful, but it's not going to solve all of your development problems by itself. There are areas where developer testing doesn't apply or doesn't work very well.

I mentioned one case already—developer tests are not very good at determining whether the application is behaving correctly according to requirements. Strict TDD is not very good at acceptance testing. There are, however, automated tools that do try to tackle acceptance testing. Within the Rails community, the most prominent of these is Cucumber; see Chapter 15, *Acceptance Testing with Cucumber*, on page 235. Cucumber can be integrated with TDD—you'll see this called *outside-in testing* or see the acronym ATDD for Acceptance Test–Driven Design. That's a perfectly valid and useful test paradigm, but it's an extension of the classic TDD process.

Testing your application assumes that you know the right answer. And although you will have clear requirements or a definitive source of correct output some of the time, other times you don't know what exactly the program needs to do. In this exploratory mode, TDD is less beneficial, because it's hard to write tests if you don't know what assertions to make about the program. Often this happens during initial development or during a proof of concept. I find myself in this position a lot when view testing—I don't know what to test for until I get some of the view up and visible.

In classic Extreme Programming parlance, this kind of programming is called a *spike*, as in, "I don't know if we can do what we need with the Twitter API; let's spend a day working on a spike for it." When working in spike mode, TDD is generally not used, but it's also the expectation that the code written during the spike is not used in production; it's just a proof of concept.

When view testing, or in other nonspike situations where I'm not quite sure what output to test for, I tend to go into a "test-next" mode, where I write the code first, but in a TDD-sized small chunk, and then immediately write the test. This works as long as I make the switch between test and code frequently enough to get the benefit of having the code and test inform each other's design.

TDD is not a complete solution for verifying your application. We've already talked about acceptance tests, but it's also true that TDD tends to be thin in terms of the amount of unit tests written. For one thing, a strict TDD process would never write a test that you expect to pass. In practice, though, I do this all the time. Sometimes I see and create an abstraction in the code, but there are still valid test cases to write. In particular, I'll often write code for potential error conditions even if I think they are already covered in the code. It's a balance, because you lose some of the benefit of TDD by creating too many test cases that don't drive code changes. One way to keep the balance is to make a list of the test cases before you start writing the tests—that way you'll remember to cover all the interesting cases.

And hey, some things are just hard. In particular, some parts of your application are going to be very dependent on an external piece of code in a way that makes it hard to isolate them for unit testing. Mock objects, described in Chapter 7, *Using Mock Objects*, on page 95, can be one way to work around this issue. But there are definitely cases where the cost of testing a feature like this is higher than the value of the tests. To be clear, I don't think that is a common occurrence, but it would be wrong to pretend that there's never a case where the cost of the test is too high.

1.6 Coming Up Next...

This book is divided into six parts.

Part I, which you are currently in the middle of, is an introduction to Rails testing. The next chapter, Chapter 2, *The Basics of Rails Testing*, on page 15, covers what you need to know to get started with unit testing in Ruby and Rails, covering Test::Unit, Test-Driven Design, and the basic workflow of a Ruby test. The following two chapters, Chapter 3, *Writing Your First Tests*, on page 33 and Chapter 4, *TDD, Rails Style*, on page 53, present a tutorial or walk-through of a basic Rails feature realized using TDD.

Words to Live By

Any change to the logic of the program should be driven by a failed test.

A test should be as close as possible to the associated code.

If it's not tested, it's broken.

Testing is supposed to help for the long term. The long term starts tomorrow, or maybe after lunch.

It's not done until it works.

Tests are code; refactor them too.

Start a bug fix by writing a test.

Part II of the book is about application data. Most of your Rails tests will cover model code, discussed in Chapter 5, *Testing Models with Rails Unit Tests*, on page 65. You'll often need sample data to run tests, and Chapter 6, *Creating Model Test Data with Fixtures and Factories*, on page 75 talks about the two most common ways to manage test data. Sometimes, though, you just need to bypass normal behavior entirely, and Chapter 7, *Using Mock Objects*, on page 95 talks about the standard way of replacing normal program behavior as needed in testing.

The models are the back room of your code, and Part III talks about testing the user-facing parts of your application. In Chapter 8, *Testing Controllers with Functional Tests*, on page 123, we'll talk about the standard Rails way of testing controllers, while Chapter 9, *Testing Views*, on page 135 discusses view testing. Increasingly, front-end code includes Ajax and JavaScript, discussed in Chapter 10, *Testing JavaScript and Ajax*, on page 151, which introduces the Jasmine framework for JavaScript testing.

The second half of the book is largely about extensions to core Rails testing. Part IV covers two of the biggest. Shoulda is covered in Chapter 11, *Write Cleaner Tests with Shoulda and Contexts*, on page 167, while RSpec gets its due in Chapter 12, *RSpec*, on page 183.

Part V of the book covers integration and acceptance testing that exercises your entire application stack. First, Rails core integration testing is covered in Chapter 13, *Testing Workflow with Integration Tests*, on page 213. Webrat and Capybara are tools that give integration tests more clarity and power, and they get their own chapter in Chapter 14, *Write Better Integration Tests with Webrat and Capybara*, on page 223. Cucumber has become a very popular tool for acceptance testing, and Chapter 15, *Acceptance Testing with Cucumber*, on page 235 tells you all about it.

The last part of the book is about evaluating your tests. The most common objective measure of tests is code coverage, which you will read about in Chapter 16, *Using Rcov to Measure Test Coverage*, on page 259. Coverage isn't everything in testing style, though, and Chapter 17, *Beyond Coverage: What Makes Good Tests?*, on page 271 talks about five other habits of highly successful tests. Adding tests to an existing application has its own challenges, discussed in Chapter 18, *Testing a Legacy Application*, on page 283. Finally, making your tests run faster is always a good thing, and Chapter 19, *Performance Testing and Performance Improvement*, on page 299 covers many different strategies.

Ready? Me too.

1.7 Acknowledgments

Over the course of the two years that I have been working on this project, I have had the guidance and support of many people. I hope I haven't forgotten anyone.

Back when this was just a DIY project, several people acted as early readers and offered useful comments including Paul Barry, Anthony Caliendo, Brian Dillard, Sean Hussey, John McCaffrey, Matt Polito, and Christopher Redinger. Alan Choyna and David DiGioia helped support the original Rails Prescriptions website. Alice Toth provided the original website design. Dana Jones made many, many valuable editorial corrections early in the life of the book.

Brian Hogan was the first person to suggest that this book might work for Pragmatic. Gregg Pollack was the second, and Gregg's kind words about this project on the official Rails blog were the push I needed to actually submit it.

Everybody I've worked with at Pragmatic has been outstanding. Dave Thomas and Andy Hunt said nice things about early chapters of the book, which was very encouraging. I doubt very much that Dave Thomas remembers when I introduced myself to him at Rails Edge in

Chicago in 2007, but he was encouraging even then. Susannah Pfalzer was the first person that I dealt with at Pragmatic, and she was helpful in guiding the transition. On a related note, David Chelimsky has also been very helpful and gracious to the "other" Chicago-based Pragmatic book about testing.

Colleen Toporek was the editor on this book at Pragmatic and has done a great job of keeping me on track and keeping the text of the book clear and consistent. It's easy when working on a book by yourself to think that you don't need an editor; thanks to Colleen for reminding me why a great editor is so very important. The copyedit was done by Kim Wimpsett, the book was indexed by Potomac Indexing LLC, and the book was typeset by Steve Peter.

Obtiva has been a great place to be, and the chance to work with and get insight from so many talented people has benefited both me and this book. Particular thanks to Dave Hoover, whose pairing session during my interview helped convince me that Obtiva was where I should be.

Technical reviewers of this manuscript include Trevor Burnham, Paul Butcher, Nick Gauthier, Brian Hogan, Dana Jones, Mike Mangino, John McCaffrey, Michael Niessner, and Christopher Redinger. Thanks to them for their feedback, along with everybody who took the time to submit errata to the Pragmatic website.

For boring technical reasons, I am 100 percent positive that Matt Polito was the first person to purchase this book from the Pragmatic website, which was awesome. Thanks to Matt, Ray Hightower, and the rest of the organizers of Chicago Ruby for giving me the opportunity to present some of this material to a live audience.

This book is a commercial product built on the time and generosity of developers who build amazing things and present them free to the world. Thanks to all of you, too many to name, who have so enriched all of our professional lives.

My family has been very supporting and encouraging throughout. My parents, Donna and Donnie, are always my biggest fans. My children, Emma and Elliot, are clever, funny, and amazing. And last in the list, but first in my life, Erin. I hope to be as good at anything as you are at everything. Thank you for your love, your friendship, and your smile.

Chapter 2

The Basics of Rails Testing

Let's start at the very beginning. For Rails testing, the beginning is the set of tools, conventions, and practices that make up the test facilities provided by Rails core. The basic Rails test functionality consists of the standard Ruby library Test:Unit, plus the Rails standard mechanisms for placing tests in the project, adding data to tests, and running tests.

All the basic features of building Rails tests are covered in this chapter. Once we have that foundation in place, we'll use these features in a Rails Test-Driven Development process in Chapter 3, *Writing Your First Tests*, on page 33.

2.1 What's a Test?

The individual test is the most basic unit of Rails testing. There are two ways to define an individual test in Rails, and they are functionally equivalent. In the older style, any method whose name starts with test_ is considered a test:

```
def test_that_a_new_user_has_a_valid_name
  # test logic here
end
```

In the newer style (Rails 2.2 and up), a more declarative syntax can be used with the method test():

```
test "that a new user has a valid name" do
  # test logic here
end
```

> ### There's Always Some Version Confusion
>
> Here's the short answer to what versions of different software we're talking about: by default, Rails 3.0.*x*, Test::Unit 1.3, and Ruby 1.8.7 (and later, RSpec 2.*x*). Where Rails 2.*x* is substantially different, I'll note that. For the most part, the differences between Ruby 1.8.7 and 1.9.2 don't significantly impact the code in this book.
>
> We're dealing with three separate entities that are in the process of transitioning between major versions. Rails is moving between the 2.*x* version stream and the 3.*x* versions. The Ruby language version 1.9.*x* is coming down the pike, and a recent fork of Test::Unit leaves 1.3 and a 2.0 version in the wild.
>
> To sweeten the deal, Ruby 1.9.2 uses a different default test library called minitest, which is mostly a smaller, faster replacement for Test::Unit 1.3. However, Ruby 1.9.2 keeps a module called Test::Unit as a wrapper around minitest, for backward-compatibility purposes.
>
> For its part, Rails smooths out the difference between minitest and Test::Unit 1.3 and adds its own features on top of both. For our purposes, we don't need to worry about the difference, and to minimize confusion (too late?), I'll continue to refer to that library as Test::Unit. Since I'm boldly assuming you are writing a Rails application, I'm not going to sweat the difference between what's in Rails and what's in Test::Unit. Test::Unit 2.0 doesn't seem to have much of a constituency at the moment, so I'm going to ignore it.

Behind the scenes, those two definitions will result in the same test being executed.[1]

You can't just slap a test method inside any old class. The tests you write need to be defined inside a subclass of Test::Unit::TestCase. Rails provides its own generic subclass called ActiveSupport::TestCase. You'd use ActiveSupport::TestCase as the parent class of any of your Rails tests. Rails also defines its own subclasses of ActiveSupport::TestCase for testing controllers and integration testing.

---

1. A beta reader points out that using a non-ASCII character in the test name may cause the test to be ignored in some environments.

2.2 What Goes in a Test?

Anything you want, followed by some assertions.

When testing from within Rails, the entire Rails environment is automatically loaded as part of test startup, so any part of your Rails application along with any required plugin or gem is available. In general, a specific test class is tied to a specific application class, and tests in that test class exist to validate the behavior of the matching application class. That's good practice and is enforced by the structure of Test::Unit within Rails. If you find yourself testing functionality outside the class your test is tied to, you should probably rethink your approach.

Inside each test, you are generally trying to do four things:

- Set up the data needed for the test. As a general rule, create as few data objects as possible for each test—it'll make the tests run faster. If you find yourself creating a lot of objects, it's often a sign you aren't testing small enough units.

- Perform the action that triggers the behavior being tested. In a Rails controller test, for example, it's generally the call to a controller action. In a model test, it's a call to the model method under test.

- Perform one or more assertions to verify that the behavior triggered in the previous step had the expected results. This usually involves making assertions about the state of the system after the action, although another style of testing, discussed in more detail in Chapter 7, *Using Mock Objects*, on page 95, makes assertions about the behavior of the application when the method under test is invoked. In either case, this is a step you want to take care to get right—a badly written assertion can leave you with a test that does not accurately reflect system behavior. A test that fails when the behavior is working is bad, but one that passes even though the underlying behavior is broken is even worse.

- Tear down any data structures that need to be removed before the next test runs. In Rails, this step is rarely needed, because most of the major bookkeeping—resetting the database state, for example—is handled by the framework. However, there are some testing tools that require a teardown statement in order to keep each individual test nicely independent.

Setup, teardown, and assertions all get some special structure from the testing framework. Let's talk about assertions first. The vanilla Test::Unit defines about twenty different methods that assert the presence or absence of a particular state. From a programmer perspective, the simplest of these methods is the plain assert() method, which takes a boolean argument. If the argument is true, the assertion passes; if the argument is false, the assertion fails, and the current test stops execution at that point. Normally, you'd have an expression evaluating to a boolean as the argument to assert(), as in this example verifying how long a man's legs should be:

```
test "ask abe the length of a man's legs" do
  @user = User.new
  assert (@user.leg.length == "long enough to reach the ground")
end
```

I'll mention this once here, and you can apply it to all the assertions discussed in the next few pages: assert() and all the other Test::Unit assertion methods take an optional last argument with a string message to be displayed on failure. In most cases, the default message and the resulting stack trace are plenty good enough to diagnose failures, so the messages are rarely used.

From a user perspective, the simplest method is assert(), but inside the Test::Unit code, almost everything is built on top of assert_block(), which takes a no-argument block and passes if the block evaluates to true.

```
test "ask abe the length of a man's legs" do
  @user = User.new
  assert_block { @user.leg.length == "long enough to reach the ground" }
end
```

The most commonly used assertion is assert_equal(), which takes two arguments: an expected value and the actual computed value. The method passes if the two arguments are equal using Ruby's == operator.

```
test "ask abe the length of a man's legs" do
  @user = User.new
  assert_equal "long enough to reach the ground", @user.leg.length
end
```

Although it is functionally irrelevant which order the arguments come in, the error message that you will receive on failure assumes that the first argument is the expected value and the second argument is the actual calculated value. Mixing up the two will cause confusion when you are trying to track down a failed test. You can negate this assertion with the converse method assert_not_equal().

Those are the most commonly used assertions, but Test::Unit defines a handful of others. All of these take an optional message as a last argument, which I'm leaving off because I want you not to use it. Let's take these in groups:

- assert_in_delta(expected, actual, delta)

  Like assert_equal(), but for floating-point numbers. Passes if the two floating-points are within the delta value of each other.

- assert_instance_of(klass, object)

  assert_kind_of(klass, object)

  Passes if the object and the class have the relationship implied by the name of the method.

- assert_match(pattern, string)

  assert_no_match(pattern, string)

  Like assert_equal(), but for regular expressions.

- assert_operator(left, operator, right)

  I've never actually seen this in the wild. Passes if the left and right objects have the relationship stated by the operator, as in assert_operator 6, :<, 10. Uses send() to send the operator to the left operand.

- assert_nil(object)

  assert_not_nil(object)

  At the risk of sounding snobby, these two really should be self-evident.

- assert_raise(*args, &block)

  assert_nothing_raised(*args, &block)

  The argument to the positive method is an exception class, and then the assertion passes if the associated block of code raises that exception. The negative method passes if the block does not raise an exception. The negative method does not care what kind of exception is raised.

- assert_same(expected, actual)

  assert_not_same(expected, actual)

  Like assert_equal(), but for actual object equality.

- assert_respond_to(object, method)

  Passes if object.respond_to?(method) is true.

- assert_send(array)

  Really odd method that takes an array of the form [receiver, method, argument_list] and passes if the snippet receiver.method(argument_list) is true.

- assert_throws(symbol, &block)

  assert_nothing_thrown(&block)

  Like assert_raise, but for Ruby's rarely used catch/throw mechanism.

2.3 Setup and Teardown

Let's look at a pair of tests. The exact functionality isn't important right now; we're interested in the structure of the test:

```
test "a user should be able to see an update within the project" do
  fred = User.new(:name => "Fred")
  barney = User.new(:name => "Barney")
  project = Project.new(:name => "Project Runway")
  project.users << fred
  project.users << barney
  barney.create_status_report("I'm writing a test")
  assert_equal("I'm writing a test", fred.project_statuses[0].text)
end

test "a user should not be able to see from a different project" do
  fred = User.new(:name => "Fred")
  barney = User.new(:name => "Barney")
  project = Project.new(:name => "Project Runway")
  other = Project.new(:name => "Project Other")
  project.users << fred
  other.users << barney
  barney.create_status_report("I'm writing a test")
  assert_equal(0, fred.project_statuses.count)
end
```

These tests share some common code. The common setup is only a few lines, but a real set of tests could wind up with far more duplication. Your first signal that something is wrong is that the setup has probably been copied and pasted from one test to the next. Copying and pasting multiple lines of code is almost always a heads-up to at least consider what you are doing to see if there is a commonality that you can refactor.

The classic way of managing duplicate setup using Test::Unit is to move the common code to the setup() method, which is automatically called by the test framework before each test:

```
def setup
  @fred = User.new(:name => "Fred")
  @barney = User.new(:name => "Barney")
  @project = Project.new(:name => "Project Runway")
  @project.users << fred
end

test "a user should be able to see an update from a friend" do
  @project.users << @barney
  @barney.update_status("I'm writing a test")
  assert_equal("I'm writing a test", @fred.project_statuses[0].text)
end

test "a user should not be able to see an update from a non-friend" do
  other = Project.new(:name => "Project Other")
  other.users << @barney
  @barney.update_status("I'm writing a test")
  assert_equal(0, @fred.project_statuses.count)
end
```

Moving the common setup code to the setup() method solves a couple of problems. The setup() code is automatically executed before each test, guaranteeing that each test is executed in the same environment. Also, moving the setup out of the test method makes it easier to write each individual test and also easier to follow the unique purpose of each test. There's some debate over whether the setup methods really are clearer; there's also a school of thought that says that moving anything into a setup method makes the test harder to follow. In general, if the setup gets too complex, you start to have problems—but in most model and controller tests, you can keep the common setup simple enough to be clear.

Over time, the setup() method, like any initializer, can become cluttered with multiple independent small setups jammed together in the same method. And don't forget that right below the sign that says "Don't Repeat Yourself" is another one that says "A Method Should Do Exactly One Thing" (the acronym AMSDEOT is nowhere near as catchy as DRY, though).[2] A confused setup method violates the AMSDEOT principle.

---

2. I'm also a big fan of CAPITROAE: "Cut And Paste Is The Root Of All Evil."

Relief for this arrived in Rails 2.2, which converted setup code to a block declaration similar to the way that before_filter() is handled in controllers. In Rails 2.2, you can declare methods to be run during setup by using the setup() call and placing something like this in your test class or in test/test_helper.rb:

```
setup :setup_users

def setup_users
  @fred = User.new(:name => "Fred")
  @barney = User.new(:name => "Barney")
end
```

What's particularly nice about this is that—as with before filters—you can have multiple setup blocks or methods, and they will all be executed before each test:

```
setup :create_fred
setup :create_barney

def create_fred
  @fred = User.new(:name => "Fred")
end

def create_barney
  @barney = User.new(:name => "Barney")
end
```

Setup methods are executed in the order in which they are declared. Calls to setup() in the test/test_helper.rb file will always be declared and thus executed before any method in the actual test file. You can also define the setup as a block:

```
setup do
  User.create(:name => "Fred")
  User.create(:name => "Barney")
end
```

This is not recommended in Rails 2, though, because the inside of the block is evaluated in class context—you can initialize global or class settings, but you can't create instance variables that are accessible from your tests. In Rails 3, the block is evaluated in instance context.

There is a similar mechanism to control what happens at the end of tests. The teardown() method has the same declaration rules as setup():

```
teardown :reset_globals

def reset_globals
  #whatever
end
```

Because Rails handles the rollback of database data in testing, it's not all that common to see teardowns used in Rails testing. Normally you'd use it to reset third-party tools outside of Rails. For example, certain mock object packages, such as FlexMock, require a method to be called at teardown to reset object status.

You're likely eventually to have one or more basic setup methods shared among multiple controller or unit tests. If the setup methods start to crowd out the test_helper.rb file, you can create a test/setup_methods.rb file with a module containing all the setup methods:

```ruby
module SetupMethods
  def setup_users
    fred = User.new(:name => "Fred")
    barney = User.new(:name => "Barney")
  end

  # put more setup methods here
end
```

Then the test class can include the module and declare any relevant methods as setups:

```ruby
class UserTest < ActiveSupport::TestCase

  include SetupMethods
  setup :setup_users

  test "my test" do
  end
end
```

The include and the setup call can also go in the test/test_helper.rb file.

2.4 What Can You Test in Rails?

When testing a Rails application, Rails specifies the default location of tests based on the class being tested. All Rails tests go in the test directory of the application. Rails assumes a consistent relationship between controllers and models on one hand and their test files on the other. This makes it easy to know where to put new tests and enables external tools like autotest (see Section 19.3, *Using Autotest*, on page 310) to know what tests to run when an application file changes. You can see the app directory of a Rails application and its associate test directory in Figure 2.1, on the next page.

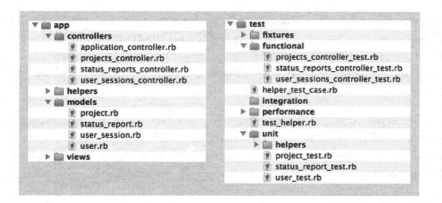

Figure 2.1: Directory comparison

Tests for Rails models are in the test/unit directory. Each test is named for its model, so by convention the test file test/unit/user_test.rb contains the class UserTest and is expected to correspond to the Rails model file in app/models/user.rb. In Rails 2.0 and up, unit tests are subclasses of the Rails ActiveSupport class ActiveSupport::TestCase, which is a subclass of the Ruby standard library class Test::Unit::TestCase. When you create a model using a Rails generator, the associated unit test class is also created for you.

Functional tests and Rails controllers have a similar relationship. Tests for Rails controllers are in the test/functional directory. The file app/controllers/users_controller.rb contains the class UsersController. The tests for that class are in test/functional/users_controller_test.rb, and the test class is named UsersControllerTest. In current versions of Rails, all controller tests are subclasses of the Rails class ActionController::TestCase, which is a subclass of the same ActiveSupport::TestCase used for models. Any time you create a controller using one of the three or four standard Rails generators that include controllers, an associated functional test file is created for you. (In Rails 2.3 and up, a test file is also created for the helper module and stored in test/unit/helpers.)

Rails also creates a file called test/test_helper.rb, which contains features and settings common to all of your tests. This file is required by any Rails test file.[3] The provided file re-opens the class ActiveSupport::TestCase to allow you to add your own methods, which are then available to all your tests. Typically, this involves initialization and teardown, complex data setups, and complex assertions. Other sections in this book will cover those possibilities in more detail.

There are two other kinds of tests in the standard Rails toolbox. The first, *integration tests*, are perhaps the most ignored feature of Rails testing. By design, integration tests are used to test sequences of events that span multiple actions or controllers. However, they don't easily map to the various test-first methodologies, and Rails developers tend to overlook them. That's unfortunate, because integration tests are a good way to validate complex interactions in an application, as well as ensure that there are no holes in the controller tests. Integration tests are created using the Rails generator script/generate integration_test, and are not automatically created by any other Rails generator. Integration tests will be discussed in more detail in Chapter 13, *Testing Workflow with Integration Tests*, on page 213.

Performance tests are different from the other automated test types. They are not intended to verify the correctness of your program; instead, they give access to profiling information about the actions called during the test. Essentially, performance tests are wrappers around the ruby-prof profiler, but if you've ever tried to get ruby-prof working, you'll appreciate the help. Performance tests are created using the Rails generator, script/generate performance_test, and are not automatically created by other Rails generators. Unlike the other Rails tests—functional, unit, and integration—performance tests are not automatically run by the Rails test runners. We'll talk about performance testing a little bit more in Chapter 19, *Performance Testing and Performance Improvement*, on page 299.

2.5 What Happens When Tests Run?

Each time you run a test task in Rails, the following steps take place. You can see the entire workflow in Figure 2.2, on the following page.

---

3. Not automatically, however: Rails places the require statement at the top of its generated files. If you create your own files, you need to add the statement yourself.

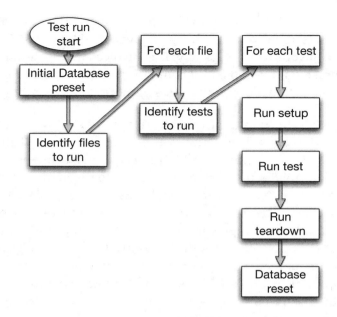

Figure 2.2: TEST FLOW

The test database, as determined by the entry with the symbol test in the config/database.yml file, is cleared of all data.[4]

Based on which test task is being run, a list of test files that matches the criteria for the task is generated. For example, running just the rake test:functionals task generates a list of all the test files in test/functionals, and no others.

Once the list of test files is created, each test file is loaded one by one. Like any other Ruby file, loading the file causes any module or class-level code to be interpreted. Although it's pretty rare to have any class-level initialization in a test file, you'll sometimes have additional classes in the file besides the test class itself (for example, a specialized mock object class).

After a file is loaded, all the test methods in the file are identified. In versions of Rails before 2.2, a test method is any method in the test class

---

4. If you run your test via the command-line rake task, then Rails will automatically apply any pending migrations. If you run via a different method—an IDE, for example— you may need to apply pending migrations to the test environment yourself.

that starts with test_. In Rails 2.2 and up, an additional test method is added that allows you to also create tests with a more natural block syntax (test "should pass this" do end). Test add-ons like Shoulda also offer different ways to define tests.

For each test method that has been identified by the test framework, the test method is executed. However, execution does not mean just running the test method itself—the test framework also executes setup code before the test method and teardown code after the test method. Here are the steps for running an individual test method:

1. Reset fixture data. By default, fixtures are loaded once per test suite, with each actual test being run inside a database transaction. At the end of each test method, the transaction is rolled back, allowing the next test to continue with a pristine state. More details on fixture loading are available in Section 6.2, *Loading Fixture Data*, on page 78.

2. Run any defined setup blocks. In versions of Rails before 2.2, there is only one setup method per test case. In Rails 2.2 and up, multiple setup methods can be declared. Note that setup blocks can be in the actual test class or in any parent classes or included modules. There are more details in Section 2.3, *Setup and Teardown*, on page 20.

3. Run the actual test method. The method execution ends when a runtime error or a failed assertion is encountered. If neither of those happens, then the test method passes. Yay!

4. Run all teardown blocks. Teardown blocks are declared similarly to setup blocks.

5. Roll back or delete the fixtures, as described in step 1. The result of each test is passed back to the test runner for display in the console or IDE window running the test. Typically, failures and errors return stacktraces from the offending point in the code.

2.6 Running the Rails Tests

Rails provides several commands to run all or part of your test suite.

The most common test to run is the Rake default testing task, invoked with either rake test or simply rake. The default task combines three subtasks, which can be individually invoked as rake test:functionals, rake test:units, and rake test:integration. Each of these tasks runs any file matching the pattern *_test.rb in the appropriate directory. The command-line output looks something like this:

```
$ rake
(in /Users/noel/Projects/huddle)
/System/Library/Frameworks/Ruby.framework/Versions/1.8/usr/bin/ruby
-Ilib:test
"/Library/Ruby/Gems/1.8/gems/rake-0.8.3/lib/rake/rake_test_loader.rb"
<ALL TESTS>
Loaded suite
/Library/Ruby/Gems/1.8/gems/rake-0.8.3/lib/rake/rake_test_loader
Started
.....EE...E.................E.E................
Finished in 2.138619 seconds.
```

Each successful test method is represented by a dot. If a test triggers an actual exception or error, it's represented by an E; if the test merely caused an assertion inside the test to fail, it's represented by an F. After the run-through, each error and failure will have a message and a stack trace.

Rails provides two helpful but often-overlooked convenience tasks for testing the files you are currently working on. The task rake test:recent looks for any controller or model file that has changed in the last ten minutes and runs the associated functional or unit test. The task rake test:uncommitted works similarly on any controller or model file that has been changed since you last committed to your source control repository. You must be using Subversion or Git to take advantage of the uncommitted task.

To run performance tests, use rake test:benchmark or rake test:profile. The two test types differ primarily in the output they present. A *benchmark test* outputs about five simple values for each performance run, including elapsed overall time and memory used. On first run, each test also generates a CSV file for output values. Further benchmark test runs append values to the CSV file, allowing for easy visualization of performance changes over time.

A *profile test* splits the timing data for each test based on the methods in which the test execution takes place and returns the amount of time spent in each method for the purpose of trying to determine where your application bottlenecks are. The output of a profile test can be either a list of methods and their data or a call graph associating each method with the methods that call it and the methods it calls.

Tests for all your plugins can be run using rake test:plugins. Individual test files can also be run just by invoking them from the command line, as in ruby test/unit/user_test.rb. (In recent versions of Rails, you may need to adjust your Ruby load path such that the require test_helper line at the beginning of the test files finds the test helper file.)

If you are using an IDE such as Eclipse or NetBeans, the IDE should provide a command to run tests within the IDE itself—typically, this will either run the rake command line in a console window (NetBeans) or invoke a custom test runner that essentially does the same thing but is prettier (Eclipse, RubyMine). The IDE should also have commands for running an individual test file or an individual test method.

2.7 More Info: Getting Data into the Test

Often, testing a feature properly requires data to be created in order to build a meaningful test setup. A reporting feature might best be tested with a number of different data items that fill different columns in a report. Or a social networking feature might require the creation of several users in various relationship permutations for proper testing.

There are a number of ways to conveniently create sample data for tests. Rails core offers an easy-to-use, if somewhat limited, feature called *fixtures*. Generically, a fixture is any predefined set of data used by multiple tests as a baseline. Fixtures in Rails are a core mechanism for defining and using known data in tests. Specifically, every ActiveRecord model gets an associated set of fixture data in test/fixtures, where data objects can be specified in YAML format.

Rails fixtures give you a consistent, potentially complex data set that is automatically created before each test. Although fixtures have been part of Rails since the beginning, most of the time I choose to use other tools that use a factory pattern for generating sample data. Although it's true that fixtures have strong limitations and factory creation methods are more flexible and generally lighter weight, we'll focus on fixtures here because they are easy to use and part of Rails core. You will find much more discussion on the why fixture data is less commonly used and what kinds of tools are used instead in Chapter 6, *Creating Model Test Data with Fixtures and Factories*, on page 75.

The directory test/fixtures is expected to contain a YAML file for each ActiveRecord model. So, app/models/user.rb is attached to test/fixtures/

user.yml. The fixture files are created automatically by the Rails generators when a model is created. If you create an ActiveRecord model manually, you'll also need to create the associated YAML file. The reverse is also true: if you remove an ActiveRecord file, you need to remove the YAML file. Otherwise, you will be unable to run tests, since Rails will try to load the fixture data into the test database for the missing ActiveRecord class. The data placed in the fixture files is automatically loaded into the test database before each test.[5]

Rails fixtures are described in YAML, which has a strict, nested format; at the top level, each individual model gets a name, followed by a colon. After that, the data for that model is indented, Python-style. Each line starts with the key, followed by a colon, followed by the value, like this:[6]

`huddle/test/fixtures/projects.yml`

```
huddle:
  name: Huddle Project
```

To start a new model, outdent back to the left edge and start again with a name for the model. Those top-level names, such as huddle in the previous file, have no particular meaning in Rails beyond being an identifier to that particular fixture within the test environment. The keys in the YAML file must be columns in the database table for that model (meaning that they can't be arbitrary methods in the Ruby code the way they can be when calling new() or create()).

Once this code is in the YAML file, then an object is generated from it, is loaded into the database before every test,[7] and is by default accessible anywhere, in any test, using the method call projects(:huddle).

Here's some sample fixture data for a status report class we'll use in a later example:

`huddle/test/fixtures/status_reports.yml`

```
ben_tue:
  project: huddle
  user: ben
  yesterday: Worked on Huddle UI
  today: Doing some testing
  status_date: 2009-01-06
```

---

5. Fixture data can also be loaded into the development database using the rake db:load:fixtures task.

6. There's more to YAML syntax, of course, but there's no need to go beyond the basics here.

7. Well... it's a little more complicated than that. See Section 6.2, *Loading Fixture Data*, on page 78 for more.

```
ben_wed:
  project: huddle
  user: ben
  yesterday: Did Some Testing
  today: More Testing
  status_date: 2009-01-07
```

There are a couple of things to note about the fixtures. We do not need to specify an id for each fixture; Rails automatically generates one for us. Also, when I said that all the keys had to be database columns, that wasn't strictly true; they can also be associations. If the key is an association, the value represents the name of a fixture in the related table (or a comma-separated list of fixture names for a one-to-many relationship). If we do specify an id in the YAML file, the nifty auto-association feature will not work.[8] Also, as you can see here, dates are automatically converted from string representations.

Fixture files are interpreted by Rails as ERb, so you can loop or dynamically generate data with the full power of Ruby. Also, when copying and pasting YAML data into a text file, remember that YAML files require a specific whitespace layout: the outdented fixture names need to be in the leftmost column of the line. Give fixtures meaningful names; it'll help later. (The Rails default names are a pain in the neck to keep straight.)

Although fixtures have many wonderful qualities—they're always available, relatively easy to set up, and consistent across all tests—they can also be kind of brittle. For example, if you are testing a reporting function, the results you are expecting are sensitively dependent on the makeup of the data in the fixtures. This dependency can cause at least two serious problems. First, if there's a lot of data in the fixtures, the results you are testing against can easily become opaque and hard to verify. Second, if anybody ever adds more data to the fixture, it can easily break all the reporting tests—a bit of a momentum-killer. As such, a number of alternatives for fixtures have been developed that make it easier to define test data specific to individual tests. We'll cover those in Section 6.4, *Using Factories to Fix Fixtures*, on page 80.

---

8. All this fancy id mapping is a Rails 2.0 and up feature. Before, we had to track the id values manually—which was a total pain for many-to-many join tables.

2.8 Beyond the Basics

Test::Unit and Rails combine to provide a common set of testing tools that are always available from any Rails application. If you've used other frameworks, particularly from a few years back, you may remember that setting up a group of tests into test cases and test suites was always something of a pain. Not so in Rails, where the design goal is to reduce unnecessary duplication of effort, especially when creating tests. Rails provides standard ways to define tests, a standard location for each test, a way to add data into the test, and easy ways to run the tests in different combinations.

With this introduction to the basic core of Rails testing in hand, it's time to see a more detailed example. Over the next two chapters, we'll take an almost new Rails application and add new features to it using a test-driven approach.

## Chapter 3

Writing Your First Tests

You have a problem. You are the team leader for a development team that is distributed across multiple locations. As an agile development team, your project has a daily stand-up meeting, sometimes called a *scrum*, where everybody briefly describes what they did yesterday, what they plan on doing today, and if anything is blocking them from getting their work done.

However, since your team is geographically distributed, you need to do these scrums via email. That's not the worst thing ever, but it does lead to annoying email threads, and I think we can all do better with a little web application magic. Let's create an application called Huddle, which will support entering and viewing these daily status messages.

Since you are a Rails developer who wants to use test-driven methods, the first thing you should ask is, "What do I test?" Test-driven developers start an application by writing tests. In that spirit, we're going to initiate our tour of Rails testing by writing lots of tests. Specifically, we're going to walk through the first few test-driven feature cycles of the Huddle application to give you the feel of Test-Driven Development (TDD) using Rails.

We'll use a hands-on approach and walk through the specifics of how to write your first tests. We'll talk about how the practice of working "test first" improves development, but more importantly, we'll show what working in a test-driven style looks like. This chapter uses the testing tools that are available in core Rails and will be limited to common Rails tasks such as creating and submitting a web form. At the end of this chapter, you should have a good sense of how TDD development

---

A Word About Best Practices

There's a tension in this section between making the introduction to Rails testing as simple and clear as possible and presenting the tests using what I would consider to be best practices. In particular, many of my regular testing practices depend on third-party tools that we're not going to cover in this walkthrough.

In this chapter, I decided to focus on making testing as easy as possible to explain while still using good coding practice, and I included some discussion of where improvements might come. We'll go over coding style and practice considerations again later in the book.

---

works in Rails, and you'll be ready to explore the third-party tools and more detailed topics in the rest of the book.

Appendix A, on page 323, contains the steps for creating the skeleton application we're starting with—including the initial setup, creation of Rails scaffolds, addition of Devise for user authentication, and other things that are necessary to the application but beside the point for our tutorial. If you'd like to start at the same place, the code samples for this chapter are available for download at http://www.pragprog.com/titles/nrtest/source_code. The code for this application was written and tested against Rails 3.0.[1]

We're going to do this in a reasonably strict test-driven style, meaning no new logic will be added to the application except in response to a failing test. We'll be a little more lenient with view code. We're assuming a basic understanding of standard Rails concepts; in other words, you don't need to be told what a controller is. For the moment, we're also going to limit ourselves to test tools provided by core Rails. Later in the book, we'll spend a lot of time covering third-party tools, especially in Chapter 11, *Write Cleaner Tests with Shoulda and Contexts*, on page 167 and Chapter 12, *RSpec*, on page 183. But in the name of keeping it simple, we'll start with vanilla core Rails.

---

1. Significant differences with Rails 2.3.*x* will be noted.

3.1 The First Test-First

The first question to ask is, "What do I test?" The answer comes from your requirements. Without some sense of what your program should be doing, it's hard to write tests that describe that behavior in code.

The form and formality of your requirements will depend on the needs of your project. In this case, you are your own client, and it's kind of a small project, and we don't have space in this book for military-level precision. So, the informal list of the first three stories in the application looks something like this:

- A user is part of a project. A user can enter his scrum status for that project.
- For the purpose of adding a testable constraint, let's say the user's status report has yesterday's status and today's expected work, and the user must include text in at least one of these items.
- Members of the project can see a timeline of status reports. This one will get covered in Chapter 4, *TDD, Rails Style*, on page 53.

Over the rest of this tutorial, we'll go after these stories one by one. Any time we add or change the logic of the application, we'll write a test. The exact starting point of the first test is not important (although it's helpful to have at least some sense of where you are going); you can start with any requirement or feature in the program that can be objectively specified.

Our starting point for Huddle is the need to have a status report that is created as part of a project. The report should have all its values, including the date, set correctly. Because I think the code for this feature might be in the StatusReportsController, I'm going to put the test for this feature in test/functional/status_reports_controller_test.rb.

```
Line 1    test "creation of status report with data" do
   -        assert_difference('StatusReport.count', 1) do
   -          post :create, :status_report => {
   -            :project_id => projects(:one).to_param,
   5            :user_id => users(:one).to_param,
   -            :yesterday => "I did stuff",
   -            :today => "I'll do stuff"}
   -        end
   -        actual = assigns(:status_report)
  10        assert_equal(projects(:one).id, actual.project.id)
   -        assert_equal(users(:one).id, actual.user.id)
   -        assert_equal(Date.today.to_s(:db), actual.status_date.to_s(:db))
   -        assert_redirected_to status_report_path(actual)
   -      end
```

Let's walk through this test in detail.

Line 3 simulates a post call to the create action of the StatusReportsController. The second argument to this call simulates the URL parameters of the call—effectively, you are setting up the params hash that will be used in the action. As part of that hash, the call references users(:one), which is a *fixture*, or set of known sample data that can be used in testing. This particular fixture set was created in Appendix A, on page 323, and it defines the data object accessed as users(:one). Section 2.7, *More Info: Getting Data into the Test*, on page 29 has more detail on fixtures.

Going back to the test itself, the block that starts in line 2 and ends in line 8 uses the assert_difference() method to assert that there is one more StatusReport object in the database at the end of the block than at the beginning. More plainly, the method is asserting that a new StatusReport instance has been created.

Line 9 uses the Rails test framework assigns() method, allowing access to instance variables set in the controller being tested—in this case, the controller variable @status_report, which should be the newly created instance. You don't need the @ symbol in the argument to assigns().

Starting with line 10, there are three lines asserting that a project, user, and status date are added to the newly created object.[2] Line 13 asserts that the result of the controller call is a redirect to the show page of the newly created StatusReport.

Although people will certainly quibble with the style and structure of this test, it is a basic, straightforward test of the desired functionality. This is the maximum amount of complexity that I'm comfortable having in a single test. In some cases, the amount of data or validation needed in a test suggests the need to refactor some of the complexity into *setup methods* or *custom assertion methods*.

Rather than start with a controller test, I could start by testing the model behavior. The model test is probably closer to the code that will be written, since good Rails style places complexity in the model. However, I sometimes find that it is easier to specify the desired result when I start testing via the controller. Another option would be to start with an integration or Cucumber-based acceptance test (described in more detail in Chapter 15, *Acceptance Testing with Cucumber*, on page 235).

---

2. If this test is run at just the right moment before midnight, 12 will fail because the date has changed during the running of the code. Section 6.11, *Managing Date and Time Data*, on page 89 discusses working around this problem in more detail.

We're testing status_date because we know new code will be needed to add that attribute to the object, and we're testing the existence of the project and user objects because the requirements need relationships to be set up between the models. We're not testing the today and yesterday texts because that's part of core ActiveRecord—we could test it, but it would be redundant. Redundancy is not always bad in testing, but right now it's unnecessary.

I often use a testing style that limits each individual test to a single assertion and might therefore separate this test into four different tests sharing a common setup. The advantage of this one-assertion-per-test style is that each assertion is able to pass or fail separately. As written, the first failure prevents the rest of the tests from running. Although it's a good point that assertions should be independent, in this case it's easier to follow the intent of the test when similar assertions are grouped. Also, single assertion tests are easier to write with a little help from third-party tools. In Section 11.7, *Single-Line Test Tools*, on page 180, we'll see some tools that make it easier to write single-assertion tests.

When we run the tests, we get an error. The stack trace for the error looks like this:

```
1) Error:
test_creation_of_status_report_with_data(StatusReportsControllerTest):
ArgumentError: wrong number of arguments (1 for 0)
    /test/functional/status_reports_controller_test.rb:58:in `to_s'
    /test/functional/status_reports_controller_test.rb:58:in
     `test_creation_of_status_report_with_data'
```

The line with the error is assert_equal(Date.today.to_s(:db), actual.status_date.to_s(:db)), and strictly speaking, the error message says that to_s, which converts the object to a string, is being called with the wrong number of arguments: (1 for 0), which means the method was called with one argument but expected zero.

This error message is technically true but misleading. The real error is that actual.status_date is nil and not Date.today. That error manifests itself as a "wrong number of arguments" because the test converts both dates to strings. The method to_s() takes no arguments for most classes, but Rails ActiveSupport overrides the method for Date with an optional format argument. Since our test results in a nil value instead of a Date, the extra argument causes an error.[3]

---

3. Why convert to strings, you ask? Because you get much more readable error messages if the values are both strings.

Also, notice that the user and project parts of the test already pass. This is a Rails feature. With the use of user:references in the script/generate command line (the exact setup commands are listed in Appendix A, on page 323), Rails automatically adds the belongs_to association to the StatusReport class. As we'll see later, it doesn't add the relationship in the other direction.

Now let's make the test pass. The classic process says to do the simplest thing that could possibly work. It's a good idea to just make the immediate error or failure go away, even if we suspect there are further errors waiting in the test. Doing so keeps the test/code cycle short and prevents the code from getting unnecessarily complex.

To get past the test failure, add a line toward the beginning of the create() method in app/controllers/status_reports_controller.rb so that the method starts like so:

```
def create
  @status_report = StatusReport.new(params[:status_report])
  @status_report.status_date = Date.today        # ==> the new line
  ## the rest of the method as before
end
```

3.2 The First Refactor

We fixed the immediate problem, and the test passes. We now enter the refactoring step. There isn't much here to refactor, but we have one detail we can tweak: it's better not to set the status_date in the controller. Good Rails practice moves complexity from controllers to models where possible. For one thing, placing code in the models tends to decrease duplication where functionality is used by multiple controller actions. For another, code in the model is easier to test.

Ordinarily, we would not be writing tests during refactoring, just using existing tests to verify that behavior hasn't changed. However, when moving code from one layer, the controller, to another, the model, it helps to create tests in the new class. Especially here, because our new behavior will be slightly different, we want the status_date to be automatically set whenever the report is saved.

The unit test goes in test/unit/status_report_test.rb:

```
Line 1  test "saving a status report saves the status date" do
     2    actual = StatusReport.new
     3    actual.save
     4    assert_equal(Date.today.to_s, actual.status_date.to_s)
     5  end
```

The test fails. As referenced in a previous footnote, in line 4 we're comparing literal string objects rather than the dates.

To pass the test, we add a before_save() callback to the StatusReport class:

```ruby
class StatusReport < ActiveRecord::Base
  belongs_to :project
  belongs_to :user

  before_save :set_status_date

  def set_status_date
    self.status_date = Date.today
  end
end
```

Now the test passes. But there's one more thing to worry about—if the status_date has already been set before the report is saved, the original date should be used. As the code stands now, the status_date will change whenever the model is edited. In the TDD process, we force ourselves to make that code change by exposing the error with a test. Here's how, in test/unit/status_report_test.rb:

```ruby
test "saving a status report that has a date doesn't override" do
  actual = StatusReport.new(:status_date => 10.days.ago.to_date)
  actual.save
  actual.reload
  assert_equal(10.days.ago.to_date.to_s, actual.status_date.to_s)
end
```

The to_date() methods in lines 2 and 5 are there to convert between 10.days.ago, which is a Ruby DateTime object, and the status_date, which is a Ruby Date object. Without that conversion, we will get an error because the string formats won't match in line 5.

The reload() call in line 4 forces ActiveRecord to re-retrieve the record from the database. ActiveRecord does not prevent a database record from having multiple live objects pointing to it. In this particular case, the controller creates a new instance from the database and saves that instance, without touching the actual variable created for the test. As a result, the database version has typecast the status_date to a Date when saving, but the live version in memory hasn't gotten that change.

In general, it's a good idea to reload any object being tested and saved. This is most commonly an issue in controller tests, where you might create an object during setup and then another object is created during the controller action that is backed by the same database record. In that case, the object you are holding on to in the test does not reflect changes made to the database during the controller action, leading to hours of fun as you try to figure out why your test is failing. Reloading will allow the object in your tests to see changes to the database made after the object was created.

One way to make the new test pass is this very slight change to the model:

huddle3/app/models/status_report.rb

```
def set_status_date
  self.status_date = Date.today if status_date.nil?
end
```

And now the scary part: removing the status-changing line from the controller and making sure that the tests pass again. This involves removing the line of code that we just added to the controller a couple of seconds ago.

It just takes a second to remove the line, and then we can rerun rake to verify that the tests still pass.

3.3 More Validations

While we're looking at the status report model, there is another one of our original three requirements we can cover, namely, the requirement that a user must enter text in at least one of the yesterday and today boxes. Back in test/unit/status_report_test.rb:

huddle3/test/unit/status_report_test.rb

```
test "a report with both blank is not valid" do
  actual = StatusReport.new(:today => "", :yesterday => "")
  assert !actual.valid?
end
```

The simplest way to pass this test is by placing the following line of code in app/models/status_report.rb:

```
validates_presence_of :yesterday, :today
```

That's great! With that line of code in place, everything will be swell. Nothing can go wrong. (Cue ominous music.) Let's run rake:

```
 1) Failure:
test_saving_a_status_report_saves_the_status_date(StatusReportTest)
[/test/unit/status_report_test.rb:9]:
<"2009-08-26"> expected but was
<"">.
```

```
  2) Error:
    test_saving_with_a_date_doesn't_override(StatusReportTest):
  ActiveRecord::RecordNotFound: Couldn't find StatusReport without an ID
      /test/unit/status_report_test.rb:17:in
      `test_saving_with_a_date_doesn't_override'
```

What? Well, you've probably figured it out, but adding the validation causes problems in other tests.[4] Specifically, status reports that were created by other tests without either text field being set are now failing their saves because they are invalid. This is admittedly annoying, because it's not really a regression in the code: the actual code in the browser probably still works fine. It's more that the shifting definition of what makes a valid StatusReport is now tripping up older tests that used insufficiently robust data.

Fixing the failing tests is straightforward. To fix the two tests in test/unit/status_report_test.rb, add the arguments (:today => "t", :yesterday => "y") to each StatusReport.new() method call, giving the following:

huddle3/test/unit/status_report_test.rb

```
Line 1   test "saving a status report saves the status date" do
    -        actual = StatusReport.new(:today => "t", :yesterday => "y")
    -        actual.save
    -        assert_equal(Date.today.to_s, actual.status_date.to_s)
    5    end

    -    test "saving with a date doesn't override" do
    -        actual = StatusReport.new(:status_date => 10.days.ago.to_date,
    -            :today => "t", :yesterday => "y")
   10        actual.save
    -        actual.reload
    -        assert_equal(10.days.ago.to_date.to_s, actual.status_date.to_s)
    -    end
```

This puts enough data in the report to make the test pass—we don't need to care what the data actually is. For Rails 2.x, a similar change needs to be made in test/functional/status_reports_controller_test.rb:

huddle/test/functional/status_reports_controller_test.rb

```
test "should create status_report" do
    assert_difference('StatusReport.count') do
      post :create, :status_report => {:today => "t", :yesterday => "y"}
    end
    assert_redirected_to status_report_path(assigns(:status_report))
end
```

---

4. In Rails 2.x, you also get a test failure in StatusReportTest for the test of the create action because of a difference in the behavior of the generated test. In Rails 3, that action is passed default values based on fixture data, so the validation works. In Rails 2, the generated test passes an empty hash to the controller.

And now we're back at all passing. This is, frankly, the kind of thing that causes people to develop an aversion to testing: sometimes it seems like a boatload of busywork to have to go back in and change all those older tests. And, well, it can be. There are a couple of ways you can minimize the annoyance and keep the benefits of working test-first.

One helpful technique is to keep a very tight loop between writing tests and writing code and to run the test suite frequently (ideally, we'd run it constantly using autotest or a similar continuous-test execution tool, Section 19.3, *Using Autotest*, on page 310). The tighter the loop and the fewer lines of code we write in each back-and-forth, the easier it is to find and track down these structural test problems.

Second, and more specific to these kinds of validation problems, using some kind of factory tool or common setup method to generate well-structured default data makes it much easier to keep data in sync with changing definitions of validity. Much more on that topic in Section 6.4, *Using Factories to Fix Fixtures*, on page 80.

Anyway, fixing the older data is a distraction: we have a larger problem. Remember, we wanted the status to be invalid only if *both* today and yesterday were blank. We need to write a couple of follow-up tests to confirm that we haven't overshot the mark. The tests go in test/unit/status_report_test.rb.

`huddle3/test/unit/status_report_test.rb`

```
test "a report with yesterday blank is valid" do
  actual = StatusReport.new(:today => "today", :yesterday => "")
  assert actual.valid?
end

test "a report with today blank is valid" do
  actual = StatusReport.new(:today => "", :yesterday => "yesterday")
  assert actual.valid?
end
```

Oops.

```
  1) Failure:
test_a_test_with_today_blank_is_valid(StatusReportTest)
[/test/unit/status_report_test.rb:36]:
<false> is not true.

  2) Failure:
test_a_test_with_yesterday_blank_is_valid(StatusReportTest)
[/test/unit/status_report_test.rb:31]:
<false> is not true.
```

At this point, we want to move to a custom validation, because the validation functions provided by Rails won't quite get this right for us.

Replace the validation line in app/model/status_report.rb with the following call to plain validate() and the associated method:

huddle3/app/models/status_report.rb

```
validate :validate_has_at_least_one_status

def validate_has_at_least_one_status
  if today.blank? && yesterday.blank?
    errors[:base] << "Must have at least one status set"
  end
end
```

And we're back to passing.[5] This, by the way, is the first line of code we've seen in this chapter that is different for Rails 3 and Rails 2. The previous is for Rails 3. In Rails 2, the error is added with the method call errors.add_to_base().

Here are a couple of points on the question of what to test and when:

- The general situation here is very important. Always try to test a boundary from both sides. If you are testing that an administrator should see a certain link, you also need to test that a regular user can't see it. Your tests will give you an accurate picture of your application only if they cover the requirement boundaries from both sides.

- Although we don't need to test the Rails validation methods as such, we do need to verify the operational behavior that a model object in a certain state is invalid. In a strict TDD process, it's the test for validity that causes us to add the Rails validation method in the first place.

- Whether to go back and add a controller test to validate behavior for invalid objects is an open question. As a matter of course, we insert a generic test into our controller scaffold using mock objects to cover the general failure case (shown in detail in Chapter 7, *Using Mock Objects*, on page 95), which means we don't need to go back and test the controller behavior for each and every different possible kind of model failure, unless, of course, each specific failure actually dictates different controller behavior.

---

5. One early reviewer pointed out that this can, in fact, be done with the core Rails validations, namely, a pair of validates_presence_of() calls with the if option.

Now, this may seem like a lot of work because we've been going through every step in excruciating detail. In practice, though, each of these test cycles is very quick—in the five- to fifteen-minute range for relatively simple tests like these.

3.4 Security Now!

Let's take a look at Huddle's login and security models that use the Devise gem. Devise has its own set of tests, so we don't need to write tests for the basic behavior of login and logout. We do need to write tests to cover parts of the application-specific security model for who can see and edit what different things. Let's say that our authentication requirements are as follows:

1. Users must be logged in to view or create a status report.

2. Users must always have a current project chosen. Right now, any user can see and create a status report on any project. Assigning users to projects may or may not happen later. At the moment, we don't care.

3. Users can only edit their own reports. Again, there may or may not be admin functionality later; we'll cross that bridge when we get to it.

To enforce a Devise login globally throughout the app, we need to add the following inside the ApplicationController. In a slight break from normal procedure, we'll implement the forced login in the code first.

huddle3/app/controllers/application_controller.rb

```
before_filter :authenticate_user!
```

Why not do this test first? It's because most of the functionality is already tested by Devise and because the authentication model is super-basic and application-wide. If and when the login model gets more complex (if, for example, there were public reports that did not require a login), we'd start adding some tests.

Despite not adding any new tests, we suddenly have no shortage of failing tests just from adding the login requirement. Running rake, the unit tests pass, but the controller tests...well:

```
15 tests, 0 assertions, 0 failures, 15 errors
```

The test failures are all due to the login requirement: every controller test is now being redirected to the login page. What we want is for all our tests to take place in the context of an active login.

There are two things we need to do to get Devise to play nicely with our tests. First, we need to add the following lines to the bottom of our test/test_helper.rb file. Note that this goes *outside* the ActiveSupport::Test-Case class already being defined in the test helper file.

huddle3/test/test_helper.rb

```
class ActionController::TestCase
  include Devise::TestHelpers
end
```

Then, in the body of the ActiveSupport::TestCase declaration in the same file, add the following method:

huddle3/test/test_helper.rb

```
def login_as_one
  sign_in(users(:one))
end
```

In the two controller tests where the controller requires a login (namely, ProjectsControllerTest and StatusReportsControllerTest), place the following line inside the test class at the top of the class declaration:

```
setup :login_as_one
```

This is the first time we've used the setup/teardown mechanism as implemented in Rails 2.2 and up; you can see the mechanism in more detail in Section 2.5, *What Happens When Tests Run?*, on page 25. The login_as_one() method is called before each and every individual test in those controllers, using the mechanism Devise provides to fake a user login. Setups are invoked in the order declared, which is why we can't just put this setup line in the test helper and declare it only once. If we try, the login_as_one() method is invoked before the setup in the actual controller test class. Since the controller test setup hasn't been called, the session object used for tests hasn't been created, and the login_as_one() method will cause an error.

The Devise mechanism is simple. The call to login_as_one() directly calls the Devise sign_in(), which simulates a fake user login.

With this setup in place, the tests pass again.

3.5 Applying Security

Now that user login is required, the form for creating a status report should no longer have the user_id as an entry in the form, since the currently logged-in user is assumed to be the creator. Similarly, although we haven't specified a mechanism for setting it, the project_id will always be an implicit current project and also doesn't need to be specified in a form. That leads us to a new test...well, actually an edit of an existing test. In test_helper.rb, add the following helper method to set a current project in the test session:

> huddle3/test/test_helper.rb

```
def set_current_project(symbol)
  @request.session[:project_id] = projects(symbol).id
end
```

Then change the previously written status report test to remove the project and user from the test we wrote a few pages ago:

> huddle3/test/functional/status_reports_controller_test.rb

```
Line 1  test "creation of status report with data" do
   -      set_current_project(:one)
   -      assert_difference('StatusReport.count', 1) do
   -        post :create, :status_report => {
   5          :yesterday => "I did stuff",
   -          :today => "I'll do stuff"}
   -      end
   -      actual = assigns(:status_report)
   -      assert_equal(projects(:one).id, actual.project.id)
  10      assert_equal(users(:one).id, actual.user.id)
   -      assert_equal(Date.today.to_s(:db), actual.status_date.to_s(:db))
   -      assert_redirected_to status_report_path(actual)
   -    end
```

The test helper method created in the first snippet and called in line 2 shown previously sets the current project in the test session; for the moment, we don't care that there's no UI way to set the current project.

Now, the first draft of this section of the book actually presented this as a separate test; as a general rule, it's not a good idea to edit existing tests unless they are actually broken by some change to the code. In this case, though, the behavior of the original test is really dangerous and must change—we don't want the user_id from the form to be acknowledged at all in order to prevent a malicious user from posting nasty things under your good name. So, we edit the existing test instead.

Preventing the malicious user is the next test, but let's pass this one first. The create() method in StatusReportsController needs to be changed so that it starts:

```
def create
  params[:status_report].merge!(:user_id => current_user.id,
      :project_id => current_project.id)
  @status_report = StatusReport.new(params[:status_report])
  ## rest of method as before
end
```

The current_user() method is defined by Devise and, since we are requiring a login to get this far, is guaranteed to be non-nil. We also need a current_project() that will always be non-nil. Put this in the Application-Controller:

huddle3/app/controllers/application_controller.rb

```
helper_method :current_project
def current_project
  project = Project.find(session[:project_id]) rescue Project.last
end
```

If there is no project_id in the session, the method returns the most recently created project. That's almost certainly not the final logic, but we can get by with it for now.

3.6 Punishing Miscreants

The time has come to punish evildoers who try to get around the site by putting somebody else's user_id into their form submit. Right now, based on the previous code, the submitted ID is ignored, and the actually-logged-in user is used instead. But why not kick out any user trying to fake a user_id? The test, in status_reports_controller_test.rb, looks like this:

huddle3/test/functional/status_reports_controller_test.rb

```
Line 1  test "redirect and logout if the user tries to snipe a user id" do
    -     noel = User.create!(:email => "railsprescriptions@gmail.com",
    -         :password => "banana", :password_confirmation => "banana")
    -     set_current_project(:one)
    5     assert_no_difference('StatusReport.count') do
    -       post :create, :status_report => {
    -         :user_id => noel.id,
    -         :yesterday => "I did stuff",
    -         :today => "I'll do stuff"}
   10     end
    -     assert_nil session[:user_id]
    -     assert_redirected_to(new_user_session_path)
    -   end
```

There are a few differences between this test and the previous one. In line 7, we've added the user_id for a newly created user to the params. In line 5, we're explicitly testing that StatusReport.count does not change—that no new report is created. Finally, lines 11 and 12 assert that the user is logged out and bounced back to the login page.

There are several things about that test that will fail at the moment (although it makes sense long term to keep it as one test). It's best to fix these things one at a time. The first failure is the assert_no_difference() call, so we need to prevent the creation of the new object.

The first attempt has two problems. First, it's ugly. Second, it doesn't work:

```
Line 1  def create
  -       if params[:status_report][:user_id].nil? ||
  -           (params[:status_report][:user_id] == current_user.id)
  -         params[:status_report].merge!(:user_id => current_user.id,
  5             :project_id => current_project.id)
  -         @status_report = StatusReport.new(params[:status_report])
  -       end
  -       respond_to do |format|
  -         if @status_report && @status_report.save
  10            flash[:notice] = 'StatusReport was successfully created.'
  -           format.html { redirect_to(@status_report) }
  -           format.xml  { render :xml => @status_report, :status => :created,
  -               :location => @status_report }
  -         else
  15            format.html { render :action => "new" }
  -           format.xml  { render :xml => @status_report.errors,
  -               :status => :unprocessable_entity }
  -         end
  -       end
  20    end
```

In lines 2–6, we're attempting to create the object only if there is a user ID; and if the ID differs from the current user, the existence of the object is a prerequisite for the save test in line 9.

It doesn't work because in the failure case, the code tries to render the new action, which assumes the existence of @status_report. We could try to make that a redirect in line 16, but that's going down a rat hole that we'd only have to walk away from in just a second. Let's try a more general solution:

```
Line 1  def create
  -       if (params[:status_report][:user_id] &&
  -         params[:status_report][:user_id] != current_user.id)
```

```
        sign_out(current_user)
  5     redirect_to new_user_session_path
        return
      end
      params[:status_report].merge!(:user_id => current_user.id,
          :project_id => current_project.id)
 10   @status_report = StatusReport.new(params[:status_report])
      respond_to do |format|
        if @status_report.save
          flash[:notice] = 'StatusReport was successfully created.'
          format.html { redirect_to(@status_report) }
 15       format.xml  { render :xml => @status_report, :status => :created,
              :location => @status_report }
        else
          format.html { render :action => "new" }
          format.xml  { render :xml => @status_report.errors,
 20             :status => :unprocessable_entity }
        end
      end
    end
```

Now the tests all pass. The if statement on line 2 grabs invalid forms, and the logout and redirect happen there, with the **return** on line 6 preventing further processing.

It would be nice to make this a more general method—the problem is that if we just convert the initial if statement into a helper method, the return statement still needs to be in the actual controller action. If it's not, the action continues to process, and we get a double-render error.

Here's one solution: the general part of method goes in the Application-Controller. It performs the same test against the current user's ID, does the logout and redirect if they don't match, and returns true:

`huddle3/app/controllers/application_controller.rb`

```
def redirect_if_not_current_user(user_id)
  if user_id && user_id != current_user.id
    sign_out(current_user)
    redirect_to new_user_session_path
    return true
  end
  false
end
```

The controller method now needs to take that result and use it to stop its own processing.

huddle3/app/controllers/status_reports_controller.rb

```
Line 1   def create
           redirect_if_not_current_user(params[:status_report][:user_id]) and return
           params[:status_report].merge!(:user_id => current_user.id,
               :project_id => current_project.id)
    5      @status_report = StatusReport.new(params[:status_report])

           respond_to do |format|
             if @status_report.save
               format.html { redirect_to(@status_report,
                   :notice => 'Status report was successfully created.') }
   10          format.xml  { render :xml => @status_report, :status => :created,
                   :location => @status_report }
             else
               format.html { render :action => "new" }
   15          format.xml  { render :xml => @status_report.errors,
                   :status => :unprocessable_entity }
             end
           end
         end
```

Line 2 is the key here: it calls the general method and then returns if the result is true. That version is the most readable, even if it's a bit Perl-ish. We could also try the following:

```
return if redirect_if_not_current_user(params[:status_report][:user_id])
```

Or:

```
if redirect_if_not_current_user(params[:status_report][:user_id])
  return
end
```

Or, we could try using a before_filter at the top of the controller:

```
before_filter :redirect_if_not_current_user, :only => [:create]
```

In that case, we don't need anything in the create() method, but the helper method needs to change in a couple of ways. First, the return value needs to flip and return false if the redirect happens in order to stop further processing and return true if the user is OK. Second, filter methods can't take arguments, so the extraction from params[:status_report][:user_id] needs to take place in the filter method itself.

With that refactoring, the tests pass again.

Testing for security is generally time well spent—security tests are relatively easy to write, since in many cases we're just testing for a redirection to a login page or that key data didn't display. The trick is to be creative and try to think of all the oddball ways that somebody might be able to submit data to flummox our application.

3.7 Road Map

In this chapter, we started a new Rails application and wrote the first couple of features of that application using Test-Driven Development. We added features to our controller, moved them to the model, and validated the model more tightly. We also tested and added authentication logic.

We're not done touring Rails core TDD procedures, though. In the next chapter, we'll look at view logic and show how to use TDD within Rails to create a feature end-to-end.

Chapter 4

TDD, Rails Style

Now that we've got some successful test/code/refactor cycles down, we'll go through a more complicated TDD example, this time adding display logic to the application. In this example, we'll cascade our tests from layer to layer, between the controller, model, and view.

4.1 Now for a View Test

We've tested some model logic and some controller logic, but we still have two view tests that need to be written to close out the initial data entry feature. We'd like to validate that the form being generated actually contains the field names that the create() method expects—this little gap is one of the easiest ways for a problem to slip through the cracks of an otherwise air-tight Rails TDD process. Then let's test that the project show page actually displays the timeline of status reports for the project.

Testing view logic is a little bit different from testing model or controller logic. It's more impressionistic and less precise. When testing views, it's important to keep the larger goal of specifying the application logic in mind and not fritter away huge amounts of time trying to get the view tests ultra-complete and correct. It's easy to write view tests that are detailed but add little to the amount of coverage in the test suite and are prone to breaking any time a web designer looks at the HTML code cross-eyed.

> ### Make Those Pop-Culture References Work for You
>
> This could well be the goofiest tip I give in this whole book, but when I create test data for users that have some kind of relationship, I find it valuable to give those users names that are meaningful in terms of some reference or other—for instance, Fred and Barney, Homer and Marge, or Lois and Clark. This simple trick helps keep the expected relationship between the various pieces of test data straight in your mind. Obviously, you can take this too far, and there will always be somebody on the team who doesn't know the reference. It sounds silly, but at the very least, it'll make you smile every now and then when looking at your code.

These issues are covered more completely in Chapter 9, *Testing Views*, on page 135, but here are three tips to keep in mind as we embark on two sets of view tests:

- Consider moving view logic to helpers where possible. In the core Rails setup, it's much easier to individually test a helper than it is to individually test a view partial (although if you use RSpec, you can test view partials directly—more on this in Chapter 12, *RSpec*, on page 183). On the other hand, moving view code from HTML/ERb and into Ruby methods could cause a web-only design team to come after you with torches and pitchforks. So beware.

- Remember that the purpose of view testing is for the developer to validate the logical correctness of the application. Automated view testing isn't (and in Rails, really can't be) a substitute for walking though the site and checking that things line up and look nice.

- Test at the *semantic* level, not the display level. Liberally assign DOM IDs and classes to the elements of the view, and test for the existence of those elements, rather than the actual text. Obviously, there are limits; sometimes the actual text is critical. But the advantage of DOM ID testing is that it doesn't break every time the content team updates the text or when the designer changes the CSS styles.

Our first view test will just validate that the form elements actually exist as we want them to, which means the attributes that will be automatically added by the controller shouldn't be in the form. With core Rails test structures, this test goes with the controller in test/functional/status_reports_controller_test.rb:

huddle3/test/functional/status_reports_controller_test.rb

```
Line 1  test "new form has expected elements" do
     2    get :new
     3    assert_select "form[id=new_status_report][action=/status_reports]" do
     4      assert_select "#status_report_project", :count => 0
     5      assert_select "#status_report_user", :count => 0
     6      assert_select "textarea#status_report_today"
     7      assert_select "textarea#status_report_yesterday"
     8      assert_select "#status_report_status_date_1i", :count => 0
     9    end
    10  end
```

This is a reasonably straightforward view test, which simulates a GET request for the new status report form in line 2 and then uses assert_select() to verify several features of the output of the call. The assert_select() method has about seventy-eleven different options, all of which are lovingly detailed in Chapter 9, *Testing Views*, on page 135. For now, the basic point to remember is that the first argument to assert_select() is a CSS-like selector, and the remaining arguments are assertions about elements in the output that match the selector.[1] For our purposes, the most useful option is :text, which is either a string or a regular expression. If this option is specified, the internal contents of tags that match the selector are checked to see whether any matches the argument. The second most useful option is :count, which is the number of elements in the view that match the selector. If :count is not specified, the expectation is that there will be at least one match. If :count and :text are specified, :count is the number of items that match both the selector and the text.

You can also nest assert_select() calls using blocks; this step adds the additional constraint that the assertions inside the block must all be true inside the body of a tag that matches the outer assert_select(). This constraint can also be described in a single assert_select() call using compound selectors like ul > li. In the previous test, the outer assert_select() matches a form tag with the ID and action that we would expect by Rails convention for a new form action. All the other assert_select() calls validate the elements inside that form tag. Specifically, we

---

1. One handy feature of assert_select() is that it parses the HTML markup and will spit out a warning if the HTML is badly formed—for instance, if it is missing an end tag.

are testing that there will not be a project, user, or date tag of any kind and also that there will be text area entry tags for the yesterday and today status report fields.

There could be some quibbling back and forth on the exact structure of these tests. We've chosen to test the form fields based on their DOM IDs, knowing that Rails has a consistent pattern for IDs and the name field of the tag. For me, DOM IDs work a little bit better with the assert_select() syntax.[2] Still, a clueless programmer who was breaking the Rails conventions could cause a bug without failing this view test. That said, chasing down every way the view could break would take all our efforts, forever: try to limit view testing to things that are likely sources of error or regression.

Passing the test is quite easy: just remove the form elements for the project, user, and date. However, unlike the model tests, even with the passing test, this view is in no way, shape, or form fit to be in a production application. You need styling; the Rails scaffold HTML is not optimal—that sort of thing. . . .

At this point, from the limited perspective of the server-side logic, the feature is essentially finished, but we *must* go into the browser and test it, no matter how complete we think the tests are. Tests are great and wonderful, but the user isn't going to care about our code coverage if it doesn't work in the browser. Writing tests minimizes the amount of time we spend cycling through the browser, but in no way does automated testing mean we can stop using the browser.

But here in tutorial world, let's move on to the display functionality for an entire project within Huddle. So far, we've covered the major features of Rails TDD, and we've tested models, controllers, and views, but we've only tested them in isolation. To close out this walk-through, let's take a slightly larger piece of functionality and show how you might move back and forth between code and tests and, between the different kinds of test, when building a complete slice of your application.

4.2 Testing the Project View: A Cascade of Tests

In Huddle, a project page should show a timeline of status reports for that project. This functionality requires at least a controller and a view

---

2. Another approach is to say that these tests should track the name directly, as in assert_select "textarea[name = ?]", "status_report[today]".

TESTING THE PROJECT VIEW: A CASCADE OF TESTS ◀ 57

test to start, and we may use some model tests later. We are going to need some status report data for this test, and we haven't discussed fixtures yet. To get these tests to work, we first need to get some sample data into our test, and then we'll use that data to specify the behavior of the application.

Testing the View

To test the view, we need some fixture data. Add the following to test/fixtures/projects.yml to create some projects:

`huddle3/test/fixtures/projects.yml`

```
huddle:
  name: Huddle Project
```

We'll also want some status reports, in test/fixtures/status_reports.yml.

`huddle3/test/fixtures/status_reports.yml`

```
one_tue:
  project: huddle
  user: one
  yesterday: Worked on Huddle UI
  today: Doing some testing
  status_date: 2009-01-06


one_wed:
  project: huddle
  user: one
  yesterday: Did Some Testing
  today: More Testing
  status_date: 2009-01-07
```

`huddle3/test/fixtures/status_reports.yml`

```
two_tue:
  project: huddle
  user: two
  yesterday: set up huddle schema
  today: pair programming with one
  status_date: 2009-01-06


two_wed:
  project: huddle
  user: two
  yesterday: sick
  today: trying to pair again
  status_date: 2009-01-07
```

We can start testing using this fixture data. The project controller method for show() should gather the reports for that project and group them by date.

This goes in test/functional/projects_controller_test.rb:

huddle3/test/functional/projects_controller_test.rb

```
test "project timeline index should be sorted correctly" do
  set_current_project(:huddle)
  get :show, :id => projects(:huddle).id
  expected_keys = assigns(:reports).keys.sort.map{ |d| d.to_s(:db) }
  assert_equal(["2009-01-06", "2009-01-07"], expected_keys)
  assert_equal(
    [status_reports(:one_tue).id, status_reports(:two_tue).id],
    assigns(:reports)[Date.parse("2009-01-06")].map(&:id))
end
```

In lines 4–5, this asserts that an object called @reports is created, and its keys are the dates of the reports that are found. Lines 6–8 assert that each key contains its reports, sorted by the name of the user (well, technically, the email of the user—we're not using name fields in the user model just yet).

That test will, of course, fail, because assigns(:reports) is nil.

Moving to the controller itself, let's just defer the assignment to the model. In app/controllers/projects_controller.rb:

huddle3/app/controllers/projects_controller.rb

```
def show
  @project = Project.find(params[:id])
  @reports = @project.reports_grouped_by_day
  respond_to do |format|
    format.html # show.html.erb
    format.xml  { render :xml => @project }
  end
end
```

That means we now need a model test in test/unit/project_test.rb:

huddle3/test/unit/project_test.rb

```
test "should be able to retrieve projects based on day" do
  actual = projects(:huddle).reports_grouped_by_day
  expected_keys = actual.keys.sort.map{ |d| d.to_s(:db) }
  assert_equal(["2009-01-06", "2009-01-07"], expected_keys)
  assert_equal([status_reports(:one_tue).id, status_reports(:two_tue).id],
    actual[Date.parse("2009-01-06")].map(&:id))
end
```

This is a direct swipe of the code we just put in the controller test, which opens up the question of whether we need both the controller and the model test. The model test is important because it's closest to the actual implementation and is the easiest place to write error-case tests. The controller test adds just the piece of information that the model method is, in fact, called by the controller—strictly speaking, the controller test does not need to revalidate the model logic. You could potentially remove the model-specific assertions from the controller test if you wanted. This is a classic place for a *mock object call* in the controller, which would prevent the controller test from depending on the specific code in the model. Mock objects are a huge topic in their own right and are covered in more detail in Chapter 7, *Using Mock Objects*, on page 95. For our purposes right now, the duplicate test is not a problem.[3]

Anyway, passing this test requires some code. In app/models/project.rb:

huddle3/app/models/project.rb

```
has_many :status_reports

def reports_grouped_by_day
  status_reports.by_user_name.group_by(&:status_date)
end
```

Previously, this model was blank: we added the has_many line here because it's needed to pass the test. Note that we don't need to separately test what has_many does—that's part of the Rails framework itself. The need for the association line came immediately as we started writing tests for the functionality of that model.[4]

The actual method uses the Rails ActiveSupport group_by(), which returns the hash structure we want. The by_user_name will be a named scope inside StatusReports() that sorts the reports based on the user's login. As I worked on this method, it became clear that the named scope was going to be complex enough to require its own test. In test/unit/status_report_test.rb:

huddle3/test/unit/status_report_test.rb

```
test "by user name should sort as expected" do
  reports = StatusReport.by_user_name
  expected = reports.map { |r| r.user.email }
  assert_equal ["one@one.com", "one@one.com",
      "two@two.com", "two@two.com"], expected
end
```

---

3. Another option is to use an integration test or a Cucumber acceptance test in place of the controller test.
4. A framework like Shoulda gives easy, one-line tests for associations—in which case, it might be worth throwing in the single line.

You only do this because the named scope crosses an association. For a simple scope, it might not be worth the trouble, since the functionality is mostly covered by Rails and is also easily covered by the existing test. Essentially, you might write the test if you're nervous that you might not write the scope correctly.

There are two overlapping issues here: when to test functionality provided by the framework and when to test private or subordinate methods that are called only by other tested methods. The guideline is that a new test needs to be written only if the logic of the application has changed. For instance, if we refactor a smaller method out of a larger, already tested method, we won't need to also write targeted tests against the smaller method—it is just a restructuring of the already-tested logic. Should the subordinate method later gain additional logic, we'll need to write tests for that method. If we find a bug in the smaller method, then it should have tests immediately.

The scope in app/model/status_report.rb looks like this:

`huddle3/app/models/status_report.rb`

```
scope :by_user_name, :include => "user",
    :order => "users.email ASC",
    :conditions => "user_id IS NOT NULL"
```

And all the tests pass.[5]

This is the order in which I actually wrote this code the first time I went through it: controller test, model test in Project, Project model implementation (after checking, the one liner was written directly), scope test, then scope code (with a little flailing in there about exactly how to manage the users table). It may not be strictly test-first, but in the entire process, I never wrote more than about five lines of code on one side of the test/code divide without jumping to the other, and I never went more than a minute or two without running the test suite.

And that's the key to success with TDD. Keep a tight feedback loop between the code and tests: don't ever let one or the other get too far out in front.

---

5. In Rails 2.x that code would start with named_scope instead of scope. In Rails 3, this can also be written as a regular class find method, since Rails 3 ActiveRecord pieces can be composed like named scopes.

Now we need a genuine view test to validate that something reasonable is going into the view layer. Back in test/functional/projects_controller_test.rb:

huddle3/test/functional/projects_controller_test.rb

```
test "index should display project timeline" do
  set_current_project(:huddle)
  get :show, :id => projects(:huddle).id
  assert_select "div[id *= day]", :count => 2
  assert_select "div#2009-01-06_day" do
    assert_select "div[id *= report]", :count => 2
    assert_select "div#?", dom_id(status_reports(:one_tue))
    assert_select "div#?", dom_id(status_reports(:two_tue))
  end
  assert_select "div#2009-01-07_day" do
    assert_select "div[id *= report]", :count => 2
    assert_select "div#?", dom_id(status_reports(:one_wed))
    assert_select "div#?", dom_id(status_reports(:two_wed))
  end
end
```

Continuing with the idea of semantic-level tests for the view layer, this test checks to see that there is some kind of div tag for each day and that inside that tag is a div tagged for each status report. Even putting in a div might be overly specific—it's possible these might be table rows or something. The count tests are to prevent more content showing up than expected, something that is not caught by just testing for the existence of known tags. In this case, we're also testing that there are exactly two days worth of reports and that each day has two reports. This is calibrated to match the fixture data we just set up and gives a quick look at one weakness of fixtures—a change to that fixture data could break this test.

Also, for this to work, add this line inside the class definition in test/test_helper.rb:

huddle3/test/test_helper.rb

```
include ActionController::RecordIdentifier
```

This allows us to use the dom_id() method in tests, which is handy.[6]

---

6. In Rails 2.x include the module with the line include ActionView::Helpers::RecordIdentificationHelper instead.

Putting aside that there are a jillion ways the view code could pass the letter of this test and violate the spirit, here's the basic structure of a passing view, in app/views/projects/show.html.erb:

huddle3/app/views/projects/show.html.erb

```
<h2>Status Reports for <%= @project.name %></h2>
<% @reports.keys.sort.each do |date| %>
  <div id="<%= date.to_s(:db) %>_day">
    <h3>Reports for <%= date.to_s(:long) %></h3>
    <% @reports[date].each do |report| %>
      <div id="<%= dom_id(report) %>">
        Yesterday I: <%= report.yesterday %>
        Today I will: <%= report.today %>
      </div>
    <% end %>
  </div>
<% end %>
```

This gives the view a div for each date and a nested div for each individual report.

4.3 So Far, So Good

At this point, we've completed our initial walk-through of Rails test-driven development. You should be able to add tests to a Rails application; use fixture data; test your controllers, models, and views; and have a feel for how the TDD quick test/code feedback loop works in practice.

The rest of the book is divided up based on what part of the application is under test. Part II deals with testing ActiveRecord models, getting data into your tests via fixtures and factories, and other data-related topics. Part III discusses testing controllers, views, and helpers, each of which has some special mechanisms to make the process easier.

The big third-party test frameworks, Shoulda and RSpec, are discussed in Part IV, while Part V covers integration testing, both using Rails itself and using external tools such as Webrat and Cucumber. Finally, Part VI talks about how to evaluate and improve your tests, using coverage testing, managing performance, and troubleshooting.

Part II

Testing Application Data

## Chapter 5

Testing Models with Rails Unit Tests

The overwhelming majority of data in a typical Rails application is accessed via ActiveRecord objects that connect to a SQL database. These objects are tested using *model tests*. Model tests, which core Rails calls *unit tests*, are the most basic level of the Rails testing functionality, by which I mean they are the closest to Ruby's Test::Unit and the foundation on which the test structures for controllers and views are built. Model tests in Rails are just Test::Unit plus the ability to set up data in fixtures; the block syntax for describing setup, teardown, and tests; and a couple of additional assertion methods. Model tests that you write are placed in the test/unit directory.[1] We're starting our tour of the Rails stack with model tests because model tests have the fewest dependencies on Rails-specific features and are usually the easiest place to start testing your application. Later, we'll move forward to controller testing, view testing, integration testing, and other Rails tools.

5.1 What's Available in a Model Test

Rails model tests are subclasses of ActiveSupport::TestCase, which is a subclass of the core Ruby Test::Unit::TestCase. Model tests also include a couple of modules from the Rails core mixed in to provide additional functionality. All told, the following functionality is added to Ruby unit

---

[1]. While I'm here, does it bother anybody else that app/controllers and app/models are plural, while test/functional and test/unit are singular?

> ### What's in a Name, Part One
>
> Tests for Rails models are usually referred to as *unit tests*, but as much as I hate being pedantic and technical, I prefer to call them *model tests*. (Who am I kidding, I *love* being pedantic and technical.) My basic problem is that *unit test* has a specific meaning that, depending on how you look at it, either includes Rails functional tests or doesn't include either kind of test. (Jay Fields, for example, argues that Rails model tests aren't really unit tests because they require an external database.) Personally, I find it less confusing to use *unit test* as a generic term for all developer testing and *model test* for tests that actually validate Rails models.

tests to make them Rails model tests (as we'll see in Chapter 8, *Testing Controllers with Functional Tests*, on page 123, controller tests have even more additions):

- The ability to load data from fixtures before each test.

- The Shoulda and RSpec-inspired test syntax: test "do something" do.

- Multiple setup and teardown block syntax, discussed in further detail in Section 2.3, *Setup and Teardown*, on page 20.

- The assert_difference() and assert_no_difference() methods.

- The assert_valid() test, which verifies that an ActiveRecord model is—wait for it—valid according to the rules of that model.

- A couple of little-known database helper methods that you can gain access to by making your test case a subclass of ActiveRecord::TestCase: assert_date_from_db(), assert_sql(), assert_queries(), and assert_no_queries(). These are used internally by the Rails core test system and don't seem have a lot of value outside core.

- The test/test_helper.rb, required by all Rails-generated model tests and part of your application, injects some additional methods into ActiveSupport::TestCase.[2] This is a good place to put common setup and assertion methods needed by all tests.

---

2. Before Rails 2.2, the injects were into Test::Unit::TestCase, even in Rails 2.1, where ActiveSupport::TestCase was already being used by the model tests.

5.2 What to Test in a Model Test

Models. Next question?

5.3 OK, Funny Man, What Is a Good Model Test Class?

The goal is to have each model's individual test file cover pretty much 100 percent of the code in that model. Other models or controller tests will probably incidentally touch code in the model, but that's not a replacement for effective tests for a particular model in its own test file. Tests should be as close as possible to the code being described.

You don't need to write a separate test for the existence of relationships like belongs_to or has_many—Rails tests those features thoroughly, and if you don't have a relationship you expect, you'll get failures all over the place.[3] The existence of the relationship should be driven by a test that needs the relationship in order to deliver functionality. You should write tests to cover validations in order to ensure that the difference between a valid and invalid object is what you expect. Named scopes are somewhere between relationships and methods. Simple named scopes can probably be treated like relationships, but anything complicated— with a lambda block, for example—should probably be tested. More on that in Section 5.5, *Testing Active Record Finders*, on page 70.

How many tests do you need? The strict test-driven answer is that all new logic should be driven by a failing test, and conversely, each new test should fail and trigger a new piece of code logic. A typical progression looks something like this (if you keep your methods smaller and simpler, you'll tend to need fewer tests for each method):

- One test of the normal, happy-path case.

- One test for each alternate branch through the code. Refactoring here often causes the method to be split into multiple smaller methods.

- At least one test for known error cases, such as being passed nil arguments, as needed.[4] My position, which is perhaps a little cranky, is that you should include this only if you either really

---

3. Brian Hogan pointed out in review—I paraphrase here—that this may be an overly optimistic view of the stability of Rails core. True enough. The place to catch that is probably at the integration test level.
4. I'm tempted to go on a rant about programmers putting too much error-checking in their code, but this really isn't the place.

need the error case to do something specific or have reason to doubt that an expected error case is really being treated as an error.

Keep each individual test small. In many cases, you only need to create a single model object for a unit test. You may find it helpful to list out all the cases you want to test before you start writing the tests. That's fine, but you still want to write and pass the tests one at a time.

If a single call to the method causes multiple changes in the model, it's fine to have all the assertions in a single test; you don't have to be a purist about keeping only a single assertion in a test method. In this example from a tracking system, marking a story complete triggers several different changes in the method. It can be awkward and hard to follow to have each of these assertions in a different method. Here's an example:

```
test "mark a story complete" do
  story = stories(:incomplete)
  assert_difference "story.task_logs.count", 1 do
    story.complete!(users(:quentin))
  end
  assert story.completed?
  assert !story.blocked?
  assert_equal(Date.today.to_s(:db), story.end_date)
  assert_equal("completed", story.most_recent_log.end_state)
end
```

By contrast, here's the one assertion per test version:

```
test "mark a story complete and add a task log" do
  assert_difference "story.task_logs.count", 1 do
    stories(:incomplete).complete!(users(:quentin))
  end
end

test "mark a story complete and the story should be completed" do
  story = stories(:incomplete)
  story.complete!
  assert story.completed?
end
```

And so on. To be fair, the one-at-a-time tests are verbose because I'm using only core Rails methods. With *contexts* and a couple of other tricks, these tests can be written more compactly (see Section 11.1, *Contexts*, on page 168 and Section 11.7, *Single-Line Test Tools*, on page 180. RSpec also has similar features described in Chapter 12,

RSpec, on page 183). Written with those tools, the one-assertion-per-test version can be more readable than the all-in-one-test version.

There's a trade-off: by putting all the assertions in the same test method, you gain clarity and cohesion benefits, but prevent the tests from running independently. In the all-in-one test, if assert story.completed? fails, you won't even get to the check for assert !story.blocked. If all the assertions are in separate tests, everything runs independently, but it's harder to determine how tests are related. (The multiple test version also runs more slowly.)

That said, when you are writing separate tests that cover different branches of the method or the error tests, they should be different test methods (unless the method setup is *extremely* simple):

```
test "full names" do
  u1 = User.create(:first_name => "Fred", :last_name => "Flintstone")
  assert_equal("Fred Flintstone", user.full name)
end

test "full names with a middle initial" do
  u1 = User.create(:first_name => "Fred", :last_name => "Flintstone"
      :middle_initial => "D")
  assert_equal("Fred D. Flintstone", user.full name)
end

test "full name where there's no first name" do
  u1 = User.create(:last_name => "Flintstone")
  assert_equal("Flintstone", user.full name)
end
```

In this case, you do want each test to run independently; trying to stuff all the branches into a single test will be very hard to read going forward.

5.4 Asserting a Difference, or Not

The two assertions that Rails adds to the basic unit test are powerful replacements for a common test pattern. The following test asserts that after a create() call, there is one more user than there was previously:

```
test "creating creates a user" do
  pre = User.count
  User.create(:first_name => "Noel")
  post = User.count
  assert_equal(pre + 1, post)
end
```

With assert_difference(), the test can be written without the duplicate call to User.count():

```
test "creating creates a user" do
  assert_difference 'User.count' do
    User.create(:first_name => "Noel")
  end
end
```

The first argument to assert_difference() is a string of Ruby code. The value of the string is calculated using eval(). The code inside the block is executed, and the value of the string is re-calculated. By default, the expectation is that the new value will be one more than the old value, but you can adjust this by passing in a second argument, such as assert_difference("User.count", 0), in order to assert no change, or assert_difference("User.count", -1), to assert the removal of a user.

If you'd like to check multiple code snippets, you have two options. The calls to assert_difference() can be nested:

```
test "create a user and a log entry" do
  assert_difference 'User.count' do
    assert_difference 'LogEntry.count' do
      User.create(:first_name => "Noel")
    end
  end
end
```

Or, if the difference number is the same for all the snippets, the snippets can be passed in a list:

```
test "creating creates a user" do
  assert_difference ['User.count', 'LogEntry.count'] do
    User.create(:first_name => "Noel")
  end
end
```

Finally, assert_no_difference('User.count') is syntactic sugar for assert_difference('User.count', 0).

5.5 Testing Active Record Finders

In Rails 3, you can write individual pieces of database logic as separate methods and compose them arbitrarily. For example, if you often find yourself needing, say, users sorted by email address or a list of all active users or to only get five users out of your database find call, you can write all of those as separate finder methods:[5]

```
def self.by_email
  order("email ASC")
end

def self.active_only
  where(:active => true)
end

def self.limit_to(x)
  limit(x)
end
```

These methods can then be used like any other ActiveRecord find() command.

```
User.by_email
User.active_only
User.limit_to(5)
```

But the best part is that these methods can be composed, which gives you a very readable way to express complex database queries:

```
User.active_only.by_email.limit_to(5)
```

Being able to compose this logic, therefore, is awesome. But these methods occupy an awkward place between methods you might write and Rails core features, leading to the question of how best to test functionality you've placed in a named scope declaration. Here are some guidelines.

Class finders are often extracted during a refactoring step. In this case, you may not need any new test to cover the scope—like any other method extracted in refactoring, it's not a change in logic, so it's already covered for TDD purposes by the original test. Even so, if the finder method winds up in a different class than the original method, it's often useful to transfer the test logic dealing with the scope to a test in the new class.

The pitfall you want to avoid when testing any database find behavior is testing the nature of the SQL call to the database rather than testing

---

5. In Rails 2, you would write these as named_scopes, which allows them to be composed the same way. You can use scopes in Rails 3, but the composable nature of all ActiveModel queries makes that less necessary.

the results of the call. In other words, it's not all that hard to extract the parameters the named scope object is going to use to contact the database. However, only testing that your method winds up with {:active => true} as its find parameters actually doesn't help you any. Just testing the parameters says nothing about the actual database behavior, and it's the actual behavior that you are normally looking to validate.

The following method can be helpful; it can be used to test any method that extracts a set of records from the database (which means that it doesn't help testing methods that just affect, say, the output sort order). This method is in Shoulda syntax and takes the finder method under test as a symbol, any arguments that get passed to the method, and then a block:

huddle/test/test_helper.rb

```
Line 1  def self.should_match_find_method(named_scope, *args, &block)
          should "match a find method #{named_scope}" do
            ar_class = self.class.model_class
            found_objects = ar_class.send(named_scope, *args)
     5      assert !found_objects.blank?
            found_objects.each do |obj|
              assert block.call(obj)
            end

    10      unfound_objects = ar_class.all - found_objects
            assert !unfound_objects.blank?
            unfound_objects.each do |obj|
              assert !block.call(obj)
            end
    15    end
        end
```

This code does three things. First, in line 3 and line 4, it extracts the model class being tested and calls the find method on that model class, resulting in a set of instances of that model. Then in lines 5–8, each instance in the list of matching objects is tested against the block and must return true for the test to pass. Just as importantly, lines 11–14 run the block against all the instances that weren't returned by the method and assert that the block is false for each one.

A sample usage of this test might look like this—notice that the test is a class-level method that assumes the user population has already been created in setup:

```
setup :create_users

def create_users
  active_user = User.create(:active => true)
  inactive_user = User.create(:inactive => true)
end

should_match_find_method :active_only { :active == true }
```

This test verifies that the named scope correctly sorts the universe of users into active and inactive groups. You don't need to create dozens and dozens of user objects for this test to work—you just need at least one in each category. Creating extra objects just slows the test down. A nice feature of this test style is that the test will be relatively robust against new objects being created. For example, if you also have fixture data in your tests, any new users created in fixtures will simply be split into the correct group and validated. The test will continue to pass.

5.6 Coming Up Next

Rails unit tests are not the only important part of testing data. Over the remaining chapters in this part, we'll compare fixture data against factory data and see when you might use one or the other. We'll show how to use mock objects to test parts of your application that might otherwise be hard to reach. And we'll cover some tricky kinds of data, such as date and times, that isn't fully test-covered.

## Chapter 6

Creating Model Test Data with Fixtures and Factories

One of the most valuable ways in which Ruby on Rails supports automated testing is through the use of easily created data that is accessible to all the tests in your system, no matter when or where you write those tests. It's sometimes hard for an experienced Rails programmer to remember just how exciting the YAML fixtures used to seem. You can just set up data once? In an easy format? And it's always there? Amazing.

Over time, the infatuation with fixtures dims a bit, but fixtures are still a quick and easy way to get data into your tests. In this chapter, we'll discuss how to use fixtures, and then we'll discuss the problems with fixtures. Many of the shortcomings with fixtures have been addressed by a variety of tools that use the *factory* pattern to create data objects. We'll discuss those factory tools and how using them differs from using fixtures.

6.1 Defining Fixture Data

A *fixture* is the baseline, or fixed state, known to exist at the beginning of a test. The existence of a fixed state makes it possible to write tests that make assumptions based on that particular set of data. In Rails, the fixtures that are available out of the box are defined in a set of YAML files that are automatically converted to ActiveRecord objects and loaded for each test.

Under normal circumstances, each model in your application will have an associated fixture file. The fixture file is in YAML format, a data-description format often used as an easier-to-type alternative to XML.[1] The details of YAML syntax are both way outside the scope of this book and largely irrelevant to fixtures—YAML contains a number of advanced features that don't need to concern us here.

Each entry in a fixture file starts with an identifier for that entry, followed by the attributes for that entry. This sample contains two entries for a hypothetical User class and would go in test/fixtures/users.yml:

```
Line 1   fred:
     2     first_name: Fred
     3     last_name: Flintstone
     4     email: fflint@slaterockandgravel.com
     5
     6   barney:
     7     first_name: Barney
     8     last_name: Rubble
     9     email: brubble@slaterockandgravel.com/
```

YAML syntax is somewhat reminiscent of Python, both in the colon used to separate key/value pairs (also a feature of Ruby 1.9) and in the use of indentation to mark the bounds of each entry. The fact that line 6, barney:, is outdented two spaces indicates to the YAML parser that a new entry has begun. Strings do not need to be enclosed in quotation marks, although it doesn't hurt if you find it more readable.[2] A multiline string can be specified by putting a pipe character (|) on the line with the attribute name. The multiline string can then be written over the next set of lines; each line must be indented relative to the line with the attribute name. Once again, outdenting indicates the end of the string.

```
fred:
  first_name: Fred
  last_name: Flintstone
  description: |
    Fred is very tall.
    He is not very small.
```

The Rails fixture creation process uses information in your database to coerce the values to the proper type. I write dates in SQL format (yyyy-mm-dd), though any format readable by Ruby's Date.parse() will work.

---

1. YAML stands for Yet Another Markup Language, which you probably figured out already.
2. Quotation marks are necessary around a string if the YAML parser would find the string ambiguous, such as if the string itself contains a colon followed by a space.

The identifier that introduces each record is then used to access the individual fixture entry within your tests. Assuming that this is the User class, you'd be able to retrieve these entries throughout your test suite as users(:fred) and users(:barney), respectively. Unless you like trying to figure out what's special about users(:user_10), I recommend meaningful entry names, especially for entries that expose special cases: users(:user_with_no_first_name).

An older mechanism for allowing access to fixtures as instance variables (in this case, @fred and @barney) can be turned on by setting self.use_instantiated_fixtures = true in the test/test_helper.rb file. This style is largely deprecated; it's rather slow, and when all fixtures are loaded, it requires all your fixture entries to have different names across all classes. The feature is still there, however, and you might occasionally see it used in (really) old legacy code.

Unlike the normal way of creating ActiveRecord models, the YAML data is converted to a database record directly, without going through the normal ActiveRecord creation methods. (To be clear, when you use the data in your tests, those are ActiveRecord models—only the original creation of the data to the database bypasses ActiveRecord.) This means you can't use arbitrary methods of the model as attributes in the fixture the way you can in a create() call. Fixture attributes have to be either actual database columns or ActiveRecord associations explicitly defined in the model. Removing a database column from your model and forgetting to take it out of the fixtures is a good way to have every single one of your tests error out. The fixture loading mechanism also bypasses any validations you have created on your ActiveRecord, meaning that there is no way to guarantee the validity of fixture data on load, short of explicitly testing each fixture yourself.

You do not need to specify the id for a fixture (although you can if you want). If you do not specify an id explicitly, the id is generated for you based on the YAML identifier name of the entry. If you allow Rails to generate these ids, then you get a side benefit: an easier way of specifying relationships between fixture objects. If your models have a relationship with models in another fixture file, the other object can be referenced using the name of the relationship and the identifier of the YAML entry in the other file. In other words, if we have a company.yml with this:

```
slate:
  name: SlateCo
```

and we also have a user model that belongs_to: company, then we can do the following in our user.yml file:

```
fred:
  first_name: Fred
  last_name: Flintstone
  company: slate
```

If the relationship is has_many, the multiple values in the relationship can be specified as a comma-delimited list. This is true even if the two objects are in a has_and_belongs_to_many relationship via a join table, although a has_many :through relationship does need to have the join model entry explicitly specified.

```
fred:
  first_name: Fred
  last_name: Flintstone
  company: slate
  roles: miner, digger, dino_wrangler
```

This is very handy and a vast improvement over the older functionality, where all the id columns had to be explicitly filled with the id number of the other model.

Fixture files are also interpreted as ERb files, which means you can have dynamic attributes like this:

```
fred:
  last_login_time: <%= 5.days.ago %>
```

Or you can specify multiple entries dynamically, like this:

```
<% 10.times do |i| %>
task_<%=i%>:
  name: "Task <%= i %>"
<% end %>
```

In the second case, notice that the identifier still needs to be at the leftmost column; you can't indent the inside of the block the way that normal Ruby style would suggest.

6.2 Loading Fixture Data

Fixture loading is covered by a few parameters that have default values, which are set in the test/test_helper.rb file. The most important is the fixtures :all method call, which ensures that all your fixture files are loaded in all your tests. Back in the day,[3] the prevailing style was to

---

3. In other words, Rails 1.x. You know, 2006.

declare which fixtures needed to be loaded in each individual test file. That got to be annoying once your models were intertwined enough to need to load bunches of them in each test file, so in the fullness of time, loading all fixtures all the time became the default. (Speculating wildly, this was about the same time that transactional fixtures were added, minimizing the performance cost of loading all that data.)

By default, fixtures are loaded just once, and every test method takes place inside a database transaction. At the end of the test method, the transaction is rolled back, and the initial fixture state is thereby restored. This dramatically reduces test time[4] unless your database doesn't support transactions (most likely because you are using MySQL with MyISAM tables).

Fixture transactions are also a problem if you are actually trying to test transactional behavior in your application, in which case the fixture transaction will overwhelm the transaction you are trying to test. If you need less aggressive transaction behavior, you can go into the test/test_helper.rb file and change the value in the assignment self.use_transactional_fixtures = true to false. That will change the value for all tests, but you can also override the value on a class-by-class basis by including the assignment (set to false) in your individual class. There's no way to change this behavior to be fine-grained enough to use the nontransactional behavior for only a single method.

6.3 Why Fixtures Are a Pain

As great as fixtures are when you are starting out, using them long-term on complex projects exposes problems. Here are some things to keep an eye on.

Fixtures Are Global

There is only one set of fixtures in a default Rails application. So, the temptation to keep adding new data points to the fixture set every time you need a corner case is pretty much overwhelming. The problem is that every time you add a user because you need to test what happens when a left-handed user sends a message to another user with a friend relationship who happens to live in Fiji, or whatever oddball scenario you need, every other test has to deal with that data point being part of the test data.

---

4. I almost wrote "This is super-nifty" but decided that wasn't professional enough.

Fixtures Are Spread Out

Fixtures live in their own directory, and each model has its own fixture file. That's fine, until you start needing to manage connections and a simple setup of a user commenting on a post related to a given article quickly spans across four different fixture files, with no easy way to trace the relationships. I'm a big fan of "small and plentiful" over "large and few" when it comes to code structure, but even I find fixtures too spread out.

Fixtures Are Distant

If you are doing a complex test based on the specific fixture lineup, you'll often wind up with the end data being based on the fixture setup in such a way that, when reading the test, it's not clear exactly how the final value is derived. You need to go back to the fixture files to understand the calculation.

Fixtures Are Brittle

Of course, once you add that left-handed user to your fixture set, you're guaranteed to break any test that depends on the exact makeup of the entire user population—tests for searching and reporting are notorious culprits here. There aren't many more effective ways to kill your team's enthusiasm for testing like having to fix twenty-five tests on the other side of the world every time you add new sample data.

Sounds grim, right? It's not. Not only are fixtures perfectly suitable for simple projects, the Rails community has responded to the weaknesses of fixtures by creating factory tools that can replace fixtures in creating test data.

6.4 Using Factories to Fix Fixtures

The goals of a fixture replacement system are to take the three largest problems with fixtures—they are global, spread out, and brittle—and turn them into strengths. We want the system to be the following:

- *Local*: Each individual test should have its setup data tuned to the needs of that test. The setup data should be defined as closely as possible to the actual test.
- *Compact*: The setup data should be easy and quick to generate; otherwise, lazy programmers (like me) just won't do it. It should be possible to generate a complex network of objects in just a few lines.

- *Robust*: Tests should not be dependent on changes made to setup data in other tests. We should even be able to specify more data in the current test without breaking other tests.

Generically, the answer to the fixture problem is a *data factory*.

6.5 Data Factories

The idea behind a data factory is that rather than specifying all the test data exactly, you provide a blueprint for creating a sample instance of your model. When you need data for a specific test, you call a factory method, which gives you an element based on your blueprint. You can override the blueprint to specify any data attributes required to make your test work out. Calling the factory method is simple enough to make it feasible to set up a useful amount of data in each test.

The original factory tool was Scott Taylor's FixtureReplacement (http://replacefixtures.rubyforge.org/). More recently, the ThoughtBot team behind Shoulda and other great tools provided factory_girl (http://github.com/thoughtbot/factory_girl/tree/master). I also like Pete Yandell's Machinist (http://github.com/notahat/machinist/tree/master).

The basic structure of all three tools is similar. Each gives you a syntax to create the factory blueprints and an API for creating the new objects. Both factory_girl and Machinist also provide a mechanism for creating unique streams of values according to a pattern, while FixtureReplacement has the most flexible creation syntax.

This chapter will use factory_girl as the primary example of how factory tools work. Specifically, we'll be using factory_girl 2.0, which is in beta as I write this. I've picked factory_girl because it's clearly emerged as the mindshare leader among these tools and the 2.0 beta because I like the streamlined syntax choices in 2.0. Machinist, also in a 2.0 beta cycle, has very similar syntax and structure, while factory_girl 1.3 is similar in functionality but with a more verbose syntax.

6.6 Installing factory_girl

To install factory_girl in a Rails 3 project, you should install the factory_girl_rails gem by placing the following in your Gemfile:

```
gem 'factory_girl_rails'
```

However, if you are trying to install factory_girl while 2.0 is still in beta, there's a little bit of a version hiccup at the moment, because the factory_girl_rails gem is tied to version 1.3. Luckily, there are some forks of the factory_girl_rails gem that just update its gem dependencies. For example:

```
gem 'factory_girl_rails',
    :git => "http://github.com/CodeMonkeySteve/factory_girl_rails.git"
```

All this should work itself out when factory_girl 2.0 becomes official.

If you're working in a Rails 2.*x* application, you can just do the following:

```
gem 'factory_girl'
```

Or, while factory_girl 2.0 is still in beta, you need to get the beta directly from GitHub, since the Rails-only extensions are specific to Rails 3.

```
gem 'factory_girl',
    :git => 'http://github.com/thoughtbot/factory_girl.git'
```

In Rails 3, factory_girl automatically loads if installed. Factory files with the following names are automatically loaded: test/factories.rb, spec/factories.rb, test/factories/*.rb, spec/factories/*.rb. Factories defined any other place need to be explicitly required into the program.

6.7 Creating and Using Simple Factories

All the definitions of your factories go inside a call to FactoryGirl.define(), which takes a block. Inside that block, factories can be declared to define default data. The factory takes a block in which you can define default values on an attribute-by-attribute basis.

A very simple example for our Huddle network might look like this; each attribute has a simple default value. We'll get to associations in a moment. By default, the blueprints go in test/factories.rb.

```
FactoryGirl.define do
  factory :project do
    name "Dog Meet Dog Dot Com"
    start_date Date.parse("2009-01-23")
  end
end
```

Note the absence of equals signs—these are not assignments. Technically, they are function calls, so if it makes it more readable to write the lines like name("Dog Meet Dog Dot Com"), go for it.

In the previous factory, all the values are static and determined when the factory file is loaded. If you want a dynamic value to be determined when an individual factory object is created, just pass a block instead of a value; the block will be evaluated when each new factory is called.

```
FactoryGirl.define do
  factory :project do
    name "Dog Meet Dog Dot Com"
    start_date { Date.today - rand(50) }
  end
end
```

You can also refer to a previously assigned value later in the factory, which is where these factories start to get powerful:

```
FactoryGirl.define do
  factory :project do
    name "Dog Meet Dog Dot Com"
    url { "#{name.downcase.gsub!(" ", "_")}" }
  end
end
```

What's nice about this is that the factory will still use the value in the name attribute to calculate the URL, even if you pass the name in yourself:

```
test "factory girl url" do
  soup = Factory.create(:project, :name => "Soups Online")
  assert_equal("soups_online", soup.url)
end
```

Inside the factory, you can call any attribute in the model that has a setter method; in other words, any virtual attribute in the model (like the password attribute of a Devise User model) is fair game.

You can use this factory in several different ways. The most common is to use the Factory.create() method.

```
setup do
  @project = Factory.create(:project)
end
```

This call to create() creates a Project instance using the default values defined in the factories file and saves it to the database. Validations on your ActiveRecord model will be called. (To be specific, factory_girl will call save!() on the object before it is returned.)

factory_girl provides three other build strategies that you can use if you don't want to actually save a new record to the database. If you want a real ActiveRecord instance, just not saved, call Factory.build(:project). The call Factory.attributes_for(:project) does not create an ActiveRecord object; it just returns a hash of the attributes defined by the factory. This is useful for use simulating an HTTP POST call in a controller test. You can also try Factory.stub(:project), which returns an object where the attributes are created as stubs. If you use the stub version, then any call that attempts to access the database via that object, for example, a call to save(), will result in an error.

Under normal circumstances, factory_girl considers create() to be the default and provides the shortcut Factory(:project). You can change the default strategy on a class-by-class basis, but I don't recommend it; the readability confusion isn't worth the slightly briefer syntax.

When you call a factory, you can override any of the default values by passing a hash to the factory_girl creation method, like so:

```
setup do
  @project = Factory.create(:project, :name => "Soups Online")
  @other_project = Factory.create(:project, :name => "Google Thumbnail")
end
```

6.8 Sequencing for Unique Attributes

Often you need to have a value in your factory that is unique, even if you specify several objects. Email addresses are a common example, since many applications will require an email address to be unique in order to validate them. While you could explicitly specify an email address every time you call your User factory, that's an error-prone pain in the neck. You can avoid this problem in factory_girl with *sequences*.

Declaring a sequence is simple. A sequence is defined inside the main FactoryGirl block and takes one argument that is incremented each time the sequence is invoked.

```
FactoryGirl.define do
  sequence :name do |n|
    "Project_#{n}"
  end
end
```

The sequence can be referred to explicitly:

```
factory :project do
  name { Factory.next(:name) }
  url { "#{name.downcase.gsub!(" ", "_")}" }
end
```

But if the attribute has the same name as the sequence, factory_girl provides an implicit shortcut:

```
factory :project do
  name
  url { "#{name.downcase.gsub!(" ", "_")}" }
end
```

If the sequence is used in only one place, you can declare it inside the factory definition where it is used.

```
factory :project do
  sequence(:name) { |n| "Project_#{n}" }
  url { "#{name.downcase.gsub!(" ", "_")}" }
end
```

6.9 Freedom of Association

It's easy to specify related objects in your factories. In this example, the factory for the Project class calls the User factory to create the associated object by explicitly noting that the user is an association. (In a one-to-many relationship, you probably want to do this from the belongs_to() side. In a many-to-many relationship, it doesn't matter what side creates the items.) However, you do need to make sure that only one side of the relationship creates items; otherwise, you can get a circular dependency and a stack-too-deep exception. This example also uses the Faker gem (http://faker.rubyforge.org/) to generate random structured data.

```
factory :user do
  first_name { Faker::Name.first_name }
  last_name { Faker::Name.last_name }
end

factory :project do
  name "Dog Meet Dog Dot Com"
  association :user, :factory => :user
end
```

You can specify values for the subordinate object by adding them to the end of the association() call just like any other factory_girl factory invocation. In this snippet, every user created from a project association will have the first name Noel.

```
factory :project do
  name "Dog Meet Dog Dot Com"
  association :user, :factory => :user, :first_name => "Noel"
end
```

If the factory name and the association name match, the factory can be left off:

```
factory :project do
  name "Dog Meet Dog Dot Com"
  association :user
end
```

If you are following Rails conventions and the model name matches the attribute name in the expected way, the factory can be simplified even further:

```
factory :project do
  name "Dog Meet Dog Dot Com"
  user
end
```

In either case, creating a Project object via factory_girl implicitly creates, verifies, and saves a User object. As with regular attributes, the value of the associated object is available for later attribute blocks:

```
factory :project do
  name "Dog Meet Dog Dot Com"
  user
  label { "#{user.first_name}'s project"}
end
```

You can pass in your own associated object just as with any other attribute defined in the factory. This is how you can create multiple sibling objects:

```
setup do
  me = Factory(:user, :first_name => "Noel",
      :last_name => "Rappin")
  my_project = Factory(:project, :user => me)
  my_other_project= Factory(:project,
      :name => "Soups Online", :user => me)
end
```

If you don't want the related object to be created, you need to explicitly set the object to nil when calling make():

```
Factory(:project, :user => nil)
```

You'll often find yourself wanting to create multiple factories from the same class. Users representing different roles or different classes of products...that kind of thing. You can specify a class name that is different from the factory name rather easily using the class option.

```
factory :cool_project, :class => Project do
  «»
end
```

You can also have one factory inherit from another factory, which keeps you from having to specify common default values in each factory.

```
factory :project do
  name "Dog Meet Dog Dot Com"
  user
  label { "#{user.first_name}'s project"}
end

factory :cool_project, :parent => :project do
  label { "A really nifty project" }
end
```

In this snippet, the cool_project factory also has a default user and a default name of "Dog Meet Dog Dot Com." Personally, I don't find the duplication of attributes to be onerous enough to justify the loss of readability—imagine that the project and cool_project factories are 300 lines apart in the factory file and trying to trace where the name value comes from.

Finally, factory_girl allows you to specify an arbitrary action after the factory is called by defining a callback method, either after_build(), after_create(), or after_stub(). These methods take a block and are called after the factory is invoked with the given build strategy, although calling a factory with create() will invoke both the after_build() and after_create() callbacks. The callback blocks take an optional argument, which is the fully created factory object.

6.10 Factories of the World Unite: Preventing Factory Abuse

The temptation when converting a project from fixtures to factories is to replicate your entire fixture setup from factory objects. You will get some benefits: the factory object will probably be easier to read and maintain than the fixtures were, and all your existing tests will pass. However, the factory tests will probably be significantly slower than transactional fixtures, and you still have the problem of global, faraway data definitions—though at least with factories, new tests can avoid using the global data.

The way to use factories is to create less data for each test. Create only the smallest amount of data needed to expose the issue in each test. This practice speeds up the test, makes the issue easy to see rather than burying it among dozens of fixtures, and makes the correctness of the test itself easier to verify.

Factories and RESTful Authentication

The RESTful Authentication gem, which is commonly used for managing user logins, has a couple of mild testing gotchas when using factories.

First, the UserTest class generated by RESTful Authentication contains a private method called create_user(). If you are using FixtureReplacement, that's a name crash with the user-generation method automatically created from your User class blueprint. In this case, you can change the name of the method in the UserTest class, adjust the tests that call it, and move on from there.

More generally, RESTful Authentication provides test user accounts as fixtures. If you are truly going to avoid fixtures and you are using an older version of RESTful Authentication, then you may run into a problem with the login_as() method provided by RESTful Authentication and used throughout tests to set up a logged-in user. The login_as() method expects to take a symbol and look up the user data using the fixture-based users(:symbol)() method. Even if you convert the RESTful Authentication fixture data to a factory-based setup method (useful if only because the RESTful Authentication accounts have known, encrypted passwords), you still need to change the login_as() method in lib/authenticated_test_helper.rb to take an actual User object rather than a symbol:

```
def login_as(user)
  @request.session[:user_id] = user ? user.id : nil
end
```

You can then use this with your factories with code like this:

```
setup do
  login_as(User.make(:role => "admin"))
end
```

6.11 Managing Date and Time Data

Calendar logic has a well-deserved reputation as one of the most annoying parts of a program that doesn't actually involve Unicode. Testing calendar logic—time-based reports, automatic logouts, "1 day ago" text displays—can be a headache, but there are a couple of things you can do to simplify the time logic beast.

You're Doing It Wrong

Picture this. You've got a YAML file with some projects:

```
runway:
  name: Project Runway
  start_date: 2010-01-20

greenlight:
  name: Project Greenlight
  start_date: 2010-02-04

gutenberg:
  name: Project Gutenberg
  start_date: 2010-01-31
```

You'd like to test some time-based code, like might be used in a search or report result; this goes in test/unit/project_test.rb:

```
test "reports based on start date" do
  actual = Project.find_started_in_last(6.months)
  assert_equal(3, actual.size)
end
```

Here's the code that makes the test pass, from app/models/project.rb:

```
def self.find_started_in_last(time_span)
  old_time = Date.today - time_span
  all(:conditions => ["start_date > ?", old_time.to_s(:db)])
end
```

On January 20, 2010, the test passes. And on the 21st it will pass, and the day after....

Six months from now, though, on about June 20th, when you've probably long forgotten about this test, this data, and maybe even this project, the test will suddenly fail. And you'll spend way too much time trying to figure out what happened, until you remember the date issue and realize that the January 20th project has moved out of the six-month time span specified in the test. Of course, changing all the dates just pushes the problem forward and gives you time to forget all about it again.

This issue may sound silly to some, but like many of the more ridiculous examples in the book, this is a mistake that happened to me and can end up costing a lot of time.

Long ago, when I was young and foolish, I solved this problem by adding an optional argument to just about every method that used Date.today(), allowing an optional time to be passed to the method and allowing an explicit date to be used for testing. This was way more work than was actually needed, so here are a couple of better ideas.

Relative Dates in Fixtures

As mentioned in Section 2.7, *More Info: Getting Data into the Test*, on page 29, fixture files are evaluated as ERb files before loading. For our purposes, that's helpful because it allows us to specify dates dynamically, like so:

```
runway:
  name: Project Runway
  start_date: <%= Date.today - 1.month %>

greenlight:
  name: Project Greenlight
  start_date: <%= Date.today - 1.week %>

gutenberg:
  name: Project Gutenberg
  start_date: <%= Date.today - 1.day %>
```

With fixtures written like this, the previous test will always work, since the start_date of the projects will never fall out of the six-month range. (If you are using a factory tool instead of fixtures, you can do something similar in your factory blueprint.)

Although this technique works quite well for keeping test data a consistent relative distance from the test time, it's less helpful if you are actually trying to test the exact value of one of the dates—when testing, say, output display. With the first, static set of fixture data, you could write the following:

```
test "that project dates are displayed in this goofy format" do
  assert_equal("2010 1 January", projects(:runway).goofy_start_date)
end
```

This test is a lot more difficult to write if you don't explicitly know the value of the project's start_date. But keep reading.

Explicit Timestamps

One trick worth mentioning when testing dates is explicitly setting the created_at attribute of your ActiveRecord model. Normally, created_at is a timestamp automatically generated by Rails, and it's often used for the kind of time-based reporting alluded to in the rest of this section. Since it's automatically created at the current time, you can get into some weird situations if other dates are specified in the past. Even without that complication, you may still need to explicitly set created_at to use the attribute to test time-based features.

You can set created_at in the fixture file, just like any other attribute, or it can be specified in ActiveRecord::create() or ActiveRecord::new(), specified in a factory blueprint, or just plain reset with an assignment or update method.

Setting updated_at is trickier. Under normal circumstances, if you try to explicitly set updated_at, Rails will just automatically reset it on save, which completely defeats the purpose. To change this behavior, set the class variable Model.record_timetamps = false sometime before you save the object with modified update time. Instead of Model, use the model class that is actually being saved. After the save, reset things to normal with Model.record_timestamps = true.*

*. See http://www.neeraj.name/blog/articles/800-override-automatic-timestamp-in-activerecrod-rails for some ways to make this call a little friendlier using Ruby Eigenclasses.

Timecop

Recently, I've been solving my time problems with the help of a nice little gem called Timecop written by John Trupiano, which you can find at http://github.com/jtrupiano/timecop. Timecop can be placed in your Bundler Gemfile with the traditional gem "timecop".

Timecop is essentially a super-specific mock object package: it stubs out Date.today(), DateTime.now(), and Time.now(), allowing you to explicitly set the effective date for your tests. Using Timecop, the original test could be rewritten as follows:

```
test "reports based on start date" do
  Timecop.freeze(Date.parse("2010-02-10"))
  actual = Project.find_started_in_last(6.months)
  assert_equal(3, actual.size)
end
```

The Timecop.freeze() command stubs the current date and time methods back to the date passed as the argument—in this case, February 10, 2010. Time does not move for the duration of the test. A separate method, Timecop.travel(), resets the time but lets the system time move forward from that point onward.

Why both options? It's because keeping time constant for the life of a test makes the test environment more consistent. (For example, RESTful Authentication has an intermittent test failure if the time rolls over in just the right way during one test.) But sometimes, it is necessary for time to move forward, so Timecop offers both options. Along those lines, it's sometimes useful to put the following line in a setup method:

```
Timecop.freeze(Date.today)
```

with the following line in a teardown block:

```
Timecop.return
```

Why? It ensures that the current time doesn't change for the duration of each test. Again, with certain kinds of timing-related issues, that consistency eliminates a possible source of intermittent test failures or just plain confusion.

The argument to freeze() or travel() is an instance of Date, DateTime, Time, or a series of arguments of the form (year, month, day, hour=0, minute=0, second=0). Both methods also take blocks such that the fake time is good only for the duration of the block:

```
test "reports based on start date" do
  Timecop.freeze(Date.parse("2010-02-10")) do
    actual = Project.find_started_in_last(6.months)
    assert_equal(3, actual.size)
  end
end
```

The time travel methods can be in your setup or in an individual test. You can also change the time in the middle of a test to speed up an ongoing process:

```
test "is the project over" do
  p = Project.new(:start_date => Date.today,
      :end_date = Date.today + 8.weeks)
  assert !p.complete?
  Timecop.freeze(Date.today + 10.weeks)
  assert p.complete?
end
```

Timecop lets you keep explicit dates in your test data without causing problems later. The only downside is that if you have many tests setting time to different days, it can get somewhat confusing in the aggregate. It's easier if you use the same start date consistently. (On a solo project, you might use your birthday, for instance, but that's probably overly cute for a team project.) A more minor problem is that the line at the end of your test runs that says how long the test suite took will be hopelessly messed up because of the continued messing with Time.now.

Comparing Dates and Times

Ruby, not content with a simple date and time system, has three separate classes that manage date and time data. The Time class is a thin wrapper around the same Unix C library that pretty much every language exposes. (Motto: "Annoying programmers since 1983!") There are also the Ruby-specific classes Date and DateTime, which are more flexible and have a more coherent API but are slower.

For testing purposes, the relevant points are that ActiveRecord uses Date and DateTime, depending on the specifics of the underlying database column; comparing a Date to a DateTime instance will always fail (as will trying to add or subtract them), and most of the Rails ActiveSupport methods (think 5.days.ago) return DateTime.

In testing, this can lead to a lot of annoying failures, especially when you have a Date column with no time information—which is recommended if the time is not important.

In general, it's a good idea to compare dates and times by converting them using to_s(:db). It avoids the irritating question of object equality, and you tend to get more readable tests and error messages. When the exact time of the time object is in question, try to force the issue by using the Rails ActiveSupport methods to_date(), to_time(), and to_datetime(). Most commonly, this means something like 5.days.ago.to_date.to_s(:db), which may read a touch on the awkward side but is a robust test with a decent error message on failure.

6.12 Model Data Summary

To sum up, Rails provides fixtures as an exceptionally simple way to create a set of test data that can be shared across multiple tests. However, fixtures are so simple that they tend to not be adaptable to more complex product needs. Factory tools, which take a little bit more initial setup, allow for more flexibility in use at some cost in test performance. The two structures don't have to be mutually exclusive. One pattern for combining them is to create exactly one complex scenario in fixtures for use in integration or complex controller tests and to use factories for unit tests or simpler controller tests.

Fixtures and factory tools allow you to get test data into your database in order to create a known baseline for testing. However, in some cases, you may not want to actually place data in the database. Using the database from a test may be undesirable for performance reasons, for philosophical reasons (some people don't consider it reasonable to touch the database in a "unit" test), or where logistical reasons make objects hard to create. In the next chapter, we'll explore mock objects, which allow tests to proceed by faking not the data but rather the actual method calls that produce the data.

## Chapter 7

Using Mock Objects

A *mock object* is a "fake" object used in place of a "real" object for the purposes of automated testing. A mock might be used when the real object is unavailable or difficult to access from a test environment—a common example is an external credit-card payment system. A mock might also be used to easily re-create a specific application state that would be otherwise difficult to trigger in a test environment, like a database or network failure. Mocks can be used strategically to limit the scope of a test to the object and method specifically under test. Used in that manner, mocks drive a different style of testing, where the test is verifying the behavior of the system during the test, rather than the state of the system at the end of the test.

7.1 What's a Mock Object?

One complicating factor in dealing with mock objects is that pretty much everybody who creates a mock framework feels perfectly free to use slightly different naming conventions than everybody else. Here are the names that I use, which are—of course—also the correct ones.[1]

The generic term for any object used as a stand-in for another object is *test double*, by analogy to "stunt double," and with the same connotation of a cheaper or more focused replacement for a more expensive real object. Colloquially, *mock object* is also used as the generic term but—confusingly—is also the name of a specific type of test double.

---

1. Actually, I believe this naming structure is the creation of Gerard Meszaros in *xUnit Test Patterns* [Mes07].

A *stub* is a fake object that returns a predetermined value for a method call without calling the actual object. We can create a stub as follows (this uses the Ruby gem Mocha, but you don't need to worry about the exact syntax just yet):

```
thing.stubs(:name).returns("Fred")
```

That line of code says that if you call thing.name, you'll get Fred as a result. Crucially, the actual thing.name method is not touched, so whatever value the "real" method would return is not relevant; the Fred response comes from the stub, not the actual object. If thing.name is not called in the test, nothing happens.

A *mock* is similar to a stub, but in addition to returning the fake value, a mock object also sets a testable expectation that the method being replaced will actually be called in the test. If the method is not called, the mock object triggers a test failure. So, when you write the following snippet to create a mock object instead of a stub:

```
thing.expects(:name).returns("Fred")
```

then if you call thing.name in your test, you still get Fred, and the actual thing.name method is still untouched. But if you don't call thing.name in the test, the test fails with what's generally called a MockExpectationError, or some such.

In other words, setting a stub on a method is passive and just says, "Ignore the real implementation of this method and return this value," while setting a mock on a method is more aggressive and says, "This method will return this value, and you better call the method, *or else!*"

The reason you might set such an expectation is that once you've stubbed the method, it makes no sense to write an assertion on it like this one:

```
thing.stubs(:name).returns("Fred")
assert_equal "Fred", thing.name
```

In this case, you're just testing that the stub works as advertised—this test can't fail. But if you use the mock:

```
thing.expects(:name).returns("Fred")
```

then your code actually has to behave a certain way to pass the test.

One of the nice side effects of Ruby's openness and metaprogramming functionality is that mock object libraries are easier to write and have more flexibility and power than similar libraries in other languages

(Java, I'm looking at you...). There are at least four widely used Ruby mock packages as I write this. All have broadly similar features with slight differences in emphasis and syntax. FlexMock (http://flexmock. rubyforge.org/) is the oldest though less commonly used these days. Mocha (http://mocha.rubyforge.org/) is in use by the Rails core team in integration testing. Double Ruby (http://github.com/btakita/rr/tree/master) is a newer library with perhaps a cleaner syntax and a couple of unique features. Finally, RSpec has its own mock library (discussed in Chapter 12, *RSpec*, on page 183), although it allows you to use any of the other three if you want.

In the absence of any compelling constituency for any of these three, we'll use Mocha in these examples, on the grounds that it's pretty close to actually being part of core Rails. However, in Section 7.7, *Comparing Mock Object Libraries*, on page 112, we'll compare and contrast the syntax of the various mock frameworks.

Thus ends the blathering. Here's how you actually use the things.

Install Mocha as a gem using gem install mocha or gem 'mocha' in a Bundler file). To use Mocha, place the following:

```
require 'mocha'
```

in any test file that will need it or in test/test_helper.rb.

7.2 Stubs

Although basically similar, stubs and mocks fit into the pattern of your tests very differently. It is easier to start by describing stubs. A stub is a replacement for all or part of an object that prevents a normal method call from happening and instead returns a value that is preset when the stub is created.

In Mocha, you can create an object that exists only as a set of stubbed methods by using the stub() method, which is available throughout your test cases. Since Ruby uses duck typing and therefore cares only whether objects respond to the messages sent to them, a stub object created in such a way can be injected into your application as a replacement for a real object.

```
test "here's a sample stub" do
  stubby = stub(:name => "Paul", :weight => 100)
  assert_equal("Paul", stubby.name)
end
```

The hash arguments to stub() list the methods that the stubbed object responds to and the values returned. So, the assertion in the second line is true because the stub has been preset to respond to the name message with "Paul." If you call the stub with a method that is not in the hash argument, Mocha will return an error. However, Mocha provides the stub_everything() method, which instead returns nil for methods not in the hash argument. Using stub_everything() makes sense in the case where there are a large number of potential methods to be stubbed, but where the values make so little difference that specifying them reduces the readability of the test.

In case it's not clear, this test is a very stupid way to use stubs; I've set up a nice little tautology, and I haven't actually learned anything about any larger system around this test.

You would use a bare stub object to stand in for an object that is unavailable or prohibitively expensive to create or call in the test environment. In Ruby, though, you would more often take advantage of the way Ruby allows you to open up existing classes and objects for the purposes of adding or overriding methods. It's easy to take a "real" object and stub out only the methods that you need. This is extraordinarily useful when it comes to actual uses of stub objects.

In Mocha, this is managed with the stubs() method, which is mixed in to any Ruby object:

huddle_mocha/test/unit/project_test.rb

```
Line 1   test "lets stub an object" do
     2     stub_project = Project.new(:name => "Project Greenlight")
     3     stub_project.stubs(:name)
     4     assert_nil(stub_project.name)
     5   end
```

This test passes: line 3 sets up the stub, and the stub_project.name call in line 4 is intercepted by the stub to return nil and never even gets to the actual project name.

Having a stub that always returns nil is a little pointless, so Mocha allows you to specify a return value for the stubbed method using the following syntax:

huddle_mocha/test/unit/project_test.rb

```
Line 1   test "lets stub an object again" do
     2     stub_project = Project.new(:name => "Project Greenlight")
     3     stub_project.stubs(:name).returns("Fred")
     4     assert_equal("Fred", stub_project.name)
     5   end
```

Line 3 is doing the heavy lifting here, tying the return value Fred to the method :name. Technically, stubs() returns a Mocha Expectation object, which is effectively a proxy to the real object. The returns() method is a method of that Expectation object that associates the return value with the method.

Since classes in Ruby are really just objects themselves, you'd probably expect that you can stub classes just like stubbing instance objects. You'd be right:

```
huddle_mocha/test/unit/project_test.rb
```

```
Line 1  test "let's stub a class" do
     2    Project.stubs(:find).returns(Project.new(:name => "Project Greenlight"))
     3    project = Project.find(1)
     4    assert_equal("Project Greenlight", project.name)
     5  end
```

In this test, the class Project is being stubbed to return a specific project instance whenever find() is called. In line 3, the find() method returns that object via the stub when Project.find() is called.

Now we may be getting somewhere...you'll notice that this test uses the results of a find() method without actually touching the database. It's not hard to find Rails programmers who would consider the database to be prohibitively expensive to use in a test environment, and this is one—admittedly, over-simplified—strategy for avoiding it. Again, remember that this stub shouldn't be used to verify that the find() method works; it should be used by other tests that need the find() method along the way to the other logic that is actually under test.

There are a couple of advanced usages of returns() that might be interesting now and again. If you have multiple return values specified, the stubbed method returns them one at a time, as the following irb sessions shows:

```
>> stubby = Project.new
=> #<Project id: nil .... >
>> stubby.stubs(:user_count).returns(1, 2)
=> #<Mocha::Expectation:0x221e470... >, side_effects[]
>> stubby.user_count
=> 1
>> stubby.user_count
=> 2
>> stubby.user_count
=> 2
```

The return values of the stubbed method walk through the values passed to returns(). Note that the values don't cycle; the last value is repeated over and over again.[2]

You can get the same effect with a little more syntactic sugar by using the then() method—you can chain together as many of these as you want:

```
stubby.stubs(:user_count).returns(1).then.returns(2)
```

A very common use of stub objects is to simulate exception conditions. If you want your stubbed method to raise an exception, you can use the raises() method, which takes an exception class and an optional message:

```
stubby.stubs(:user_count).raises(Exception, "oops")
```

You can even chain returns() and raises():

```
stubby.stubs(:user_count).returns(1).then.raises(Exception)
```

Another common use case is if you want all instances of a class created during a test to respond to the same stub. This is managed with the class method any_instance(), followed by any returns() or raises() expectation you care to add. As in:

```
Project.any_instance.stubs(:save).returns(false)
```

With this little trick, you can rectify a nagging annoyance in the standard Rails scaffolds. As currently constituted (at least, as of this writing), the Rails-generated tests for a standard script/generate scaffold controller do not cover 100 percent of the controller methods. Specifically, the failure conditions for create() and update() are not covered. I've always assumed, with no real justification, this oversight was because the easiest way to test these is with a mock package, and the Rails team didn't want to mandate one particular package.[3]

Since we've already mandated a mock package, here are a couple of sample tests that use the any_instance() call to validate the error behavior for create() and edit().

---

2. For some reason, the Mocha RDoc says that returns([1, 2]) is the same as returns(1, 2)—not true, according to my testing. returns([1, 2]) returns the array [1, 2], and returns(1, 2) returns 1 and then 2 on successive calls.

3. Alternate possibility: they just figured it was too minor to care about.

This is for the Huddle Project class—you'll need a slight tweak for your own classes:

`huddle_mocha/test/functional/projects_controller_test.rb`

```
Line 1   test "fail create gracefully" do
           assert_no_difference('Project.count') do
             Project.any_instance.stubs(:save).returns(false)
             post :create, :project => {:name => 'Project Runway'}
   5         assert_template('new')
           end
         end

         test "fail update gracefully" do
  10         Project.any_instance.stubs(:update_attributes).returns(false)
             put :update, :id => projects(:huddle).id, :project => {:name => 'fred'}
             assert_template('edit')
             actual = Project.find(projects(:huddle).id)
             assert_not_equal('fred', actual.name)
  15       end
```

These two tests have the same basic format. The first command in each one sets an any_instance() expectation (lines 3 and 10); then the actual controller command is run (lines 4 and 11). After that, validation: first that the error-appropriate template is used (lines 5 and 12) and then that the actual creation or update did not take place. For create, that's the assert_no_difference() call validating that Product.count doesn't change, and for update, it's validating that the :name => 'fred' in the update form doesn't actually get sent to the database.

The truly sharp-eyed among you have probably realized that, while the create() version of this test needs to use any_instance() because the exact instance being created is not known at runtime, the update() version could, in fact, include a stub on project(:huddle).id, since that's the only instance under consideration, and its identity is known before the controller call. Fair point. In practice, though, there's no guarantee that the find() method in the controller will return the exact same object as is used in the test—it will most likely create a new instance that is a copy of the fixture data but loaded from the database. If so, a stub limited to the particular instance created in the test would not apply to the instance created in the controller. After we introduce with() in the next section, we'll see one potential hack/workaround for this issue.

A related gotcha to watch out for when using any_instance() is that a stub or mock declared via any_instance() applies only to instances that are created after the declaration. Specifically, Rails fixture objects, accessed via one of the special fixture methods like users(:fred) that have already been generated when the test starts will not reply to the stub or mock—the object needs to be re-created from the database for the double to apply.

In addition, the find() method call in line 13 is required in order to force a check all the way back to the database to see whether the database record is changed—you could get the same effect by calling reload() on projects(:huddle). Otherwise, changes made to the database won't have been reflected on the instance already created and in memory. And, last and perhaps most obviously, when you adapt this to your own classes, the form part of the call in line 11 needs to have attributes that are actually part of the class under consideration.

7.3 Stubs with Parameters

The next level in tuning the stub is to have it return different values based on the input parameters. In Mocha, this is managed using the with() method:

```
huddle_mocha/test/unit/project_test.rb
test "let's stub a class again" do
  Project.stubs(:find).with(1).returns(
      Project.new(:name => "Project Greenlight"))
  Project.stubs(:find).with(2).returns(
      Project.new(:name => "Project Blue Book"))
  assert_equal("Project Greenlight", Project.find(1).name)
  assert_equal("Project Blue Book", Project.find(2).name)
end
```

In its simplest form, shown in the previous example, the with() method takes one or more arguments. When the stub() method is called, Mocha searches for a match between the arguments passed and the declared stubs and returns the value matching those arguments.

One thing to be careful of is that by setting expectations tied to specific input values, you are limiting the Mocha stub to only those input values. In other words, if we were to try Project.find(3) in this test, the test would fail—which is a counterintuitive result for a stub. The failure triggers the following rather cryptic error message:

```
test_let's_stub_a_class_again(ProjectTest)
    [/test/unit/project_test.rb:43]:
unexpected invocation: Project(id: integer, name: string,
created_at: datetime, updated_at: datetime, start_date: date,
end_date: date).find(3)
satisfied expectations:
```

```
- allowed any number of times, already invoked once:
Project(id: integer, name: string, created_at: datetime,
updated_at: datetime, start_date: date, end_date: date).find(2)
- allowed any number of times, already invoked once:
Project(id: integer, name: string, created_at: datetime,
updated_at: datetime, start_date: date, end_date: date).find(1)
```

The guts of this message will perhaps be a little clearer after we've discussed mocks a little bit more, but the gist is simple: we did something Mocha didn't expect, and Mocha doesn't like surprises.

A with() descriptor can be attached to either return values or raised exceptions:

```
Project.stubs(:find).with(1).returns(
    Project.new(:name => "Project Greenlight"))
Project.stubs(:find).with(nil).raises(Exception)
assert_equal("Project Greenlight", Project.find(1).name)
assert_raises(Exception) { Project.find(nil).name }
```

The with() declaration can be made more complicated in several ways—frankly, practical application of some of these eludes me, but we'll run through them quickly.

Most generally, we can pass a block to with instead of an argument:

```
proj = Project.new()
proj.stubs(:status).with { |value| value % 2 == 0 }.returns("Active")
proj.stubs(:status).with { |value| value % 3 == 0 }.returns("Asleep")
```

When the stubbed method is called, if the with() block returns true, then the expectation is considered matched:

```
>> proj.status(2)
=> "Active"
```

If more than one block returns true, it seems as though the last one declared wins:

```
>> proj.status(3)
=> "Asleep"
>> proj.status(6)
=> "Asleep"
```

If none of the blocks returns true, we get a unexpected invocation error, as we did just a second ago.

Mocha also defines a bunch of parameter matchers that give more flexible with() behavior. This is an incomplete list of the ones that seem most useful. Note that all of these behaviors can be implemented using the block syntax.

The instance_of() matcher and its related cousin is_a() match any incoming parameter that is of the given class. Use instance_of() like this:

```
proj = Project.new()
proj.stubs(:tasks_before).with(instance_of(Date)).returns(3)
proj.stubs(:tasks_before).with(instance_of(String)).raises(Exception)
```

This or any other Mocha matcher can be negated with the Not() method. (Yes, it's capitalized, presumably to avoid weird parse collisions with the keyword **not**.)

```
proj = Project.new()
proj.stubs(:tasks_before).with(Not(instance_of(Date))).returns(3)
```

We can apply a stub to more than one possible argument with the any_of() matcher:

```
proj.stubs(:thing).with(any_of('a', 'b')).returns('abababa')
```

which would match against either of the following:

```
proj.thing('a')
proj.thing('b')
```

We can also nest any_of() with other matchers, though we can quickly get tangled in a pile of syntax:

```
proj.stubs(:thing).with(any_of(instance_of(String),
    instance_of(Integer))).returns("Argh")
```

Another useful matcher is regexp_matches(), which allows us to match against—guess what?—a regular expresssion:

```
proj.stubs(:thing).with(regexp_matches(/*_user/)).returns("A User!")
```

A hash argument can be matched against the existence of a specific key/value pair with the has_entry() matcher.

```
proj.stubs(:options).with(has_entry(:verbose => true))
```

The stub in this snippet will match any hash argument that contains a :verbose => true entry, no matter what the other contents of the hash might be.

There's about a dozen more of these matchers, many of which seem to be, shall we say, somewhat lacking in real-world practical value. Rather than cluttering your head with a bunch of stuff you'll never use, I invite you to check out the Mocha docs at http://mocha.rubyforge.org for a full listing.

One possible use of with() is to help work around the issue with Active-Record objects mentioned in the previous section. Anthony Caliendo came up with the following clever solution for creating a mock or stub on an ActiveRecord object in your test and getting it to still be applied to the ActiveRecord object created by the controller.[4]

Remember, the problem is that the database call from the controller creates a completely different Ruby object than the one you've attached a stub to. But you can dig into the ActiveRecord internals and define this in your test helper:

```
Line 1  def mock_active_records(*records)
     2    records.each do |record|
     3      record.class.stubs(:instantiate).with(
     4          has_entry('id' => record.id.to_s)).returns(record)
     5      record.stubs(:reload).returns(record)
     6    end
     7  end
```

The key phrase here is stubs(:instantiate).with in line 3. That method is called with a set of key/value pairs used to create an ActiveRecord object. Then in line 4, Mocha's has_entry decorator is used to declare that if the set of key/value pairs contains an entry for the id that matches the known record's ID, then return that object directly. The instantiate() method is called from ActiveRecord::Base::find(), so any mechanism for trying to retrieve this object from the database will be caught here such that if the ID of the object you are requesting matches one of the known objects, that object is returned without a new trip to the database. The reload() method is similarly stubbed.

A sample usage might look like this:

```
test "My projects might be properly saved" do
  @bluebook = Project.make(:name => "Project Bluebook")
  @runway = Project.make(:name => "Project Runway")
  mock_active_records(@bluebook, @runway)
  @bluebook.stubs(:save => true)
  @runway.stubs(:save => false)
end
```

Note that you have to mark the records you are going to use with the mock_active_records() method as well as actually specify any other stub or mock on those objects. There are a couple of things to watch out

---

4. This method is described in more detail at http://www.pathf.com/blogs/2009/08/using-mocha-for-activerecord-partial-mocks-with-finders/.

here, the most glaring of which is that all ActiveRecords you might find
in your test need to be in the mock_active_records() call, since an attempt
to call the stubbed instantiate() method with a nonmatching hash would
trigger an expectation error. In a factory universe, with only a couple of
object defined, that may not be a difficult constraint to live with. Also,
the internals of ActiveRecord may change in the future, causing this
mechanism to stop working.

There is a simpler option if you have only one or two objects to mock
and a simple method under test.

```
test "My projects might be properly saved" do
  @bluebook = Project.make(:name => "Project Bluebook")
  Project.stub(:find).return(@bluebook)
  @bluebook.stubs(:save => true)
  post :update, :id => @bluebook.id
  «»
end
```

All this does is stub the Project class to always return @bluebook when
find() is called. That ensures that the controller method that looks up
the object using find() returns the same object that you've set up in the
test. There are sharp limitations here—basically, we're assuming that
only one Project object needs to be created for the test. But there are a lot
of cases, like a simple update or create method, where that assumption
holds, and this is a reasonably clean way to share a stubbed object
between the test and the method being tested.

7.4 Mock, Mock, Mock

A true mock object retains the basic idea of the stub—returning a specified value without actually calling a live method—and adds the requirement that the specified method must actually be called during the test.
In other words, a mock is like a stub with attitude, expecting—nay,
demanding—that its parameters be matched in the test or else we get a
test failure.

As with stubs, Mocha provides a way to create a mock object from whole
cloth, as well as a way to add mock expectations to an existing object.
The method for bare mock creation is mock():

```
test "a sample mock" do
  mocky = mock(:name => "Paul", :weight => 100)
  assert_equal("Paul", mocky.name)
end
```

As it happens, this test fails:

```
 1) Failure:
test_a_sample_mock(ProjectTest) [/test/unit/project_test.rb:46]:
not all expectations were satisfied
unsatisfied expectations:
- expected exactly once, not yet invoked:
    #&lt;Mock:0x25550bc&gt;.weight(any_parameters)
satisfied expectations:
- expected exactly once, already invoked once:
    #&lt;Mock:0x25550bc&gt;.name(any_parameters)
```

It fails because the first line sets up two mock expectations, one for mocky.name() and one for mocky.weight(), but only one of those two mocked methods are called in the test. Hence, it's an unsatisfied expectation. To pass the test, add a call to mocky.weight():

```
test "a sample mock" do
  mocky = mock(:name => "Paul", :weight => 100)
  assert_equal("Paul", mocky.name)
  assert_equal(100, mocky.weight)
end
```

The method for adding a mock expectation to an existing object is expects():[5]

`huddle_mocha/test/unit/project_test.rb`

```
test "lets mock an object" do
  mock_project = Project.new(:name => "Project Greenlight")
  mock_project.expects(:name).returns("Fred")
  assert_equal("Fred", mock_project.name)
end
```

All the modifiers we've seen so far were applied to stubs, like returns(), raises(), any_instance(), and with(), or all the pattern matchers can be added to a mock statement. For example, the controller test for create and update failure can be changed to use true mocks:

`huddle_mocha/test/functional/projects_controller_test.rb`

```
test "mock fail create gracefully" do
  assert_no_difference('Project.count') do
    Project.any_instance.expects(:save).returns(false)
    post :create, :project => {:name => 'Project Runway'}
    assert_template('new')
  end
end
```

---

5. I have no idea why they didn't use *mocks*, which would seem more consistent.

```
test "mock fail update gracefully" do
  Project.any_instance.expects(:update_attributes).returns(false)
  put :update, :id => projects(:huddle).id, :project => {:name => 'fred'}
  assert_template('edit')
  actual = Project.find(projects(:huddle).id)
  assert_not_equal('fred', actual.name)
end
```

Again, the behavior of these tests is identical to the stub version, except for the additional, implicit test that the save() and update_attributes() methods are, in fact, called during the test.

By default, mock() and expects() set a validation that the associated method is called exactly once during the test. If that does not meet your testing needs, Mocha has methods that let you specify the number of calls to the method. These methods are largely self-explanatory:

```
proj = Project.new
proj.expects(:name).once
proj.expects(:name).twice
proj.expects(:name).at_least_once
proj.expects(:name).at_most_once
proj.expects(:name).at_least(3)
proj.expects(:name).at_most(3)
proj.expects(:name).times(5)
proj.expects(:name).times(4..6)
proj.expects(:name).never
```

In practice, the default behavior is good for most usages.

7.5 Mock Objects and Behavior-Driven Development

The interesting thing about using true mocks is that their usage enables a completely different style of testing. In the tests we've seen throughout most of this book, the test validates the result of a computation: it's testing the end state of a process. When using mocks, however, we have the opportunity to test the behavior of the process during the test, rather than the outcome.

An example will help clarify the difference. Back in Section 4.2, *Testing the View*, on page 57, the Huddle application had a controller test that was largely based on the results of a call to the model.

Without mock objects, the test looked like this (from test/functional/ project_controller_test.rb):

huddle_mocha/test/functional/projects_controller_test.rb

```
test "project timeline index should be sorted correctly" do
  set_current_project(:huddle)
  get :show, :id => projects(:huddle).id
  expected_keys = assigns(:reports).keys.sort.map{ |d| d.to_s(:db) }
  assert_equal(["2009-01-06", "2009-01-07"], expected_keys)
  assert_equal(
      [status_reports(:ben_tue).id, status_reports(:jerry_tue).id],
      assigns(:reports)[Date.parse("2009-01-06")].map(&:id))
end
```

As the process played out in that section, the assertions in this test wound up being copied more or less identically to the model test that actually exercised the model call that is made by the controller show() action being tested here. At the time, we mentioned that a mock object package would be a different way of writing the test. The mocked version of the test could look something like this passing test:

huddle_mocha/test/functional/projects_controller_test.rb

```
Line 1   test "mock show test" do
     2     set_current_project(:huddle)
     3     Project.any_instance.expects(:reports_grouped_by_day).returns(
     4         {Date.today => [status_reports(:aaron_tue)]})
     5     get :show, :id => projects(:huddle).id
     6     assert_not_nil assigns(:reports)
     7   end
```

At first glance, that looks ridiculously minimalist. It doesn't seem to actually be asserting much of anything. The trick is the combination of the mock expectation set in lines 3–4, along with the rest of the tests that presumably exist in this system. This test validates that the controller calls the model method reports_grouped_by_day() exactly once, and it validates that the reports variable is set to some value. It also validates that the controller and view run without error, but that's secondary. The test is validating a behavior of the controller method—namely, that it calls a particular model method, not the state that results from making that call.

What this test doesn't do is attempt to validate features that are actually the purview of other tests. It doesn't validate the response from the model method; that's the job of the model test. What the view layer does with this value is the job of a view test. This test validates that a particular instance variable is set to a value using a known model method, on the theory that the job of the controller method is to produce a set of known values for use by the view. But validating the exact value of the :reports variable would be pointless (at least in this case), since the value is completely generated by the mock expectation.

Using mock objects in this style of testing has advantages and disadvantages. Speed is a significant advantage: getting values from mocks is going to be a lot faster than getting values from either a fixture or a factory database. Another advantage is the encapsulation of tests. In the previous example, if a bug is introduced into the model object, the only tests that will fail will be the model tests—the controller tests, protected by the mock, will be fine. The nonmock version of the controller test, however, is susceptible to failure based on the results of the model method. Done right, this kind of encapsulation can make it easier to diagnose and fix test failures.

However, there are a couple of potential problems to watch out for. One is a mismatch between the mocked method and the real method. In the previous controller example, the mock call causes the method to return a hash where the key is a Date object and the values are lists of StatusReport objects. If, however, the model method really returns a hash with the keys as strings, then you can have a case where the controller method passes, the model method passes, but the site as a whole breaks. In practice, this problem can be covered by using integration or acceptance tests; see Chapter 13, *Testing Workflow with Integration Tests*, on page 213 and Chapter 15, *Acceptance Testing with Cucumber*, on page 235.

It's also not hard to inadvertently create a test that is tautological by setting a mock to some value and then validating that the mocked method returns that value (the earlier examples that show how stubbed methods work have this flaw).

Finally, an elaborate edifice of mocked methods runs the risk of causing the test to be dependent on very specific details of the method structure of the object being mocked. This can make the test brittle in the face of refactorings that might change the object's methods. Good API design and an awareness of this potential problem go a long way toward mitigating the issue.

I have to say, as much as I love using mocks and stubs to cover hard-to-reach objects and states, my own history with very strict behavior-based mock test structures hasn't been great. My experience was that writing all the mocks around a given object tended to be a drag on the test process. But I'm wide open to the possibility that this method works better for others or that I'm not doing it right. Or, to quote Stephen Bristol:[6] "RSpec, done properly, isn't testing. It is designing."

7.6 Mock Dos and Mock Don'ts

Here are some guidelines on the best usage of stubs and mocks:

- If you are using your fake objects to take the place of real objects that are hard or impossible to create in a test environment, it's probably a good idea to use stubs rather than mocks. If you are actually using the fake value as an input to a different process, then you should test that process directly using the fake value rather than a mock. Adding the mock expectation just gives you another thing that can break, which in this use case is probably not related to what you are actually testing.

- When you are using a true mock to encapsulate a test and isolate it from methods that are not under test, try to limit the number of methods you are mocking in one test. The more mocks, the more vulnerable the test will be to changes in the actual code. A lot of mocks may indicate that your test is trying to do too much or might indicate a poor object-oriented design where one class is asking for too many details of a different class.

- I've come to use mocks frequently in controller testing to isolate the controller test from the behavior of the model, essentially only testing that the controller makes a specific model call and using the model test to verify model behavior. Among the benefits of using mocks this way is you are encouraged to make the interface between your controllers and models as simple as possible. However, it does mean that the controller test knows more about your model than it otherwise might, which may make the model code harder to change.

---

6. http://twitter.com/stevenbristol/statuses/1221264618

- You also need to be careful of mocking methods that have side effects or that call other methods that might be interesting. The mock totally bypasses the original method, which means no side effect and no calling the internal method. Pro tip: saving to the database and outputting to the response stream are both side effects.

- Be very nervous if you are specifying a value as a result of a mock and then asserting the existence of the very same value. One of the biggest potential problems with any test suite is false positives, and testing results with mocked values is a really efficient way to generate false positives.

- A potentially larger problem is the type mismatch issue between the real method and values being used for mocks. Integration or acceptance testing can help with this problem, but that's not much help during development. I don't know that there's an automated way to ensure that mock values are actually valid possible results and still get the benefits of using mocks, so it's something to keep an eye on.

7.7 Comparing Mock Object Libraries

Now that we've spent some time exploring how mock objects work using Mocha, let's take a brief look at the various ways that the other popular Ruby mock libraries manage similar tasks. There are four packages that are currently popular:

FlexMock
> This is the original Ruby mock object package.

Mocha
> We've already discussed this at some length. It's quasi-official for Rails in that it is used in Rails core.

RSpec
> The RSpec library, described in more detail in Chapter 12, *RSpec*, on page 183, defines its own mock object package

RR
> Pronounced "Double Ruby," it's the newest entry, with a more concise syntax than the other packages and unique advanced features.

This is a quick tour of common features and not a complete look at each of these packages. Check the documentation for all the details and quirks—RR, in particular, has features that don't map to the other tools.

Loading into Test Suite

The first part of using any of these packages is installing and integrating with Test::Unit. The RSpec mocks, of course, can't be integrated with Test::Unit; however, any of the other packages can be integrated with RSpec by adding the line config.mock_with :rr or :flexmock, or :mocha in the spec_helper.rb file.

FlexMock

```
% sudo gem install flexmock
```

Then, in test_helper.rb, add this:

```
require 'flexmock/test_unit'
```

Mocha

```
sudo gem install mocha
```

Then, in test_helper.rb, add this:

```
require 'mocha'
```

RSpec

N/A

RR

```
sudo gem install rr
```

Then, inside the test case declaration in test_helper.rb, add this:

```
include RR::Adapters::TestUnit
```

Creating Blank Stubs

The most basic function of any of these packages is creating a simple stub object in which you can specify the return value of one or more methods. When those methods are called, the specified value is returned. If the methods are not called, nothing happens. Here's the syntax to create a stub object that is not connected to any preexisting object in the application.

FlexMock

```
stub = flexmock("name", :method => result)
```

Mocha

```
object = stub(:method => result)
```

The method/result pairs can also be specified in a block argument as shown in the next section.

RSpec

```
stub = stub("name", :method => value)
```

RR

```
double = stub(Object.new).method { value }
```

This can be abbreviated as as follows:

```
double = stub!.method { value }
```

Creating Stubs from Existing Objects

Most of the time, though, you'll want to create stubs that replace methods on existing objects. In FlexMock and RR, this involves calling a special method with the object as an argument, as in FlexMock's flex-mock(object), while in Mocha and RSPec, this involves calling a method of the object itself, as in object.stubs. In either case, further information about the method being stubbed, and its return value, is usually chained after the declaration of the stub.

Remember, classes are just another kind of object in Ruby, so class methods can be treated like any other method, as in stub(User).should_receive(:find).

FlexMock

```
stub = flexmock(project).should_receive(:method).and_return(value)
```

If the object being mocked is a string or symbol, use :base as the first argument to prevent confusion with a simple test double containing just the name. In other words, the call flexmock("fred") is ambiguous. As written, it is just a bare FlexMock object with the name fred. If you actually want to stub methods on the string "fred", then use flexmock(:base, "fred").

The :safe argument is used in the case where your object being mocked might already define methods with the same name as the ones used by FlexMock. When called via :safe, FlexMock will not add extra methods to the existing object. Since those methods don't exist, a FlexMock object declared with :safe can be used only by having any expectations defined in an attached block.

```
mock = flexmock(:base, object)
mock = flexmock(:safe, project) { |mock| mock.should_receive(:a) }
```

Multiple should_receive calls can be chained to a single stub, in which case they cycle in the same way as Mocha values. Values can also be set in a block argument to flexmock(), as follows:

```
flexmock(obj) do |m|
  m.should_receive(:method).and_return(value)
end
```

To specify errors, and_raise(exception) is used. The syntax :method => value can be used as a shortcut for and_return() in either of the following forms:

```
flexmock(obj).should_receive(:method => value)
flexmock(obj, :method => value)
```

Mocha

```
obj.stubs(:method).returns(value)
obj.stubs(:method, value)
```

The previous two methods are identical. To specify errors, use raises(exception) instead of returns. Multiple values in the returns method cycle can also be written returns(1).then.returns(2).

RSpec

```
project.stub!(method).and_return(1)
```

The and_return() method can also take a block or a list of values, which is treated as Mocha or FlexMock. Use and_raise() to raise an error.

RR

```
stub(project).method { value }
```

This can also be written as follows:

```
stub(project).method.returns(value)
```

Creating Mocks with Expectations

All these packages allow you to create a mock object with an expectation that the method will be called a specified amount of times. The biggest difference here is that FlexMock does not have a separate syntax for creating objects with expectations; any doubled object can have an expectation added by appending a method like once() to the description chain. In Mocha, RSpec, and RR, test doubles that will have expectations must be declared as such, using mock() or (in Mocha) expects(). In those libraries, specifying an method with mock() implicitly assumes that the method will be called exactly once.

Each library offers options to change the expected number of times a method will be called.

RR has a unique feature called a *proxy*, where the method is actually called (as opposed to the return value being set by RR), but you can still specify an expectation on how many times the method is called.

FlexMock

```
mock.should_receive(:method).and_return(value).once
```

Other options include zero_or_more_times(), twice(), never(), and times(n). You can also use combination methods, as in at_least. once() or at_most.twice().

Mocha

Bare mock objects are just like bare stub objects, except all methods are expected to be called once. Existing objects use the expects() method to be converted to mocks.

```
mock = mock()
project.expects(:method)
```

The default is that the method is called exactly once, equal to project.expects(:method).once. Other options include twice(), at_least_once(), at_most_once(), at_least(x), at_most(x), times(x), times(x..y), and never().

RSpec

```
obj.should_receive(:method).and_return(1)
```

The default expectation is that the method will be called once. If the method should never be called, use this:

```
obj.should_not_receive(:method)
```

Other method count expectations can be set with once(), twice(), exactly(n).times(), at_least.once(), at_least(n).times(), at_most.once(), at_most(n).times(), and any_number_of_times().

RR

> This sets an expectation for a single call. The expected value is the result of the block.
>
> ```
> mock(obj).method { value }
> ```
>
> To set an expectation that a method is called more than once, use this:
>
> ```
> mock(obj).method.times(n) { value }
> ```
>
> To set an expectation that a method is not called, use this:
>
> ```
> do_not_call(obj).method
> ```
>
> RR lets you create a *proxy* that creates an expectation that a method will be called, but unlike a mock, it actually calls the method. A block argument to the proxy call allows you to post-process the output of the actual method:
>
> ```
> mock.proxy(project).method { |actual| "#{actual}_mocked" }
> ```

Filtering Methods by Argument

All four libraries offer similar syntax for specifying arguments that must match for the doubled method to be invoked. This allows you to specify different return values based on the arguments. For example, you could specify multiple stubs of the find method, each returning a different model object. In addition to matching based on the exact value of the arguments, each library offers some more generic matchers based on class or matching a regular expression or whatnot.

FlexMock

> ```
> mock.should_receive(:method).with("a")
> ```
>
> Also with_any_args() and with_no_args(). If the argument to with() is a class, any instance of the class matches. If it's a regular expression, any string matching the regular expression matches. There is also a mechanism for more complex logic.

Mocha

> ```
> project.expects(:method).with(1)
> ```
>
> If with() is passed a block, the method matches if the block returns true. Several other matchers can be combined with the argument, including instance_of(), Not(), any_of(), and regexp_matchers().

RSpec

```
project.should_receive(:method).with(1)
```

Other filters include anything(), any_instance_of(), hash_including(), boolean(), duck_type(:message), or a regular expression.

RR

```
mock(project).method(1) { value }
```

Just set the arguments to the method when defined. There are special matchers that can be placed as an argument, including anything, is_a(), numeric, boolean, and duck_type. You can also put in a range or a regular expression.

Doubling Any Instance of a Class

Three of the libraries also have special syntax that allow you to specify stub or mock behavior for any instance of the class that is created subsequent to that declaration. (Be careful, instances of the class previously created will not have the double behavior.) Typically, after the method declares that this double applies to all new instances, any other filter or expectation can be applied. In each example, the Project class is being decorated to return false when save() is called.

FlexMock

```
flexmock(Project).new_instances.should_receive(:save => false)
```

After new_instances(), any FlexMock expectation or filter can be used.

Mocha

```
Project.any_instance.expects(:save).returns(false)
```

RSpec

RSpec doesn't have an exact match for this feature; the closest workaround seems to be this:

```
Project.stub!(:find).and_return(
    mock_model(Project, :save => false))
```

RR

```
mock.instance_of(Project).save(false)
```

ActiveRecord Mock Features

A couple of the libraries offer special features for ActiveRecord.

FlexMock

```
flexmock(:model, Project)
```

Works like a normal stub, with the methods id(), to_params(), new_record?(), errors(), is_a?(), instance_of?(), kind_of?(), and class() already stubbed to consistent defaults.

Mocha
    N/A

RSpec

```
mock_model(Project, :method => value)
```

This requires the rspec-rails plugin and stubs id(), to_param(), new_record?(), and errors().

RR
    N/A

Method Chains

Some of the libraries offer the ability to set a stub or mock on an entire chain of method calls in one line, without having to explicitly set the intermediate mock object. This can make code clearer in the odd case where you need to mock across several objects.

FlexMock

```
flexmock(project).should_receive("project.leader.address.city")
```

The resulting mock acts like any other FlexMock object.

Mocha
    N/A

RSpec

```
stub_chain(project.leader.address.city).and_return("Chicago")
```

RR

```
stub(project).leader.stub!.address.stub!.city { "Chicago" }
```

7.8 Mock Object Summary

In this part of the book, we covered model testing. First, we talked about the services Rails provides for testing models, and we discussed fixtures and factories as mechanisms for creating consistent test data. With this chapter, we've started to transition from testing models to testing the user-facing parts of the application. Mock testing is useful for testing models, but it becomes especially useful when trying to shield the various layers of your application from each other.

In the next part, we'll be discussing testing the controller and view layers. Mock objects can be a very important part of controller testing; creating mock models allows the controller tests to proceed independently of the model test.

Part III

Testing User-Facing Layers

## Chapter 8

Testing Controllers with Functional Tests

Even more than model testing, Rails controller testing depends on Rails-specific structures and methods. The goal of controller testing is to simulate a single request to a specific controller method and make assertions about the result. This may or may not include assertions about the view output, depending on your taste. Standard Rails functional testing includes both controller and view tests, but third-party add-ons allow for separate testing of views and partials.

8.1 What's Available in a Controller Test?

Rails-generated controller tests are subclasses of ActionController:: TestCase, itself a subclass of the ActiveSupport::TestCase used for model

---

What's in a Name, Part Two

I don't want to belabor the point (too late), but as much as I try to hold to standard Rails naming conventions here, *functional test* still doesn't sit right with me. I'll stick to *controller test* and *view test* in order to be specific about what the actual goal of the test is.

testing.[1] All the features available for model testing are still present in controller and view testing. In addition, some additional toys are added to ActionController::TestCase via a few modules that are mixed into it. This is what is at your disposal:

- Three instance variables that are the mock object versions of the @controller, the @request, and the @response. Functionality that would require a real user request or client browser is stubbed out. My experience is that I don't use those directly a whole lot, except for @response.body, which is helpful for view testing and debugging by inspecting the body text from inside a test method.

- Four pseudo-hash variables representing control structures. You have session, cookies, and flash, each of which represents the Rails construct of the same name, such as session[:user_id]—although the cookie variable has string keys, not symbol keys. And you have assigns, which allows access to any instance variable set in the controller method so that, say, @user in the controller method can be verified in the test by using assigns(:user). You're supposed to access that as a method and not as a hash—assigns[:user] won't work (but assigns["user"] will...).

- A method to simulate each HTTP verb for the purpose of pretending to call a controller: get(), post(), put(), delete(), plus the bonus xhr() for Ajax calls.

- Several assertions aimed at the specifics of controller and view testing, the most valuable of which will be covered in more detail in Chapter 9, *Testing Views*, on page 135.

8.2 What to Test

The controller part of controller tests is generally straightforward. If you are following good development practice, the complicated functionality is in the model and is being tested in your model tests; one of the reasons this is a best practice is that models are easier to test. Views, which are genuinely a pain in the neck to test, we'll cover in Chapter 9, *Testing Views*, on page 135.

---

1. Before I let go of the naming topic entirely, why is it *Action*Controller and *Action*View, but *Active*Support and *Active*Record?

A controller test should have one of the following goals:

1. Verifying that an normal, basic user request triggers the expected ActiveRecord calls and passes the necessary data to the view.

2. Verifying that an ill-formed or otherwise invalid user request is handled properly, for whatever definition of "properly" fits your app.

3. Verifying that your security roles work as expected, such as requiring logins for pages as needed and testing that users who enter a URL for a resource they shouldn't be able to see is blocked or diverted. These tests often have a view component: admins should see a Delete button, but nobody else should.

8.3 Simulating a Controller Call

The general structure of a controller test includes a setup method that puts the data and session context in place and then an individual test method that simulates a call to the controller and validates the controller response.[2] The most simplified version of this structure looks something like this:

```
setup :generic_setup

def generic_setup
  @task = Task.create
  login_as :admin
end

test "should show a task" do
  get :show, :id => @task.id.to_s
  assert_equal(@task.id, assigns(:task).id)
  assert_response :success
  assert_template :show
end
```

Rails provides a test method for each HTTP verb: get(), post(), put(), and delete(). Each of these methods works the same way. The first argument to the simulated call is the controller method to invoke. The second argument contains the key/value pairs that become the params of the call. The Rails conventions for placing complex data types into parameter names holds here, so :task => {:project => {:id => "3"}} creates params[:task][:project][:id] = "3".

---

2. If you are heavily into contexts, then the simulated call can go in the context. See Section 11.1, *Contexts*, on page 168 for a look at this structure.

In most cases, the parameters argument is the only one passed to the controller and so is written as a list of key/value pairs rolled into a hash by Ruby. However, there are optional third and fourth arguments to these test methods that set hashes for the session and flash, respectively. In the following snippet, the session is getting a user ID and current project, and the flash is getting a notice:

```
get :show, {:id => @task.id.to_s}, {:user_id => "3",
    :current_project => @project.id.to_s}, {:notice => "flash test"}
```

The xhr() method simulates an Ajax call to the controller. The signature of the method is a little different; the first argument is the HTTP verb, the second is the controller method, and the remaining arguments match the order of the other HTTP mimic methods:

```
test "my ajax call" do
  xhr :post, :create, :task => {:id => "3"}
end
```

The controller will respond to a test call made with the xhr() exactly the way it would respond to an actual Ajax request. That is to say, if you use the more modern respond_to blocks, then the request will match the format.js block. Alternately, the controller method xhr? will return true for the action being tested.

There are two gotchas in simulating controller calls. The first is that the controller method is called directly without working through the routes file. This means the test is not verifying whether the method in question is actually reachable using the given HTTP verb—that can be done via a separate routing test that we'll cover later in Section 8.6, *Testing Routes*, on page 132. This can be particularly annoying for RESTful controllers, where the HTTP verb is salient, and the test can mask a potential issue by using an unexpected HTTP verb without catching the problem.

I get snared by this trap when testing the intersection of Ajax and REST If the method called via Ajax in the previous example actually doesn't expect an HTTP POST (for example, it's a standard RESTful edit method), the test passes, but the code fails in the browser.

Another distinction between the test environment and the real request is that real request parameters are always strings, whereas these test invocations do not convert the key/value values to strings before calling the controller method. Under many circumstances this isn't a big deal— if you are just doing, say, a find() on an ID parameter, ActiveRecord does

---

Testing File Uploads

When you want to fake a file upload in a test, Rails provides the helper method fixture_file_upload() to help. It takes two arguments: a path to an actual file relative to the Rails root and a MIME type. You use this as the value part of a key/value pair being passed to a Rails method in a controller test, as in post :upload_icon, :icon => fixture_file_upload('/public/images/test_icon.png', 'image/png'). The controller treats that value as though it was an uploaded file.

---

the right thing regardless. However, if you are depending on an exact match of the variable (for example, directly comparing the parameter to an ID), the type may matter, and you might have a test that passes in the test environment, while the code in the browser fails.

This may become an issue in security testing. If the controller method looks like this:

```
def create
  if current_user.id == params[:id]
    # allow
  else
    # deny
  end
end
```

and the test looks like this:

```
test "I can create"
  login_as(@user)
  put :create, @user.id
  #assert that allowed branch was taken
end
```

the test will pass because params[:id] in the test is an integer, but the create() method will fail in the browser because params[:id] will be a string. The workaround is to ensure that the test values are converted to strings in the test. One recommendation is to use @user.to_param as the argument to put(); this method is preferable to the @user.id.to_s because it gives you some flexibility if you override the to_param() method later.

8.4 Testing Controller Response

The most basic thing you usually want to verify in a controller method is that it returns the HTTP status code you expect and that the appropriate Rails template is placed in charge of returning the response. Rails provides three assertion methods to help: assert_redirected_to(), assert_response(), and assert_template().

When you're expecting a normal HTTP response and not a redirection, you can indicate your expectation in the test with a combination of assert_response() and assert_template(), like so:

```
test "successful index request" do
  get :index
  assert_response :success
  assert_template "index"
end
```

Let's break that down. assert_response() actually verifies the response code sent by Rails to the browser. Typically, the expected value from the test is :success, meaning code 200, or :redirect, which matches any of the 300–399 range that indicates a redirect of some form or other. Other special values are :missing to match a 404 error, and :error, which matches any of the 500–599 error range. Instead of a special value, the expected argument can also be the exact integer of the expected response. All the individual response codes also have their own specific, if rarely used, symbolic equivalent.[3]

The assert_template() verifies which template Rails uses to generate the response. The template name is specified exactly as it would be in the controller using render :action—the template name can be a string or a symbol. If the argument is just a single string or symbol, then it is checked against the name of the main template that rendered the action. If you call assert_template() with a key value argument of the form assert_template :partial => '_user_data_row', then you are testing whether the specified partial is called when the controller action is rendered. The partial name in the test method must include the leading underscore. Adding the :count option verifies that the specified partial was called a specific number of times, which is potentially useful for a partial that is rendered inside a loop.

---

3. There are about 50 different status codes; the entire list can be found in the Rails source in actionpack/lib/action_controller/status_codes.rb.

For a redirect, Rails provides assert_redirected_to(), which takes as an argument any object that can be resolved into a URL. (assert_redirected_to() implicitly makes a call to assert_response :redirect, so you don't need to write a separate assertion for that.)

If the argument to assert_redirected_to() is a hash, as in:

```
assert_redirected_to :controller => :task, :action => :show, :id => 3
```

then if the actual redirect URL as specified in the controller also uses a hash, the Rails test checks only the keys that you actually use in your assertion, allowing you to check for a partial match. However, if the actual redirect URL is specified via a named route or RESTful route mechanism, Rails will insist on an exact match.

You can check against a named or RESTful route method:

```
assert_redirected_to new_task_url
```

Or an object that corresponds to a RESTful route:

```
assert_redirected_to @task
```

A Rails controller test does not—repeat, does not—follow the redirect.[4] Any data validation tests you write apply only to the method before the redirect occurs. If you need your test to follow the redirection for some reason, you are cordially invited to try something in an integration test; see Chapter 13, *Testing Workflow with Integration Tests*, on page 213.

8.5 Testing Returned Data

Rails allows you to verify the data generated by the controller method under test through the four collections mentioned earlier: assigns, session, cookies, and flash. Of these, assigns, which is a hash of instance variables created in the controller, is the most commonly used. A typical use might look like this, with a common use of assigns, and a frankly contrived use of session:

```
test "should show task" do
  get :show, :id => @task_1.id
  assert_response :success
  assert_equal @task_1.id, assigns(:task).id
  assert_equal "task/show", session[:last_page]
end
```

---

4. Prior to Rails 2.2, there was a method that let you follow a redirect from a test, but only within the same controller. It was deprecated in Rails 2.2.

> ### Gotcha: Requiring a Login
>
> Here's something that happens to me with disturbing fre-
> quency. On sites that require user logins, I often code the site up
> a little bit before adding the filter that requires a user login, usu-
> ally to get the site architecture correct before forcing the secu-
> rity. I add the line before_filter :authenticate_user! for Devise, and
> boom—all the controller tests fail because they are redirected
> away from the controller because the test does not have a
> valid login. It seems it always takes me longer to remember why
> this has happened than it should (since it should, by now, take
> only about ten seconds). To sum up, remember to put the login
> in your tests. With Devise, by default that means putting include
> Devise::TestHelpers in a setup block, along with some other setup
> that is specified in Section 3.4, *Security Now!*, on page 44.

The cookies and flash special variables are used similarly, though I don't
write tests for the flash very often.[5]

When testing the model data in a controller, keep in mind that you usually don't want to duplicate the actual model tests, and you definitely
don't want the controller test to replace the model test. It's easier and
more effective to test the model in the model test—there's less setup,
and the test is generally clearer and more focused. See Section 4.2,
Testing the Project View: A Cascade of Tests, on page 56 for a description of how to interleave controller and model tests with a Test-Driven
Development process.

To Mock or Not to Mock

While you want to make sure and cover any error conditions specific to
the controller itself, you don't need to test all the error and condition
paths of the model: again, that is best managed in the model test. However, you do want to verify that the controller gets the expected object.
In many cases, it's enough to know that the controller object is calling the expected model method and sets the expected variable. Since
the model test covers the result of the model method, knowing that the

---

5. One thing to note about cookies: in Rails 2.3 and up, cookies in controller tests are
just strings. In prior versions, you could also specify them as CGI::Cookie objects if you
wanted to test cookie attributes. It doesn't seem like you can test cookie attributes in
Rails 2.3 without manually accessing the request header.

method is called with the expected arguments is enough to verify the state of the controller.

This is a potentially great use case for mock objects. Mock object tests are covered in more detail in Chapter 7, *Using Mock Objects*, on page 95, but here's a sample of how they can be used in controller testing, with the Ruby mock object tool Mocha:

```
test "should show task" do
  task = Task.new
  Task.expects(:find).with(1).returns(task)
  get :show, :id => 1
  assert_response :success
  assert_equal task, assigns(:task)
end
```

The Task.expects line has two separate functions:

- The stub function. Bypassing the real find() method so that if the object receives a call for find(1), it will return task without calling the actual Task.find() method. Note that this bypasses the database entirely.
- The mock function. Setting up an expectation that find(1) will be called exactly once during this test. If that method is not called, the test will fail.

The upshot of this is that you can test the controller behavior without having to worry about the finer points of the model implementation— in fact, you can test the controller before the model method is even written. There's a downside, common to any mock testing. Setting up the mocks can be time-consuming and brittle, and if the object that you return from the mock doesn't match the real method, you may be obscuring bugs in the controller or view.

One compromise is the concept of a *spy*, which the Double Ruby mock object framework allows.[6] Essentially, you can identify the model method as being of interest, then set an assertion that the method has actually been called. In Double Ruby syntax, the test might look like this:

```
Line 1  test "should show task" do
     2    stub.proxy(Task).find('1')
     3    get :show, :id => 1
     4    assert_response :success
     5    assert_received(Task) { |t| t.find('1') }
     6    assert_equal task, assigns(:task)
     7  end
```

---

6. Spies can also be added to Mocha using an extension gem called Bourne.

There are just two special lines in this snippet. In line 2, a special Double Ruby construct called a *proxy* is created. Basically, this just calls the method normally but marks the method as one for Double Ruby to keep track of.[7] Since Double Ruby is now tracking calls to the method, you can make assertions based on method counts, in this case asserting that the Task class actually received a method call find('1'). I find this to be a nice way to split the difference between real mocks and actually testing the model method in the controller.

There's much, much more on the costs and benefits of mock object testing in Chapter 7, *Using Mock Objects*, on page 95. Also, see Section 7.2, *Stubs*, on page 97 for a description about how mock objects can be used to shore up test coverage of the failure states in code generated by standard Rails scaffolds.

8.6 Testing Routes

Although the basics of Rails routing is simple, the desire to customize Rails response to URLs can lead to confusion about exactly what your application is going to do when converting between an URL and a Rails action, and vice versa. Rails provides two core methods that you can use to specify or validate routing behavior.

The two Rails methods, assert_generates() and assert_recognizes(), are mirror images of each other. Let's take them in alphabetical order.

The assert_generates() method takes an expected path string as its first element and a hash of key/value pairs as the second. The test passes if the Rails router would convert the key/value pairs into the expected string—it's doing a string comparison. Here's an example from Huddle:

```
assert_generates "/status_reports/1",
    {:controller => "status_reports", :action => "show", :id => "1"}
```

In this case, Rails runs the router against the hash and compares it to the string.

The inverse method, assert_recognizes(), flips the order of the arguments and also flips the execution.

```
assert_recognizes {:controller => "status_reports",
    :action => "show", :id => "1"}, "/status_reports/1"
```

---

7. You can also choose to post-process the returned result, though an obvious use case doesn't leap to mind.

In this case, the second argument is run through the Rails router, and the parameters that it converts to are compared against the hash in the first argument.

There's a little bit more flexibility to the arguments in assert_recognizes(). The second argument can also be a hash with two keys, a :path key and a :method key, which allows you to test RESTful routing like this:

```
assert_recognizes {:controller => "status_reports",
    :action => "update", :id => "1"},
    {:path => "/status_reports/1", :method => :put}
```

For the purposes of this test, the first argument can be written as a RESTful method or named route method, though it's not immediately clear to me why this is an improvement:

```
assert_recognizes new_status_report_url, 'status_reports/new'
```

If you want to test items that would be in the query string, you must pass them as a hash in an optional third argument—just appending them to the string path argument won't work:

```
assert_recognizes {:controller => "status_reports",
    :action => "show", :id => "1", :all => true},
    "/status_reports/1", {:all => true}
```

RSpec automatically generates route tests as part of its controller scaffold, but the default tests don't. I don't usually make a habit of including these tests, but they are handy in cases where the routing instructions get complicated.

8.7 Coming Up

In this chapter, we covered how to simulate controller actions for test purposes. Next, we're going to run through other user-facing parts of the Rails stack. The next chapter will talk about view testing and when and why you need it. After that, we'll discuss testing helpers; nearly every Rails application I've ever seen has untested helpers, and we'll show some ways to tackle them. In the following chapter, we'll close with an example of how to integrate JavaScript Ajax testing with your Rails test suite.

Chapter 9

Testing Views

View testing is fundamentally different from testing controllers and models in that it's prohibitively time-intensive to fully test the view output, and even when that's accomplished, it's still hard to validate the actual in-browser look of the view. Not to mention that overly detailed view tests are notoriously brittle in the face of consistent redesign of the look of your application. Using Rails' tools, you are best served by trying to specify and verify the logical and semantic structure of your application's output.

9.1 The Goals of View Testing

Successful view testing is an art—it's hard to find the appropriate balance between testing so little that the tests have minimal value and testing so much that they break every time your HTML designer looks at them cross-eyed.

Create a view test when you want to do one of the following things:

- Validate that the view layer runs without error. This is of course the bare minimum you'd expect from a view test. That said, you can save yourself some production deployment embarrassment if you know that every branch of your views actually runs.
- Validate that the data gathered by the controller is expressed as expected in the view. You'll especially want to test that any view logic dependent on the presence or absence of particular data works as expected.
- Validate security-based output; for example, administrators may have links on pages allowing them access to edit mode. Or users may be able to edit their own posts but not a different user's. And so on.

A view test, within Rails itself, should not attempt to do any of the following:

- Validate the exact text or HTML markup of the response. This is susceptible to random breakage.

- Validate the user-facing look of the site. Even if you could figure out a reasonable way to do this automatically in Rails, again, it's too easily broken. Other tools, such as Selenium, can handle some of this testing.

9.2 Keys to Successful View Testing

The lists in the previous section demonstrate that view testing is somewhat different from model or controller testing. View testing is more impressionistic than model or controller testing. To keep view testing manageable, you need to assume that the HTML keeps true to the spirit of the test. That is, if you are testing for the existence of an element with a DOM ID project_description, then for your own sanity, you need to assume that the content of that DOM ID will actually be something related to the project description and not, say, the phase of the moon.

With that in mind, here are some guidelines for keeping your eye on the ball when writing view tests:

Try not to test for the existence of specific inner text of the HTML tags. If you feel the need for this kind of double-check, odds are your test is too specific. Testing for more general regular expression matches is sometimes useful, though. You may be tempted to say that testing for the inner text of an HTML tag is OK if you are testing for the exact contents of a field that you have specifically created in your test data. Maybe, but don't blame me when somebody decides to add the phrase "date of birth" into the actual text field and you have to fix a bunch of tests. You know your code better than I do, but I've seen this movie, and it rarely ends well.

Instead, test views at the semantic level. Put DOM IDs on HTML tags all over the place and test for the existence or nonexistence of tags with the expected DOM IDs. Alternately, consider tagging with CSS classes that describe the semantic role of some output, even if the CSS class doesn't have specific styling associated (for instance, giving all the data rows of a table a data_row CSS class). This lets you verify the structure

> ### Validating HTML
>
> A very strong side benefit of assert_select() is that the method parses the HTML and will emit warnings if the HTML is badly formed—for example, if an end tag is missing. (Unfortunately, the warning message doesn't come with a stack trace, so if a warning suddenly pops up in the middle of your test suite, it can be hard to track down.) For this reason, assert_select() is valuable to run on your output even if you aren't doing any other validations in the call. If you want to test for valid markup more formally, you can check out the html_test plugin on GitHub.

of your output without being caught up in the content. The extra DOM IDs also help in Ajax, CSS, and browser debugging later.

The only exceptions to testing for DOM IDs are form elements; you can test those using their name attribute (which allows you to directly verify the key that will be in the ensuing POST call). You can even test the value attribute, at least sometimes.

In addition to testing for what is in the response, testing for what is not in the response is very useful, especially when dealing with users who have different roles and therefore different output.

9.3 Using assert_select

The assert_select() method is a powerful and flexible method of validating HTML content. We use the syntax of CSS selectors to specify HTML structures to be found in the output. The assert_select() method automatically looks at @response.body to find the output to test against. Once you've found matching structures, you can further test for the content of the structures or the number of matches found. The basic structure of assert_select() is copied with slight variation in the acceptance test frameworks Webrat and Capybara; see Chapter 14, *Write Better Integration Tests with Webrat and Capybara*, on page 223.

The simplest use of assert_select() is merely to test for the existence of a specific HTML tag:

```
assert_select("form")
```

This assertion is true if there is at least one HTML form element in the response body. (By the way, the tag selector must be a string, not a symbol.)

There are three ways to make an assert_select() test more specific. You can augment the selector using various CSS-style syntax decorations, you can specify the content of the tag, and you can specify the number of matching tags that should exist, based on the selector and content. Or you can do all three.

The least complicated of these three options is to specify the content of the tag. If the next argument to assert_select() is a string or regular expression, then the assertion is true only if there is at least one matching HTML tag with inner content that matches the argument. String arguments must match the content exactly. Regular expression arguments must =~ match the contents. The following two examples both match against Happy Birthday:

```
assert_select("span", "Happy Birthday")
assert_select("span", /Birthday/)
```

If the second argument after the selector is a number or a range, the test validates that the number of matching elements in the response is either the exact number or in the range. In practice, I use this to validate that, say, an table in an index view has one row for each element being displayed:

```
assert_select("tr", 5)
assert_select("tr", 2 .. 3)
```

You can also write the tests with true and false as the second argument. True indicates the default "one or more" behavior, and false indicates that there are no matching elements: assert_select(:form, false). A common scenario is a view in which different text elements display for different users. Testing for just the existence of options leaves a hole in the tests: a view that displays all options at all times will pass the tests. Testing for the nonexistence of text that shouldn't exist exposes that particular bug.

If you want to be bold and specify both text and a count, the final argument is a hash or some key/value pairs. The keys :text and :count match the features you've already seen:

```
assert_select("span", :text => "User Name", :count => 5)
```

Personally, I find the keys more readable, and I tend to use them even when specifying only one option. You can also specify range behavior with the keys :minimum and :maximum.

That brings us to modifying the selector. There are many different selector modifiers, most of which don't get used very often. The modifiers boil down to five types, described in the following sections.

Specify the DOM ID of the Element

You can specify an element by DOM ID using an #, as in "div#user_name_3". You can leave off the HTML tag if you want; "#user_name_3" matches any DOM element with that ID, regardless of tag type. In any assert_select() selector, a ? behaves as it does in an ActiveRecord SQL condition string, as a placeholder for a value specified later. So, the common use case of specifying an element using the Rails dom_id() method can be written as follows:[1]

```
assert_select("div#?", dom_id(@user, :name))
```

This is often easier to read than duplicating the hash symbol to interpolate the string. As mentioned previously, I recommend testing for IDs frequently.

Specify the CSS Class of the Element

The CSS class of the element being searched for can be specified using ., as in "div.headline". Again, you can leave off the HTML tag. Aside from looking at class rather than ID, the behavior is exactly as described earlier.

Specify the Value of an Arbitrary HTML Attribute

An assert_select() method can be made to look for any arbitrary HTML attribute. This is most useful when searching for the name attribute of input tags. Other, noncontrived examples include the action attribute of a form tag, the src attribute of an img tag, and the href attribute of an a tag. The basic syntax looks like this:

```
assert_select("input[name=user_id]")
```

---

1. Remember that you need to include ActionView::Helpers::RecordIdentificationHelper in order to use dom_id() in your test class.

Note than when testing forms that use Rails naming conventions, you probably want to use the ? syntax for the case where the name actually contains a bracket; otherwise, you can put the entire name in quotes:

```
assert_select("input[name=?]", "user[email]")
assert_select("input[name='user[email]']")
```

The = operator indicates an exact match with the value of the attribute. There are a couple of modifiers to the = for different match behavior. The one I use most often is *=, which is true if the attribute value contains the specified text, as in assert_select("input[name *= email]"). You can also use ^= and $= for starts with and ends with, respectively.

Use a Pseudoclass

There are a number of pseudoclass modifiers that can be added to a selector, including the following:

```
assert_select("div:first-child")
assert_select("div:last-child")
assert_select("div:only-child")
assert_select("div:nth-child(3)")
assert_select("div:nth-last-child(3)")
```

To clear up any confusion: you read these as "a div element that is a first child of its parent," not as "the first child of a div element." I find these helpful when I am testing for output that is in a specific order, such as a sorted list. It's easier to test for "li:nth-child(2)" than to try to extract all the list element text via regular expression and test for the elements of that resulting list. Also, notice those are dashes and not underscores in those pseudoclass names. It seems like I'm always typing them as underscores and then being surprised when the pseudoclass is not recognized.

Each of these has a more specific modifier, replacing child with of-type, such as first-of-type, which means the matching tag must be the first of its siblings of the given HTML type. Read div:first-of-type as "a div element that is the first div element child of its parent." (Do I need to mention that you can use any number as the argument to the nth modifiers?)

Other modifiers that aren't in the first/last/only genre include the following:

```
assert_select("div:root")
assert_select("div:empty")
assert_select("div:not(.headline)")
```

The first modifier in the list checks for an element of the given type that also happens to be the root element. The second looks for an empty tag, while the not modifier looks for an element of that type that does not match the given selector—in this case, a div element that does not have a CSS class of headline. I tend to feel the first two of these are too fiddly for useful tests, but I'm sure there's a valuable use case out there somewhere. The not construct can be helpful for negative testing.

Combine Multiple Selectors

You can use assert_select() to test for different combinations of tags. Again, the syntax is similar to standard CSS.

```
assert_select("div.headline span")
```

That snippet finds all span elements that are inside a div with the class `headline`. Putting a > operator between the two elements means that the second element must be a direct child of the first, not an arbitrary descendant. The + operator means the second element must come immediately after the first in the document, while the ~ operator means that the second element comes somewhere after the first.

You can do further testing on the elements that match your selector. This is most valuable when you want to perform a second match that is limited to only a particular part of your HTML body, such as if you want to test for the existence of a particular text input field but only within a specific form on the page. The most common way to do this kind of search is by nesting assert_select() calls. Nested assert_select() calls have an explicit form that shows the general idea:

```
assert_select("div.headline") do |matching_elements|
  matching_elements.each do |element|
    assert_select(element, "span")
  end
end
```

To begin with, this example exposes a feature of assert_select() that hasn't been mentioned yet. If the first argument to the assert_select() call is a Rails HTML::Node class, then the search is limited to content within that HTML node. If no HTML node is specified, then as you have seen, the default is the response body for the response being tested.

If assert_select() is passed a block element, then the argument to the block is an array containing all the HTML nodes that match the selector: in this case, any div element with the DOM class headline. Inside the block, the matching elements can be iterated on. In this case, they are iterated on for the purpose of verifying that all headline elements contain a span subelement.

This pattern is so common that it has a shortcut, which is used by passing a block that takes no arguments:

```
assert_select("div.headline") do
  assert_select("span")
end
```

In this case, any assert_select() method called within the block is automatically applied to all the matching elements and must pass all those elements in order for the entire assertion to pass—meaning that this snippet and the previous one are exactly equivalent, and each verifies that every div.headline element contains at least one span element.

The form where the block takes an argument is more flexible, although to be honest, I've used assert_select() for years without needing that flexibility—frankly, without even knowing that flexibility existed. If you need even more flexibility, assert_select() also returns the same array of matches, so the same test could be written like this:

```
matching_elements = assert_select("div.headline")
matching_elements.each do |element|
  assert_select(element, "span")
end
```

That's arguably an improvement over the first form: it's shorter. This structure is most helpful to debug an assert_select() test that's failing.

Using assert_select() well is the difference between view tests that actually help you and view tests that make you tear your hair out, so point it at those DOM IDs and take advantage of the shortcuts, and you're off to a great start.

9.4 Testing Outgoing Email

The process of testing outgoing email is closely related to view testing. Typically, you are interested in validating two separate pieces of logic: first, that your application sends an email when expected; and second, that the email content is what you want. The somewhat indirect nature of the Rails ActionMailer makes testing email somewhat less obvious than it might be, but it's not that hard. This section assumes that you are using ActionMailer—if you're using a third-party tool for managing email, you may need to find a different way to test.

To test emails in Rails, configure your test setup so that ActionMailer saves emails in a queryable data structure rather than actually mailing them. This step should be done for you in the Rails config/environments/test.rb file:

```
config.action_mailer.delivery_method = :test
```

Remember to put this next line in your test setup; doing so ensures that the data structure holding the mailings is emptied. Otherwise, emails from other tests will linger and make your test results invalid:

```
ActionMailer::Base.deliveries.clear
```

The quickest email test you can create is one to find out if an email has been sent. The method ActionMailer::Base.deliveries.size() returns the number of emails that have been sent since the last time the Action-Mailer::Base.deliveries object was cleared. So, a simple way to determine whether an email has been sent is just to query it:

```
assert_equal 1, ActionMailer::Base.deliveries.size
```

Rails provides a shortcut, along the lines of assert_difference. This method takes a block and determines how many emails are sent in the course of executing the block:

```
assert_emails 1 do
  get :forgot_password
end
```

The argument to the assert_emails() method is the number of emails that need to be sent in the block for the assertion to pass. The assert_emails() method does not depend on the clear() method having been called; it does its own tracking of count before and after the block. There's also an assert_no_emails(), which is equivalent to assert_emails(0).

If you want to specify the content of the email messages and not just the count, Rails provides the assert_select_email() method, which you might use like this:

```
assert_select_email do
  assert_select "div", :text => "Email Reset"
end
```

What assert_select_email() allows you to do is make assert_select() assertions that will be applied to the body of every email currently in the ActionMailer::Base.deliveries repository. All emails must pass the assertions in the block for the whole thing to pass. This method works only if your outgoing emails are of content type text/html, which is a significant limitation.

You can test the features of the sent emails directly using code like this:

```
email = ActionMailer::Base.deliveries.first
assert_equal "Forgot Password Notice", email.subject
assert_equal @user.email, email.to
assert_match /new password/, email.body
```

The basic accessors have expected names. You can find out more about how to inspect a mail object at http://guides.rubyonrails.org/action_mailer_basics.html.

Outside of core Rails, Shoulda provides a couple of helper methods for testing email; these are described in Section 11.4, *Shoulda Assertions*, on page 173. The most robust way of testing emails, though, is linked to RSpec (see Chapter 12, *RSpec*, on page 183) and also works great with Cucumber (see Chapter 15, *Acceptance Testing with Cucumber*, on page 235). The email-spec library provides a number of very useful helpers. For the most part, they are nice, RSpec ways of performing the tests we've already examined, but the library also provides the ability to follow a link in an email back to the site, which is very helpful for acceptance testing of user interactions that include email. The library's home is http://github.com/bmabey/email-spec.

9.5 Testing Helpers

Helper methods are the storage attic of most Rails applications. Typically, helper modules contain reusable bits of view logic, such as the logic to control what output is printed or change the display based on model data. In practice, helper modules tend to get filled with all kinds of clutter that doesn't seem to belong anywhere else. Worse, since the Rails mechanism for testing helpers was underpowered and underpublicized, helper methods often aren't tested even when they contain significant amounts of logic.

Unfortunately, helpers occupy a somewhat ambiguous place in the Rails MVC pattern structure. Helpers are sort of in the view layer, but they are frequently used as a conduit between views and models, or even views and controllers. Helper tests have a lot in common with model tests—for instance, individual helper methods can be unit-tested one at a time. However, in order for helper methods to be properly run in a test context, at least *some* of the test controller framework used for Rails functional tests needs to be loaded, and getting the setup correct takes a couple of extra steps.

There is a core Rails mechanism for testing helpers, added in Rails 2.1 or so; it's one of the best kept secrets in the entire core stack. (Or was...as of Rails 2.3, helper tests are generated whenever you generate controllers.) You can find it in ActionView::TestCase. This class creates a fake controller environment so that helpers can be loaded, called, and tested.

For helper tests to work if you're using anything prior to Rails 2.3, you must explicitly require 'action_view/test_case' either in your test/test_ helper.rb file or in the helper test itself. Your actual helper test class is a subclass of ActionView::TestCase. The Rails-generated test shell looks like this:

```
require 'test_helper'

class UsersHelperTest < ActionView::TestCase
end
```

The naming convention is just like everything else in Rails: add Test to the end of the name of the helper module to get the class name, and add _test to get the filename. So, your UsersHelper module is tested in users_helper_test.rb and is declared as class UsersHelperTest < ActionView:: TestCase. As of Rails 2.3, Rails places helper tests in the test/unit/helpers directory.

At this point, you are good to go and can test helper methods exactly as though they were regular model methods (with an exception or two described in a moment). For example, if you have the following helper module:

```
module UsersHelper
  def display_name(user)
    "#{user.first_name} #{user.last_name}"
  end
end
```

the test is straightforward:

```
class UsersHelperTest < ActionView::TestCase

  test "a users display name" do
    @user = User.new(:first_name => "Ron", :last_name => "Lithgow")
    assert_equal("Ron Lithgow", display_name(@user))
  end

end
```

Inside your test class, you should have access to all the helpers in your project as well as all the regular Rails helpers, which are automatically loaded by ActionView::TestCase.

9.6 Testing Block Helpers

In Rails 2.2, the private _erbout variable in templates that stored the output stream was changed to a public instance variable. This change caused very little stir outside of _erbout's immediate family, but it did have two very nice effects. It made it possible to inject text from a helper directly into the ERb output without fussing around with block variables, and it also made it easier to test block helpers.

A *block helper* is a helper function that, when invoked in the ERb file, takes a block made up of ERb text. Two common uses of block helpers are as access control, in which the logic in the helper determines whether the code in the block is invoked, and as wrapper code for HTML that might surround many different kinds of text—a rounded rectangle effect, for example.

Here's a small example of a block helper:

```
def if_logged_in
  yield if logged_in?
end
```

which would be invoked like so:

```
<% if_logged_in do %>
  <%= link_to "logout", logout_path %>
<% end %>
```

and which you would test like this (in Rails 2.2 and higher):

```
test "logged_in" do
  assert !logged_in?
  assert_nil(if_logged_in {"logged in"})
  login_as users(:quentin)
  assert logged_in?
  assert_equal("logged in", if_logged_in {"logged in"})
end
```

What we're taking advantage of here is that the last value in the block becomes the return value of the block, which becomes the last value in the method, which becomes the return value of the method. So if nobody is logged in, the block doesn't fire, and the method returns nil. If a user is logged in, then whatever gets passed in the block—in this case, the literal string logged in—is the returned value of the helper.

This also works for helpers that concat values directly into the ERb stream. The somewhat contrived helper:

```
def make_headline
  concat("<h1 class='headline'>#{yield}</h1>")
end
```

And the test:

```
test "make headline" do
  assert_dom_equal("<h1 class='headline'>fred</h1>",
      make_headline { "fred" })
end
```

Again, we're taking advantage of concat() returning the final string as well as placing it into the ERb output. Be careful when using this kind of testing: you aren't actually testing the ERb output—just the return value of the helper method.

If that's not good enough, you can actually test against the ERb output by taking advantage of the fact that concat adds its text to an output buffer that you can also access in your test:

```
test "make headline with output buffer" do
  make_headline { "fred" }
  assert_dom_equal("<h1 class='headline'>fred</h1>", output_buffer)
end
```

In this test, the helper call places the text in the output_buffer, which is then validated in the final line of the test. The method assert_dom_equal() tests whether two strings of HTML are equivalent even if their attribute lists are differently formed.

9.7 Using assert_select in Helper Tests

The output buffer trick is kind of neat, but it would be even nicer if you could bring the full flexibility of assert_select() to bear on the output. Under normal circumstances, assert_select() looks to @response.body to get the text to parse. There are two ways to work around this. You can fake a @response.body object, or you can point assert_select() at an arbitrary string.

The arbitrary string mechanism is perhaps simpler—include the following method in your test/test_helper.rb.

```
def assert_select_string(string, *selectors, &block)
  doc_root = HTML::Document.new(string).root
  assert_select(doc_root, *selectors, &block)
end
```

This method creates an HTML selector object of the kind that Rails accepts as the selector first argument of assert_select(). Using this method would look like this:

```
test "make headline with response body" do
  assert_select_string(display_name(user) "div.first_name")
end
```

In other cases, you might want to have a more complete controller setup, because you are testing session logic. You might also want to call assert_select() directly. If so, you can add the controller setup easily. Place this module somewhere, then require it instead of action_view/test_case:

huddle/test/helper_test_case.rb

```
require 'action_view/test_case'

module ActionView
  class TestCase

    setup :setup_response
    def setup_response
      @output_buffer = ""
      @request       = ActionController::TestRequest.new
      @response      = ActionController::TestResponse.new
      @session = {}
      @request.session = @session
    end

    def session
      @request.session
    end

    def make_response(text)
      @response.body = text
    end
  end
end
```

This adds a TestResponse object; it also gives you a session object, if you need that for testing. The new class now has the make_response() method, which takes arbitrary text and slaps it right into @response.body for you. All you need to do is call make_response() with whatever text you want to assert:

```
test "make headline with response body" do
  make_headline { "fred" }
  make_response output_buffer
  assert_select("h1.headline")
end
```

> ### Gotcha: url_for
>
> Although all core helpers are automatically loaded into the ActionView test environment, there are one or two that have significant dependencies on the real controller object and therefore fail with opaque error messages during helper testing. The most notable of these is url_for( ). One workaround is to override url_for( ) by defining it in your own test case (the method signature is def url_for(options = {})). The return value is up to you; I find a simple stub response is often good enough.

I'm not prepared to defend this as the most elegant way to get assert_select() into your helper tests, but it does work. I think this mechanism probably results in more readable tests for block helpers or for nested assert_select() calls. Note that the ActionView::TestCase() creates its own new TestResponse object every time you call a helper method—so if for some odd reason you have a test that depends on the exact @response object in a helper, you could run into problems with the response object not holding values from helper call to helper call.

9.8 How Much Time Should You Spend on Helpers?

The amount of time you spend testing helpers really depends on the helper or, more generally, on how you use helpers. If you have a lot of view logic in helpers and they are shading toward being presenters of one kind or another, it's a good idea to validate any complex logic. Simple HTML methods, like the make_headline() example here, don't require a lot of testing (certainly not if the testing is bogging you down). However, if you do find a bug in a helper, pull the method into the garage and cover it with tests.

9.9 When to View Test

It's important to test view logic in a considered, careful way. In all TDD, any change to the logic of the program should be driven by a test. Although you shouldn't have the bulk of your logic in the view layer, you'll need to have some logic surrounding display, and that should be tested.

However, complex view logic should be moved to helpers,[2] which are easer to test; see Section 9.5, *Testing Helpers*, on page 144. A strict TDD process often breaks down a little in the view. View programming sometimes feels more exploratory to me, so I usually do a little bit of view code and then cycle back to write a test. As long as the feedback between test and code is relatively tight, that process won't hurt you. View testing can also be managed in an integration test layer using Cucumber (see Chapter 15, *Acceptance Testing with Cucumber*, on page 235) or Rails integration tests; see Chapter 13, *Testing Workflow with Integration Tests*, on page 213. Find the workflow that works best for you.

---

2. A number of third-party tools enlarge the helper concept to a full-fledged object called a *Presenter*, which effectively mediates between a view and one or more models.

## Chapter 10

Testing JavaScript and Ajax

I've had this conversation more than once:

ME: *What test tools do you use?*

SOMEBODY ELSE: *Oh, you know, Shoulda, factory_girl.*

ME: *Do you test your views?*

SOMEBODY ELSE: *Sometimes. When necessary.*

ME: *How do you test your Ajax?*

SOMEBODY ELSE: *[With sad resignation] We don't.*

To be fair, sometimes the roles are reversed, and it's me observing that we don't test our JavaScript.

And really, can you blame me? Testing JavaScript and Ajax is a pain. For one thing, JavaScript is frequently, well, written in JavaScript. It's a nice language, but it has not historically had anywhere near the level of test framework support and commitment as Ruby.[1] Not only that, but Ajax actions often only happen in the browser. The actions are difficult to extract for a user test if they exist only in the view layer. Then there's the whole browser dependence thing. It's hard to blame somebody for chucking the whole testing thing and just writing the code already.

Yet, as more application logic moves to the browser to create cool and useful user experiences, leaving that code untested becomes a bigger

---

1. For some reason, JavaScript tool support has always lagged a few years behind similar languages, probably because of the mistaken impression that JavaScript is just some kind of toy language. This has started to change over the last few years as frameworks like Prototype and jQuery have enabled really powerful JavaScript tools.

and bigger risk. In this chapter, we'll walk through some strategies and tools for testing JavaScript and Ajax from within a Rails application.

This is not meant to be a complete guide to all possible JavaScript tools; we simply don't have the space for that. The tool structure that is outlined in this chapter is one method that I've had some success with and that I think you can be successful with as well. The advantage of the tool chain described in this chapter is that it allows you to test your Ajax both in the browser and as part of your regular command-line Ruby testing. Outside your Rails application, you should also consider browser-level acceptance tools like Selenium as a way to test your web application as a whole.

10.1 First Off, RJS

Even in the notoriously fickle-about-new-tools Rails community, the rise and fall of Ruby JavaScript (RJS) from "cool new tool for writing Ajax" to "tool whose usage is a slightly embarrassing admission that you don't like writing JavaScript" seemed to happen quickly. RJS came along at a time when the JavaScript toolkits were so clunky that it made sense to make what was potentially an extra server call and write simple client-side commands in Ruby so as to avoid writing scary JavaScript. Since then, the JavaScript tools have made legitimate strides, the idea of unobtrusive JavaScript has spread, and the Ruby and Rails community has gotten more comfortable with the need to write more complex client-side interactions in JavaScript, all of which have combined to make RJS seem unneeded at best.

That said, RJS is still nice for quick Ajax features that are inside the limited RJS feature set and are simple enough not to need the weight of an entire JavaScript framework, such as a simple dynamic update of a specific point on the page based on current server data. Plus, since RJS executes essentially as a Rails controller action, it's much easier to test than other JavaScript that exists exclusively in the browser. Also, legacy Rails projects may still have some RJS that you might want to bring under test.

Your weapon of choice in testing RJS is the assert_select_rjs() method. This method is less like the normal assert_select() than you might imagine. The meaning of an assert_select_rjs() call depends slightly on the number of arguments the method is called with. In what I think of as the standard way of calling the method, it takes two arguments, the first of which is a symbol matching an existing RJS Rails method, and the second of which is a DOM ID.

The DOM ID can be static, or can be calculated, as in this example:

```
assert_select_rjs :replace, dom_id(@project)
```

This assertion passes if the controller call in question returns an RJS JavaScript snippet and that snippet contains a call to the RJS replace() method with a DOM ID matching dom_id(@project). This does not make any claim—yet—about the text that is being injected into that DOM element. If the first argument is the RJS method :insert, then the second method can be the position of the insertion (:top, :bottom, :before, or :after), in which case the assertion passes only if the method and the position are called from the RJS. If there is no position argument, any insertion to the given DOM ID will match.

The assertion in assert_select_rjs() can be made weaker. If there's no method symbol, any RJS call to the DOM ID will pass the assertion. If there are no arguments to assert_select_rjs(), the assertion will pass if any RJS call is made in the output—not the most helpful assertion in terms of actually saying something useful.

Clearly, though, the RJS assertion is more valuable, or at least more detailed, if you can specify details about the HTML being sent back to the client page. In order to manage that, you need to pass a block to assert_select_rjs(). As a block container, assert_select_rjs() behaves just like plain old assert_select(), meaning that you can place assert_select() calls inside the block and they will be evaluated against the HTML extracted from the RJS call sent to the client.

```
assert_select_rjs :replace, dom_id(@project) do
  assert_select "div#project_name", :text => @project.name
end
```

In addition to testing for the existence of the RJS call, the previous snippet also tests that the HTML sent to replace the existing text contains a div element with @project.name as its content. This works for any RJS call that is associated with sending text back to the browser—so, for example, remove() doesn't need a block call.

If you happen to be using RJS, then the RJS should be tested as though it was a view, and since RJS pretty much always indicates a change in application logic, then that means RJS calls nearly always should have tests. Exactly how detailed the tests need to be is up to you—normally I do test for the specifics of the text coming back to the browser, but then most of the time I only use RJS if the call is on the simple side. When the call gets more complicated, then we move to actual JavaScript, which needs its own test framework.

10.2 Testing JavaScript from Rails with Jasmine

Once you outgrow the RJS training wheels and start riding the big-kid bicycle that is actual JavaScript, the testing awkwardness becomes apparent. Many JavaScript test frameworks run in a browser, which is certainly nice for assuring fidelity in that browser but is slow and unwieldy for TDD-style tight-feedback testing. If only you could work in both modes...well, you can, using a BDD test framework for JavaScript called Jasmine, along with a gem that wraps Jasmine in Ruby and another gem that produces nicer command-line output.

If you are using Jasmine, you are also going to be much happier if you write using the *unobtrusive* JavaScript style, which I'll define as the separation of JavaScript from the HTML markup. When writing JavaScript unobtrusively, no JavaScript behavior is specified in the body of the HTML page. Instead, event handlers are bound to DOM IDs in functions written elsewhere and injected to the page on load.

There are a number of advantages to an unobtrusive style—generally speaking, it opens browser client JavaScript up to the full range of modern software techniques. For our purposes here, the biggest advantage is that JavaScript separated from the HTML view layer is much easier to isolate and test.

10.3 Getting Started with Jasmine

Jasmine for Rails is distributed as a gem, which gives you access to the Jasmine test framework from within your Rails application. You can then add Jasmine to your Bunder Gemfile with gem 'jasmine' and then use a bundle install to make sure that everything is in place. With the gem installed, you can generate Jasmine files:

```
% bundle exec jasmine init
Jasmine has been installed with example specs.

To run the server:

rake jasmine

To run the automated CI task with Selenium:

rake jasmine:ci
```

In Rails 2, the startup command is script/generate jasmine.

Behind the scenes, Jasmine has created a few files. It has created a spec/javascripts directory—even if you are using Test::Unit, Jasmine creates a spec directory. In that directory, Jasmine has placed a sample file, PlayerSpec.js, which you don't need to keep, and three other files that you do need to keep. The file helpers/SpecHelper.js is the Jasmine analog of Test::Unit's test_helper.rb, and the support directory has a jasmine_runner.rb script and a jasmine.yml configuration file. We'll talk about the config file in a bit.

Jasmine also adds two sample files to the public/javascripts directory, which again you can delete if you don't need them. Finally, it adds a Rake file defining two different tasks for running Jasmine.

10.4 Running Jasmine Tests

The Jasmine gem defines two tasks that let you run your Jasmine specs. The first is simply rake jasmine.

```
$ rake jasmine
your tests are here:
  http://localhost:8888/
```

The Rake task uses Selenium to allow you to run the tests in a browser. All you need to do is hit that http://localhost:8888 address helpfully provided by the Rake task, and the suite will run, as shown in Figure 10.1, on the following page.[2]

The in-browser display shows you every test in the Jasmine suite—green for pass, red for fail. Clicking any test or test group will rerun those tests.

If you'd like to actually run your tests from a command line, Jasmine provides the rake jasmine:ci task. Depending on how strict your definition of "from a command line" is, this task does run tests from a command-line prompt. Sort of. The output looks like this:

```
% rake jasmine:ci
Waiting for jasmine server on 49421...
«Some boring stuff»
==> Waiting for Selenium RC server on port 49427... Ready!
Waiting for suite to finish in browser ...
```

---

2. I suspect it might be annoying if I was creating new Jasmine projects every day, but right now, as an author, I'm really happy that the Jasmine team provides a working sample in their general distribution.

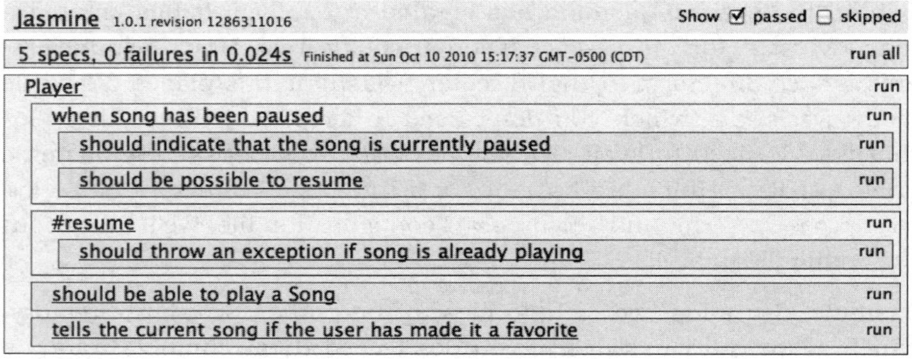

Figure 10.1: Jasmine

```
Player
- should be able to play a Song
- tells the current song if the user has made it a favorite

Player when song has been paused
- should indicate that the song is currently paused
- should be possible to resume

Player#resume
- should throw an exception if song is already playing

Finished in 0.048983 seconds
```

What you can't see from that session transcript is that the Jasmine task has actually opened a Firefox browser, is running the tests in that browser, and is reporting the results back to the terminal session. If you have a failing test, you will see a stack trace pointing to the offending line. Since the task needs to start the Jasmine server, a Selenium remote server, and a Firefox browser window, you can safely surmise that the 0.048 seconds it takes to actually run the tests is but a small fraction of the total time the test takes from start to finish.

As the ci suffix indicates, this task is intended to be integrated into your continuous integration server, where it would be run every time there's a new check-in to the code base. If you want something a little more suitable for regular development, you can try the jazz_money gem,[3] which uses the harmony gem to execute JavaScript from a Ruby process, meaning that your Jasmine tests really do run in a terminal session.

10.5 Writing Jasmine Tests

It doesn't help to know how to run a Jasmine test unless you know how to write one. Jasmine's syntax is as much like RSpec as you can imagine, given that it's JavaScript and not Ruby. If you aren't already familiar with RSpec's basics, it might be worth going to Chapter 12, *RSpec*, on page 183 and then coming back here.

As with RSpec, the basic units of a Jasmine test are denoted with describe() and it(). Where Ruby uses blocks, JavaScript uses anonymous functions, giving you something like this:

```
describe("on my edit page", function() {

  beforeEach(function() {
    clearMyValues();
  });

  it("should do something neat on start", function() {
    initValues();
    expect(userCount).toEqual(2);
  });

});
```

As with RSpec, describe() creates a group of several related tests, the beforeEach() function defines a callback that is executed before each test, and it() describes a test. The method pair expect() and toEqual() are the Jasmine equivalent of a matcher. To negate the matcher, you chain in a not() method, as in expect(userCount).not.toEqual(2).

You can nest describe() methods, and the semantics of defining multiple beforeEach() functions are exactly as with the Ruby libraries we've discussed—outermost first. There is an analogous afterEach() method that is performed after each test, and that, as you'd expect, is executed in innermost first order. Both the beforeEach() and afterEach() methods can also be placed outside any describe() method, in which case the

---

3. As I write this, the jazz_money gem is, wait for it...between versions strongly enough that I don't think it's going to be helpful to provide detailed installation instructions. See http://github.com/pivotalexperimental/jazz_money for current updates.

function applies to all tests in the file. One twist unique to Jasmine is that any individual spec can define its own after functionality by defining a this.after method anywhere within its body that takes a function argument:

```
it('does something' function() {
  this.after(function() { cleanUp(); })
});
```

Cleanup at the individual spec level is sometimes necessary to clear global information about the DOM or event handlers that would otherwise be persisted between tests.

Jasmine defines about a dozen default matchers. See the Jasmine docs at http://pivotal.github.com/jasmine/matchers.html for a full list. Here are the most useful. These should be reasonably self-explanatory.

```
expect(obj).toBeFalsy;
expect(obj).toBeGreaterThan(value)
expect(num).toBeLessThan(value);
expect(obj).toBeNull;
expect(obj).toBeTruthy;
expect(array).toContain(value);
expect(obj).toEqual(value);
expect(str).toMatch(regex);
```

Jasmine makes it easy to add your own custom matchers. The first step is to define the matcher. You have two different parameters to worry about. The actual value, meaning the argument to the expect() method, is exposed as this.actual. Any arguments you want to pass to the matcher itself as part of the matcher logic you can just pass as a straightforward argument list. The matcher function needs to return true if the matcher passes. So, a sample matcher might look like this:

```
function(expected_name) {
  return this.actual.name == expected_name;
}
```

To actually use the matcher, it needs to be registered with Jasmine using the addMatcher() function, which is available inside any before() or it() method. The matcher can be defined inline inside addMatcher(), as follows:

```
beforeEach(function() {
  this.addMatchers({
    toHaveTheName: function(expected_name) {
      return this.actual.name == expected_name;
    }
  })
});
```

You don't actually have to define the matcher function inline, of course. The function can be defined anywhere, assigned to a variable, and referenced within the addMatchers() function. For that matter, beforeEach() here can also be defined globally in a helper file.

Of course, saying that we can define the method globally begs the question of exactly how the Jasmine gem determines what files to load, both for testing and as the application to be tested. Unlike Test::Unit and RSpec, which infer these items from the file system, the Jasmine gem determines the boundaries of the test suite from entries in the spec/javascripts/support/jasmine.yml file.

The first thing you can do in the jasmine.yml file is specify the JavaScript source libraries to load from:

`huddle3_rspec2/spec/javascripts/support/jasmine.yml`

```
src_files:
  - public/javascripts/prototype.js
  - public/javascripts/effects.js
  - public/javascripts/controls.js
  - public/javascripts/dragdrop.js
  - public/javascripts/application.js
  - public/javascripts/**/*.js
```

Each line here is a different pattern, and any JavaScript files that match the pattern are loaded and available to be accessed from Jasmine files. The files are loaded in order, which explains why you'd specify individual files even though the wildcards in the last line cover all of them. By specifying what files go first, you can make sure that any dependencies between the files are managed.

Although the JavaScript file list is probably what you would need to edit the most, the jasmine.yml file also allows you to specify CSS files that can be used for DOM testing, helper files with, say, custom matcher functions, and the location of the actual Jasmine spec files.

Jasmine has a very flexible and feature-rich mock framework, which Jasmine refers to as *spies*. You declare a spy with the spyOn() method, which takes two arguments. The first argument is an object, and the second argument is a string that is the name of a method to which the object responds. You can also declare an empty spy with Jasmine's create_spy() method. So:

```
var User = {
  username: 'zachp',
  authenticate: function(password) {
    return someWebServiceCall(this.username, password);
  },
```

```javascript
    authWithCallback: function(password, callbackFunction) {
      if authenticate {
        return callbackFunction(password);
      }
    }
};

describe("user stuff", function() {
  it('should call authenticate', function() {
    var myUser = Object.create(User);
    spyOn(myUser, 'authenticate');

    // do something
  });

  it('should authenticate with callback', function() {
    var myUser = Object.create(User);
    spy = jasmine.createSpy();
    myUser.authWithCallback('password', spy);

    //do something
  });
});
```

In the previous fragment, I create an object named myUser that knows about an authenticate() method and then use the spyOn method to create a spy for that method. At this point, the only thing the spy does is block the actual call to the authenticate() method and just return null. In the second spec, a bare spy is created and passed to the authWith-Callback() method as the callback function.

So far, that's not very helpful, but there are a few different ways to add useful behavior.

We can create an expectation on the spy, effectively testing to see if the mocked method has been called. Note that when using spyOn(), the spy is actually part of the object's namespace, but the bare spy created using createSpy() can be used directly. So, you'd add the basic expectation like so:

```javascript
expect(myUser.authenticate).toHaveBeenCalled()
expect(myUser.authenticate).toHaveBeenCalledWith('password')

expect(spy).toHaveBeenCalled()
expect(spy).toHaveBeenCalledWith('password')
```

We can augment the spy when it is created to change the default behavior of just returning null. These methods work with spies created with either spyOn() or createSpy().

```
spyOn(myUser, 'authenticate').andCallFake(aFunction);
spyOn(myUser, 'authenticate').andCallThrough();
spyOn(myUser, 'authenticate').andReturn(arg);
spyOn(myUser, 'authenticate').andThrow(exception)
```

The andCallFake() method takes a method as an argument and invokes that method when the spy is called, exactly analogous to a Ruby mock package taking a block as an argument. The andCallThrough() method is unusual in that it allows for spy-like watching behavior and also calls the original method as though there was no spy. Both andReturn() and andThrow() specify the behavior of the fake method when called, again similar to the Ruby mock packages we've already seen.

10.6 Integrating Jasmine with Dynamic Rails

If you are reading about Jasmine in this particular book, then you probably are most interested in testing JavaScript that interacts with your Rails application. Meaning that much of what you want to test will be dependent on the particular DOM structure of your pages and the event bindings that you create. Jasmine is designed to be DOM and framework agnostic, so it doesn't offer out-of-the-box support for tight Rails integration. However, with a little elbow grease, it is possible to write Jasmine specs that use the output of your Rails app as DOM fixtures. There are a couple of ways to do this; the mechanism outlined here comes from JB Steadman on Pivotal's blog at http://pivotallabs.com/users/jb/blog/articles/1152-javascripttests-bind-reality-.

The idea here is to write a script that does nothing but generate HTML and put it in a temporary file for later loading by Jasmine. The original Pivotal version used RSpec for this purpose, on the theory that the files would then be generated as part of your regular test suite. But there's nothing magical about RSpec here except that RSpec already has the Rails environment loaded and primed for easy querying. What you need is to add a line like the following to any RSpec spec, integration test, or whatever, which is generating HTML that you'd like to use in a later Jasmine test.

```
save_fixture((response.body, 'body'), 'project_file')
```

The save_fixture() method is a helper method from JB's blog post that I have tweaked very slightly here:

`huddle3_rspec2/spec/spec_helper.rb`

```
def save_fixture(raw_markup, name, parent_element="body")
  markup = html_for(raw_markup, parent_element)
  fixture_path = File.join(RAILS_ROOT, '/tmp/js_dom_fixtures')
  Dir.mkdir(fixture_path) unless File.exists?(fixture_path)
  fixture_file = File.join(fixture_path, "#{name}.fixture.html.erb")
  File.open(fixture_file, 'w') do |file|
    file.puts(markup)
  end
end
```

The save_fixture() method gets its HTML text from a method that uses Nokogiri to extract and clean up the HTML.

`huddle3_rspec2/spec/spec_helper.rb`

```
def html_for(html, selector)
  doc = Nokogiri::HTML(html)
  remove_third_party_scripts(doc)
  content = doc.css(selector).first.to_s
  return convert_body_tag_to_div(content)
end
```

The exact details of the cleanup methods called here aren't that important. It cleans up third-party scripts by removing a known DOM element from the output. More importantly, it changes the body tag to a regular div tag because, as we'll see, we'll be injecting this text into an already existing Jasmine page. One important fact is that if you are trying this call from an RSpec controller method, you need to have called render_views (in RSpec 1.x, that's integrate_views) in the RSpec describe block so that RSpec will generate output.

From Jasmine, you can then use the fixture with the assistance of some helper methods that you can find online at http://github.com/pivotaljb/js-fixture-example or in the code samples for this book at code/huddle3_rspec2/spec/javascripts/helpers/load_fixture.js. The Github repository is a full application that shows how to incorporate the fixtures into a Rails apps. The downside is that it was written for RSpec 1.3, and the RSpec helper code needs a little bit of tweaking to work in RSpec 2.[4]

---

4. Most notably, the RSpec 1.3 helper code is implemented inside the class Spec::Rails::Examples::ControllerExampleGroup, and in RSpec 2, the fully qualified class name is RSpec::Rails::ControllerExampleGroup.

```
describe("huddle project behavior", function() {
  it("does some fancy ajax thing", function() {
    spec.loadFixture("project_file");
    $(".project").click();
    // and then some expectations
  });
});
```

There are a couple of notes here. Once the fixture is loaded, you can use jQuery or your framework of choice to interact with the DOM. Any event bindings that are generated as part of that particular page are also loaded and can then be triggered from the spec. Any event bindings that are part of an external script that would normally be loaded before the body of the fixture, such as in an application.js file, need to be separately loaded in the Jasmine test after the fixture is loaded. So, for example, if your JavaScript event handlers are nicely separated into functions, you need to call those functions after loading the fixture in order for the event handlers to be honored by the Jasmine code.

Also, you need to clear the global event bindings and DOM after each test:

huddle3_rspec2/spec/javascripts/helpers/SpecHelper.js

```
beforeEach(function() {
  $('#jasmine_content').empty();
  spec.clearLiveEventBindings();
});

spec.clearLiveEventBindings = function() {
  var events = jQuery.data(document, "events");
  for (prop in events) {
    delete events[prop];
  }
};
```

Granted, this isn't exactly a simple process, and I'd hope that a future version of the Jasmine gem will move some of this into the framework, at least as an option. That said, this is pretty close to having everything you'd want in a Rails/Ajax framework: you can use your actual application code to drive your JavaScript test, you can run the tests in a browser or at the command line, and everything is reasonably easy to create and run. JavaScript testing has gotten a lot better over the past year, from prohibitively irritating to actually feasible and valuable. As JavaScript continues to be a big part of dynamic web apps, increased testing is a very good thing.

Part IV

Testing Framework Extensions

## Chapter 11

Write Cleaner Tests
with Shoulda and Contexts

The core testing tools distributed with Rails are great, and I would have killed for them back when I was doing Java applications. Even so, there are extensions, add-ons, and frameworks that make the tools even more powerful and allow us to write tests that are even more concise and clear. We've seen a couple of these categories already: data factories in Section 6.5, *Data Factories*, on page 81 and mock object tools in Chapter 7, *Using Mock Objects*, on page 95.

Data factories and mock tools expand the reach of what we can cleanly do in a test. Over the next two chapters, we'll talk about test add-ons that change the structure of our tests as a whole. In this chapter, we'll talk about *contexts* as a way of denoting groups of related tests and how the ability to organize tests can lead to a different style of testing where each test has a single assertion. A Rails add-on called *Shoulda* adds this style of testing on top of the standard-issue Test::Unit. In addition, Shoulda bundles up a lot of common test patterns into one-line macros that can easily be inserted into our tests.

As we talk about single assertion test styles, we'll show how Shoulda implements them on top of Test::Unit while still being useful inside RSpec. The single-assertion style is more appropriate in some settings than others, and we'll also cover some tools that make writing single assertion tests inside Test::Unit a little bit easier.

In the following chapter, we will look at RSpec. RSpec is not built on Test::Unit but is a completely parallel testing tool with its own structure, syntax, and style. RSpec is designed to allow us to specify system behavior with an emphasis on making our code read as naturally as possible.

11.1 Contexts

In Section 2.3, *Setup and Teardown*, on page 20, we saw how Test::Unit and Rails allow us to extract common setup and teardown behavior to methods that are automatically run before or after each test. It's a handy feature, with one flaw: the setup methods are common to all tests in a given class. Since Rails tends to prefer that we keep all tests for a single controller or model in one file, this can cause problems.

Often, you'll find that in addition to having setup common to the entire class, you'll have subordinate setup common to only a cohesive subset of the tests. For example, you might be writing controller tests for a user that is logged in, for one that is not logged in, and for an admin. While there is common setup to all these tests, each set of tests has a separate user initialization not shared by the others. If only tests could be grouped with their own startup method, one not shared by all the other tests....

Enter the idea of contexts. Contexts are not part of the core Rails test tools but are implemented very similarly by three different add-ons: RSpec, Shoulda, and a gem by Jeremy McAnally conveniently called Context.[1] For this discussion, we'll be using the Shoulda syntax. RSpec contexts will be discussed in Section 12.2, *Contexts with describe*, on page 187.

The context() method is used to group a set of tests into a single set for the purpose of giving them a common setup and teardown block that is not shared by other tests in the test class.

The basic idea is that each context has its own methods, run before and after each test in that context—the Context gem uses before() and after() as the names of these methods, and Shoulda uses setup() and teardown(). Not to spoil the next chapter or anything, but RSpec uses before(:each) and after(:each).

---

1. As I write this, Shoulda's status as a stand-alone tool is in flux, and by the time you read this, there is a pretty good chance that the context part of Shoulda will have also been extracted into a stand-alone gem.

Within a context, we define the setup and teardown blocks by calling the methods setup() and teardown(). We can have as many different setup or teardown blocks as we want; they will be executed in the order they are defined. Here's an example:

```ruby
class ProjectControllerTest < ActionController::TestCase

  context "with an admin user" do
    setup do
      login_as_admin
    end

    teardown do
      logout
    end

    test "admin features"
      # something administrative
    end
  end

  context "with a regular user" do
    setup do
      login_as_normal
    end

    test "normal features"
      # something normal
    end
  end
end
```

The tests in each context have the setup() methods for that context run before each test. We can still use the standard Test::Unit setup and teardown blocks outside of any context. Those methods would be called first, before the context setup method, at the beginning of each test.

Since a simple Ruby method creates contexts, we can generate them dynamically in the same way that tests can be generated dynamically:

```ruby
["admin", "root"].each do |role|
  context "with a #{role} user" do
    setup do
      @user = User.new(:role => role)
    end

    test "can login"
      # this test is run twice, once in each context
    end
  end
end
```

I'm not saying I recommend this in general, mind you, but it can be done. You need to be careful with this kind of metaprogramming in tests, because the added complexity makes it easier for bugs to get into the tests, and the metaprogramming will make the test less clear to future readers.

Contexts can also be nested, which we can accomplish by simply declaring a new context inside the old one. We normally do this when we have a setup that we want shared by other tests that will extend the setup. In this example, both inner contexts share the @product object, but one tests for what an administrative user would see, and the other tests for what a normal user would see:

```ruby
context "for the product show page" do
  setup { @product = Product.create(:name => "Wonderflonium") }

  context "with an administrative user" do
    setup { User.create(:admin => true) }
    should "see an edit link" do
      get :show, :id => @product.id.to_s
      assert_select "a", "edit"
    end

  end

  context "with a normal user" do
    setup { User.create(:admin => false) }
    should "not see an edit link" do
      get :show, :id => @product.id.to_s
      assert_select "a", "edit", :count => 0
    end
  end
end
```

The setup blocks are called in the order you'd expect, from the parent context down to the children—contexts can be nested as deeply as you want. However, it's hard to think of a real-world example where you'd want more than three levels, maybe four. In any case, teardown blocks, if they exist, are resolved in the reverse order, from child up to parent.

Nested contexts are great in that they can reduce duplication in our tests, specifically duplication in test setup, which can make it easier to focus attention on the part of the test that is actually, you know, testing. However, if the contexts or the tests within get long, it can easily become hard to follow the execution thread through the various layers of nested contexts. Sometimes it's worth it to have a little duplication in tests in order to make it clear what's going on.

11.2 Basics of Shoulda

Let's take a brief moment to talk about the basics of Shoulda. It's distributed as a gem, so for Rails 3 all we need to do is include it in the Bundler Gemfile:

```
gem "shoulda"
```

In Rails 2.*x*, we need the following line in the config.rb file:

```
config.gem 'shoulda', :lib => 'shoulda'
```

Once installed, it will insert itself into Test::Unit, so there is no further include or require needed to use Shoulda. In addition to working with Test::Unit, the matcher and assertion features of Shoulda can also be integrated with RSpec. For that to work, require 'shoulda' in the spec/spec_helper.rb file somewhere before the RSpec configuration block.

We have already seen the Shoulda syntax for defining contexts. In Test::Unit, Shoulda gives us the should() method to define a test, which is analogous to the Rails standard test() method or to the older-style Test::Unit construct def test_. This was a lot cooler before Rails added the test() method, which does effectively the same thing. The method takes a string name for the test and a block that defines the test. A simple example follows:

```
should "actually work" do
  @user = User.new
  assert @user.valid?
end
```

This creates a method called test_should_actually_work(), which is incorporated into the standard Test::Unit test runner.

Within the body of a context, we can define as many should() tests as we want. To clarify, should() tests don't need to be in contexts; contexts just turn out to be a handy way to group related tests together.

11.3 Single Assertion Testing

When added to Test::Unit, Shoulda has a lot of functional similarities to RSpec. However, Shoulda popularized a different style of structuring tests that depends on contexts and nested contexts. The defining feature of this style is the idea that each test should contain only a single assertion. In essence, what would otherwise be a test with some setup and a series of assertions has the setup placed instead in the context setup, and each assertion becomes a separate test.

To put it another way, a test consists of three basic steps: setting up the test data, performing some action, and verifying the result. In a traditional-style Test::Unit test, the setup is in the setup block, and the action and verification are in the actual test. Typically, a test has more than one assertion.

In a single-assertion style test, the setup and action are in the context setup, leaving just the verification in the actual test. As you'll see in the next section, Shoulda comes with a lot of macros that are designed to be used in the body of a context where the action under test has been performed. The design goal is that each test contain only a single assertion, but obviously that's not always feasible. A sample set of tests about an index page might look like this:

```
Line 1    context "with the index page" do

            setup do
              @p1 = Product.create(:name => "product 1")
        5     @p2 = Product.create(:name => "product 2")
              get :index
            end

            should "be successful" { assert_response :success }
       10   should "set the users" do
              assert_same_elements([@p1, @p2], assigns(:users))
            end
            should "display the table rows" do
              assert_select "tr.product_row", :count => 2
       15   end
          end
```

The action of this test, get :index, is in the context setup in line 6. Each should() test has one assertion, so the context is effectively what would have been one test in the more classic test style. In Section 11.4, *Shoulda Assertions*, on the facing page, we'll see that Shoulda has some macros to simplify writing these tests, and in Section 11.7, *Single-Line Test Tools*, on page 180, we'll see some other tools for single-line tests.

This style has one significant advantage: each individual assertion will now run independently. If they were all in the same test, a failure in one assertion prevents later assertions from being evaluated. This gives us a somewhat more accurate view of our code from the test suite. The major disadvantage to this style is a loss of speed, since the setup block is now being called once for each assertion. If the setup adds a lot of objects to the database, there can be a significant slowdown. As far as readability goes, I personally don't see a huge difference between the two styles, although the one-assertion test may be clearer in simple cases. It is true, though, that the one-assertion style tends to lead to more deeply nested contexts that can be hard to wade through.

11.4 Shoulda Assertions

In addition to the context() and should() helpers, Shoulda defines a set of additional test methods that can make tests easier to read.

First are a couple of methods that could be described as assertions that should really be in Rails core. Two that are particularly useful are assert_same_elements() and assert_contains(). The assert_same_elements() method takes two array arguments and returns true if the arrays contain the same elements, even if the order of the elements differs. So, the following test will pass:

```
should "have the same elements" do
  assert_same_elements([1, 1, 3, 4], [4, 1, 3, 1])
end
```

If one array contains an element multiple times, the other array must contain the same element the same number of times.

Also helpful is assert_contains(), which takes an array and an object. The assertion passes if the array contains the object. If the object happens to be a regular expression, the assertion passes if any of the elements in the array matches the regular expression. The flip side is assert_does_not_contain():

```
should "contain things"
  assert_contains([1, 2, 3, 4], 2)
  assert_does_not_contain([1, 2, 3, 4], 7)
end
```

For ActiveRecord, we get assert_valid() and assert_save(), both of which take an ActiveRecord model and return true if the model is either currently valid or able to be saved. We also get assert_good_value(), the basic form of which takes three arguments. The first argument is an ActiveRecord model, the second is an attribute, and the third is a value. The assertion passes if the value is valid for the attribute, given the validations defined in the model. An optional fourth argument consists of a string or regular expression that causes the assertion to check that any validations errors do not match that argument; it limits the "good" check to a single validation error. The complementary method, assert_bad_value(), is the exact opposite. In both methods, the first argument can be a class, in which case a new instance of that class is created and used for the assertion.

11.5 Shoulda One-Liners

Shoulda is famous for its one-line test matchers, which are powerful tests that can be expressed in a single line. In most cases, these tests are designed to be placed inside contexts or the top-level class, not inside should() tests. The tests then validate certain conditions based on the context setup.

Shoulda defines specific one-liners for ActionController, ActionMailer, ActionView, ActiveRecord, and ActionMailer. In earlier versions of Shoulda, these tests were effectively class methods that started with should_. Over time, however, the Shoulda team switched to a more RSpec-like matcher structure, in which the tests are methods that can be used after the more generic should or should_not methods, as in the following ActiveRecord test:

```
Line 1   class CalendarTest < Test::Unit::TestCase
     2     should have_many(:tasks)
     3   end
```

Notice that the call in line 2 is not inside a context or test. Instead, it generates a test that contains one assertion, namely, that the Calendar class has a Rails has_many association with the Task class.

Also, every method that can be called after should can also be called after the method should_not, which reverses the effect of the method: should_not have_many(:tasks) passes if the class does not have the association. Rather than take arguments, many of the matchers have further methods that can be chained after them to produce the same effect. If you're familiar with RSpec, you'll recognize these features from the RSpec syntax. (Those of you who are not familiar with RSpec will be after reading the next chapter.) In fact, it's an important feature of the Shoulda matchers that they are fully compatible for inclusion in RSpec specifications.

Action Controller Macros

The ActionController methods are generally designed to be used inside a context that makes a controller call in its setup, and they validate common side effects of controller actions. The following code sample shows the most useful ones, in a really contrived way. This is not the complete set; check out the Shoulda documentation at http://dev.thoughtbot.com/shoulda/ for the whole shebang.

```
context "with the index page"
  setup { get :index }

  should assign_to(:projects)
  should render_template(:index)
  should render_with_layout('application')
  should respond_with(:success)
  should respond_with_content_type('application/pdf')
end

should route(:get, '/index', :action => :index).to(
    :action => :index)

context "with a redirect"
  setup { get :an_action_that_redirects }
  should redirect_to('route_path')
  should set_session(:user_id).to(nil)
  should set_the_flash.to(/Sorry/)
end
```

Let's look at this a little more closely. First, should assign_to() passes if the controller sets an instance variable of that name to any value. We can make the test more specific with two chain methods. The method with() (as in should assign_to(:project).with(@project)) makes the assertion pass only if the variable is assigned to that particular value, while the method with_kind_of() takes a class as an argument and passes if the assigned value has a kind_of?() relationship with the class.

The should redirect_to() takes any Rails url-convertable() object as the argument; alternately, the method can take a block that evaluates to a URL-like object. The should_respond_with_content_type() method takes a string, which must match the MIME type exactly; a symbol, which is mapped to a MIME type using Ruby's standard lookup table; or a regular expression, which must match the string for the MIME type.

The should set_session() method is analogous to should assign_to() but checks the session list. The to() chain method takes the expected value in the session. The should set_the_flash_to() takes either a string or a regular expression as its argument.

The should route() method is a little special, in that it checks general routing, rather than anything specific to the particular controller. The first argument is an HTTP verb; the second is a URL string. Remaining arguments are key/value pairs representing the options set by Rails during the routing process. If we don't specify the controller in the option list, Shoulda will infer the controller from the name of the current test class. The to chain method contains the expected route, and the expected and actual routes are compared using the same logic as the standard Rails routing tests described in Section 8.6, *Testing Routes*, on page 132.

ActiveRecord Macros

There are many ActiveRecord macros, most of which are designed to be run outside of a context and check the relationships or validations of the ActiveRecord model. Again, I'll present sample usage of the most useful in a slightly contrived test class and put any special notes at the end:

```
class ProductTest < ActiveSupport::TestCase
  should allow_mass_assignment_of(:name)
  should allow_value("123").for(:serial_number)
  should belong_to(:company)
  should ensure_inclusion_of(:price).in_range(0 .. 100)
  should ensure_length_of(:name).is_at_least(5).is_at_most(10)

  should have_and_belong_to_many(:orders)
  should have_many(:categories)
  should have_one(:brand)
  should validate_acceptance_of(:agreement)
  should validate_numericality_of(:price)
  should validate_presence_of(:password)
  should validate_uniqueness_of(:email)
end
```

Some general notes: remember that all of these matchers also work with the negating should_not() method. All of the matchers that would expect an error, such as should_not allow_value, take an optional chain method with_message(), which allows us to test the exact error message. In older versions of Shoulda, many of these methods took an optional list of arguments. That functionality seems to have been removed.

The ensure_length_of() matcher has a series of chain methods to specify the length, including is_at_least(), is_at_most(), and is_equal_to.

ActionMailer Macros

Shoulda defines one matcher for testing ActionMailer behavior; it is called should have_sent_email(). With no chain methods, it passes if an email has been sent. One or more chain methods can be added on: from(), to(), with_body(), and with_subject().

```
should have_sent_email.to("mom@mommy.com").with_subject(/laundry/)
```

All the chain methods take a string, which must be an exact match, or a regular expression, which must match the email part in question. For from() and to(), the string or regular expression needs to match only one of the list of addresses. If multiple email addresses are sent by Action-Mailer, all the email addresses must match for the entire expression to pass.

11.6 Writing Your Own Shoulda Matcher

The Shoulda team's decision to move Shoulda to a higher degree of RSpec compatibility had undeniable positive benefits—such as, well, RSpec compatibility and also a more consistent syntax. However, the ability to easily create our own Shoulda matchers was clearly a casualty. What was once a simple, three-line class method is now about a page of code. To be fair, if you are in RSpec, you can use RSpec's tools for creating custom matchers simply, as shown in Section 12.6, *Creating Your Own Matchers*, on page 208. If you aren't in RSpec-land, though, you don't have a lot of tools to hold your hand through the process. It's doable, though, and here's an example. If you are going to start writing your own Shoulda matchers for Test::Unit, I recommend digging into the Shoulda source for examples.

We'll build this Shoulda matcher from the top down. The first thing we need is the method that will actually be called from the Shoulda test. The example we're going to walk through is the ActionController render_template matcher, which is called something like this:

```
should render_template(:index)
```

The first thing we need to define is the actual render_template() method. Although Ruby syntax flexibility is disguising it, the render_template() method is actually an instance method of TestCase—which might be easier to see if we wrote the line fully parenthesized:

```
should(render_template(:index))
```

So, the render_template method has to be defined as an instance method of TestCase, and it needs to return a Matcher object—more about this in a second.

The actual Shoulda definition of the method looks like this:

```
module Shoulda
  module ActionController
    module Matchers
      def render_template(template)
        RenderTemplateMatcher.new(template, self)
      end
    end

    class RenderTemplateMatcher
      # Full definition of matcher here
    end
  end
end
```

The arguments passed to the matcher class must include the context in which the matcher was called, handled here by passing self. This allows the matcher to work both when called from the top level and when called from within a context and ensures the correct context startup and teardown are executed around the matcher.

Now, we have to make that method visible to TestCase. As a short example, we can just include it inside the test_helper.rb file. For a larger example, we can have a separate file that opens the class and manages the include:

```
module Test # :nodoc: all
  module Unit
    class TestCase
      include Shoulda::ActionController::Matchers
    end
  end
end
```

The render_template() method returns an instance of RenderTemplateMatcher. What's that? Nearly anything we want, within some constraints. For example, notice that RenderTemplateMatcher, as listed earlier, does not have a parent matcher class of any kind.

The rest of the Shoulda system does expect the Matcher class to define a specific set of methods. To wit:

- A description() method that returns a string. This string is used to give the test a name for the Test::Unit system, so the method typically uses some of the arguments to the matcher to create a unique string for each matcher, as in "render template #{@template}".

- A method matches?, which takes one argument, the eventual subject of the test at runtime. It returns true if the matcher matches and false otherwise. If this method is complex, it will often defer to private methods of the class to define its logic.

- Methods failure_message() and negative_failure_message(), which return strings and are used as the display message when the matcher doesn't return the expected value. We can make these plain attributes, in which case default messages are used.

- Any other methods that we want to chain with the matcher would be defined as instance methods of the matcher class. Typically, those methods set instance variables that are referred to by the matches?() method when determining whether the matcher should pass.

The entire matcher looks like this, a slightly edited code sample straight from the Shoulda source:

```ruby
class RenderTemplateMatcher

  attr_reader :failure_message, :negative_failure_message

  def initialize(template, context)
    @template = template.to_s
    @context  = context
  end

  def matches?(controller)
    @controller = controller
    begin
      @context.send(:assert_template, @template)
      @negative_failure_message = "Didn't expect to render #{@template}"
      true
    rescue Test::Unit::AssertionFailedError => error
      @failure_message = error.message
      false
    end
  end

  def description
    "render template #{@template}"
  end
end
```

Shoulda matchers aren't that complicated, but if you find yourself creating a bunch of them, it might be time to check out RSpec and its more simplified ways of creating matchers.

11.7 Single-Line Test Tools

The single assertion per test style has a lot of nice features, but it can be kind of verbose, since each single-line test needs its own description string. In this section, we examine two different tools for writing more concise one-assertion tests. One tool, Zebra, works nicely within Shoulda, while the other, Testbed, is more of a stand-alone tool. Again, the following chapter discusses RSpec's own mechanisms for single-line tests.

One-Line Tests with Zebra

Zebra, by James Golick, is dedicated to the proposition that test names are basically just comments and therefore inherently untrustworthy. With Zebra, we can write very succinct one-line tests.

Install Zebra as a gem by putting it in the gemfile for Rails 3 (gem 'zebra'); or, in Rails 2.3, with the following in an environment file:

```
config.gem 'giraffesoft-zebra', :lib => 'zebra',
```

Once installed, Zebra is pretty straightforward to use. Here's an example from within a Shoulda controller test—you can use Zebra outside of Shoulda, but it works really nicely inside it:

```
context "GET new" do

  setup do
    get :new
  end

  expect { assert_response :success }
  expect { assert_select "form[action *= password_resets]" }
  expect { assert_select "input[name = email]"}

end
```

Effectively, what we get here is an anonymous test by calling expect() with a block argument. Zebra creates regular Test::Unit tests with names based on the context of the block. In this case, the first Zebra test will be named test: assert_response :success; if the test fails, that's the name we'll see.

Other than that, the expect() block behaves just like any other test. The code in the block is executed after the setup; if the assertions fail or error, they'll be reported just like any other test. There's no explicit requirement that the test block be just one line, but it makes little sense to use Zebra for longer tests.

I don't know about you, but to me, these tests read great. They are easy to write and easy to read. I suspect I may like Zebra even more than James Golick does.

Creating Quick Case Tests with Testbed

Testbed was written by, well, by me. Originally it was just an experiment in metaprogramming, but I find it useful from time to time, so I've continued to use it where appropriate. Testbed is a Rails plugin, and you can get it at http://github.com/noelrappin/testbed.

Testbed is useful when we need to write a series of tests that validate the same method or series of methods for a variety of input values—in other words, something like this, taken from tests I wrote for extensions to Enumerable:

```
test "lowest missing number" do
  assert_equal([1, 2, 3].lowest_missing_number, 4)
  assert_equal([1, 2, 4].lowest_missing_number, 3)
  assert_equal([].lowest_missing_number, 1)
end
```

That test isn't horrible by any means, but it does put all the assertions in a single test, and in some sense it duplicates the call to lowest_missing_number(), somewhat obscuring the point of the test. And this is something of a best case for this kind of test—if the common test feature is more than one line, these tests can get kind of verbose.

Testbed allows us to put the common method in a block and then pass each individual input as a separate test. Here's the same set of tests using Testbed:

```
testbed "should return lowest missing number" do |list|
  list.lowest_missing_number
end
verify_that([1, 2, 3]).returns(4)
verify_that([1, 2, 4]).returns(3)
verify_that([]).returns(1)
```

The testbed() method takes a descriptive string and a block. Any verify_that() methods between that block and the next testbed() creates a test with a name like test_should return lowest missing number_[1, 2, 3].

When the test is run, the arguments to verify_that() are passed to the block and can then validate the return value of the block against the argument to the returns() method. The generic returns() method can take any argument. There are also specific methods: returns_true(), returns_false(), and returns_nil().

The key to using Testbed is to pass literals or simple objects to the test-bed and let the block do the heavy lifting. In this example from a timesheet application, Testbed uses Timecop (described in Section 6.11, *Timecop*, on page 91) to freeze a date and then creates a factory object and calculates a resource's anniversary in a given year:

```
testbed "calculate anniversary" do |start_date, year|
  Timecop.freeze(2009, 6, 1)
  resource = Resource.make(:start_date => start_date.to_date)
  resource.start_date_anniversary(year).to_s(:db)
end
verify_that("May 6, 2007", 2008).returns("2008-05-06")
verify_that("May 6, 2007", nil).returns("2009-05-06")
```

11.8 When to Use Shoulda

Originally, Shoulda was let into the world as a way to get many of the advanced features of RSpec without the heavy commitment that RSpec entailed and without some of the more magical features of RSpec syntax that some people don't like. Over time, the Shoulda team became more comfortable with RSpec, and now Shoulda is probably best understood as a way to make single-assertion testing easier, no matter which other tools are in your toolbox.

I love the clarity of the single-line style, especially in simple cases, and that's the way I work by default. That said, it's possible for those tests to get so tangled in nested contexts that they become hard to read. If you start to have test failures because other people on your team can't trace the flow of action in tests, that's a real problem and an indication that you need to dial the nested contexts back. Also, keep an eye on test speed, and watch out for slow running setups that have to be run for multiple single-assertion tests.

Now that we've seen how contexts and single-line testing work within Test::Unit, it's time to see how they play out in RSpec, a library written from scratch to support a very strongly natural-language way of specifying application behavior.

Chapter 12

RSpec

RSpec is a Behavior-Driven Development alternative to Test::Unit for Ruby applications. I haven't spent a lot of time parsing the difference between the original term *Test-First Programming*, the later term *Test-Driven Development* (TDD), and further derived terms like *Test-Driven Design* (also TDD) and *Behavior-Driven Development* (BDD), let alone more esoteric acronyms like *Example-Driven Development* (EDD) or *Acceptance Test–Driven Development* (ATDD).[1]

By featuring the word *test* so prominently, the initial terminology put the emphasis on testing in and of itself, and certain folks got the idea the sole point of the process was to verify program correctness. Of course, as I've already quoted once in this book, Kent Beck knows that "Correctness is a side benefit." Suggesting that TDD is about correctness may seem a minor point, except that the same folks then had a tendency to buy into two somewhat more pernicious corollaries:

- If the whole point of Test-Driven Whatever is to verify correctness, then if the process isn't 100 percent perfect at proving correctness, it must be worthless.

- If the whole point of Test-Driven Whatever is verifying correctness, then it doesn't matter when I write the tests; I can write them after I write the code.

In point of fact, the goal of TDD is to improve the quality of your code in many ways; verifying correctness is only one of them. And it makes

---

1. The acronym I prefer, Failure-Driven Development (FDD), has never really caught on. I also like to refer to my preferred Agile process as Boring Software Development, but that's another story.

> **What's a Spec?**
>
> What do you call the things you write in an RSpec file? If you are used to TDD and Test::Unit, the temptation to call them *tests* can be overwhelming. However, as we've discussed, the BDD theory behind RSpec suggests it's better not to think of your RSpec code as tests, which are things happen after the fact. So, what are they?
>
> The RSpec docs and code refer to the elements of RSpec as *examples*. Maybe I'm not going to the right parties, but I've never heard an actual person use that term. (I have, however, heard people use *example group* to refer to RSpec's version of contexts.) The term I hear most often is simply *spec*, as in: "I need to write some specs for that feature." I've tried to use that term in this section. But I suspect I'll slip up somewhere. Bear with me.

a big difference when you write the tests, because the process is much more effective when the tests come first. That's why the original name for the process explicitly called out *test-first*.

I'm in danger of disappearing into a huge rant here, but here's the important part: names like Test-Driven Development tended to lead people to the conclusion that the TDD process was mainly about verifying existing behavior. This led to a lot of frankly irritating online debates with people talking past each other because of different interpretations of what *testing* meant in *test-driven*. The term Behavior-Driven Development was coined to help win those arguments. Well, an argument like that can't really be won, but it was coined to help clarify the terms. Where the word *test* implies verifying already written code, the terms like *behavior* and *specify* imply describing the workings of code that has yet to be written. Ideally, then, discussing your process in BDD terms makes you more aware of the reason why you are using the process in the first place. Eventually, RSpec was created as a tool for implementing BDD in Ruby.

12.1 Getting Started with RSpec

RSpec is a large, involved framework, with uses that go well beyond Rails. We'll cover the basics here, with special emphasis on uses within

Rails and also on the contrast between RSpec and Test::Unit. We have already alluded to various differences in naming conventions, but RSpec also tends to favor a different style than Test::Unit, with more mock objects. This chapter can only scratch the surface of what's possible with RSpec; for more details, check out *The RSpec Book* [CAD⁺09].

Installing RSpec

Navigating the various RSpec and Rails versions to install RSpec correctly is a little complicated. For the rest of this chapter, we're going to assume Rails 3 and RSpec 2. Where advisable, differences between RSpec 2 and RSpec 1.3.*x* will be noted.

Installing older versions of RSpec or installing into older versions of Rails can get a little dicey. Instructions for different combinations of Rails and RSpec can be found at http://wiki.github.com/dchelimsky/rspec/rails.

One initial difference between RSpec 1 and Rspec 2 is that RSpec 2 is split across multiple gems. For our purposes, however, the most interesting one is rspec-rails. Since the other gems are dependencies on rspec-rails, importing that gem into a project brings the others along for the ride.

To get RSpec into your project, include it in your bundler Gemfile like so:

```
group :test, :development do
  gem "rspec-rails"
end
```

The rspec-rails gem must be in both the development and test groups in order for the RSpec generators to be available from the default command line. As I write this, the current version is 2.3.

Run a bundle install to install the RSpec gems. After that is done, you can run the initial RSpec generator, which creates the RSpec skeleton files:

```
% script/rails generate rspec:install
      create  .rspec
      create  spec
      create  spec/spec_helper.rb
```

You'll get this:

- The .rspec file, where RSpec run options go. Initially, the only option is --colour.[2]

- The spec directory, where your specs go. RSpec does not automatically create subdirectories like controller and model. Those are created by the generators when you build specs in those directories for the first time.

- A spec_helper.rb file that is the RSpec analogy to test_helper.rb. It contains some setup options and is a good place to put methods you want to be available to all tests.

In addition, the rspec-rails gem does a couple of other things when loaded via a Rails 3 Railtie subclass:

- Adds a Rake file that resets the default Rake task to run the RSpec spec files and also defines subtasks such as spec:models to run part of the specs at once.

- RSpec sets itself up as the test framework for the purposes of future generators. Later, when you set up, say, a generated model or resource, RSpec's generators are automatically invoked to create appropriate spec files. This process is different from in Rails 2.*x*, where RSpec has to provide its own custom generator tasks.

Now that RSpec is installed, let's go over the basic concepts. They boil down to four words: *describe*, *it*, *should*, and *mock*.

12.2 RSpec in Ten Minutes

Here's just about the smallest RSpec file that still shows off RSpec's main features:

```ruby
describe Project do
  it "should be able to abbreviate its name" do
    mock_project = mock_model(Project, :name => "My Big Project")
    mock_project.abbr.should == "MyBP"
  end
end
```

As small as this example may be, it demonstrates four of the key features of RSpec.

---

2. In RSpec 1.3.*x*, these options were located in spec/spec.opts.

Contexts with describe

While Shoulda uses the term *context* to refer to a set of related tests, RSpec formally calls them *example groups*, although the term *context* is not unheard of informally. An example group is normally declared by using the describe() method, although RSpec also defines the method context() as an exact alias.[3]

The describe() method takes either a String or a Class argument (or both) and a block containing whatever specifications are being grouped together, as in the previous example. If the argument to the describe() method is a class, the specifications described in that block are expected to relate to that class—we'll see in a moment how RSpec uses that information to determine what code is being exercised.

Setup and teardown behavior is accomplished via the before() and after() methods, each of which take a single argument. If the argument is :each, the block is executed before or after each specification, as opposed to the much less often used :all, which indicates the block is executed once before or after all specifications in the common description are executed.

As with Shoulda contexts, RSpec describe() blocks can be nested, with a similar meaning for combining before and after blocks. Unlike Shoulda contexts, all RSpec specifications must be inside a describe() block. In a related note, in RSpec you don't need to explicitly declare a subclass as a wrapper for your specifications the way that all Test::Unit files contain a subclass of Test::Unit. The outermost describe() block implicitly creates an instance of a class, including RSpec's ExampleGroupMethods module, which has all the actual specification behavior.[4]

Support methods can be defined inside a describe() block using normal Ruby syntax and can be used by any spec within the block.

Writing Specs: The "It" Factor

The it() method is used to define actual RSpec specifications or examples. The it() method takes an optional string that describes the behavior and a block that is executed. RSpec also defines specify() as an alias

---

3. Stylistically, context() is sometimes used to refer to an inner block with multiple sibling blocks that test different situations: for example, an administrative user vs. a regular user.

4. Inner nested describe() calls refer to a method defined by ExampleGroupMethods, which has slightly different behavior than the outermost describe(). As an RSpec user, you normally don't need to be concerned about that implementation detail.

to it(). Normally, it() is used when the method takes a string and is used to give the method a readable natural-language name. For single-line tests in which a string description is unnecessary, specify() is used to make the single line read more clearly, as follows:

```
specify { user.name.should == "fred" }
```

RSpec has a handy mechanism for marking that a particular specification has not yet been implemented in the code. You can define an it() method without a block. In this case, the test will appear in the RSpec output as "pending":

```
it "should bend steel in its bare hands"
```

Or you can use the method pending() in the spec block:

```
it "should bend steel in its bare hands" do
  pending "Not implemented yet"
  steel.should be_bent
end
```

This test stops when the pending() method is reached and returns its result as "pending." (If the test fails before the pending() is reached, the failure is treated normally.)

You can also have pending take a block:

```
it "should bend steel in its bare hands" do
  pending "Not implemented yet" do
    steel.should be_bent
  end
end
```

The behavior may not be what you expect. The code inside the pending() block is executed, but any failure there is treated as a "pending" result, rather than a failure result. However, if the code in the block actually passes, you'll get a failure that effectively means, "You said this was pending, but lo and behold, it actually works. Maybe it's not actually pending anymore; please remove the pending block."

Matching Expectations with "should"

Perhaps the signature part of RSpec syntax is the *expression matchers* that RSpec uses to specify specific features of the program. Where Test::Unit uses assertions that look like this:

```
assert_equal(expected, actual)
```

RSpec uses expression matches to specify desired behavior:

```
actual.should == expected
```

Note the shift in tone from an assertion, potentially implying already implemented behavior, to "should," implying future behavior. The RSpec version, arguably, reads more smoothly, especially given the other tricks RSpec has for matchers. I find it difficult to remember the order the expected and actual parameters are supposed to have in the assert_equal version, but I have very little trouble remembering the order in the RSpec version.[5]

The way this works is that the should() method is defined for all Ruby objects. The should() method takes one argument, a matcher. Normally, you would use one of the functions that RSpec makes available to return a specialized matcher. Here's an example:

```
actual.should be_true
```

It's a easier to see what's going on if you fully parenthesize, although in practice, RSpec is written without the parentheses. As in the previous snippet, showing the parentheses makes it clearer that the matcher is an argument to should():

```
actual.should(be_true)
```

As we'll see, the matcher itself can have methods chained to it but remains the argument to should:

```
actual.should(have(1).user)
```

When the example is run, the should method evaluates the matcher based on the criteria that the matcher defines and determines pass or failure behavior based on the result. With should, if the matcher is true, the specification passes. With should_not, the behavior is reversed.

RSpec lets us do a lot of different things when defining a specification. First, we have should_not(), which reverses any matcher, as follows:

```
actual.should_not == expected
```

On the matcher side, there are a couple of predefined special matchers:

```
actual.should be_true
actual.should be_false
actual.should be_close(100, 0.01)
actual.should change(object, :attribute) { block }
actual.should eql("Fred")
actual.should match(regex)
actual.should raise_error(SomeError)
actual.should satisfy { "block value" }
```

---

5. This cute little boast did not prevent me from mixing up the actual and expected parts of the RSpec lines in an early draft of this chapter. I really don't mess it up in practice. Really. When the expected value is a literal, it's much clearer.

Most of these are straightforward: be_close() is for floating-point numbers within a delta, change() passes if the value for object.attribute changes when the block is evaluated, satisfy() passes if the arbitrary block passed to it returns true, and so on. One of the previous examples used ==, and you can use other comparison operators, such as ===, =~, >, >=, <, and <=. You should not use the negative operators, like !=. Instead, use should_not ==.

The most significant piece of RSpec's magic may be the name mangling that RSpec does for matchers that it doesn't recognize. Any matcher of the form be_whatever() evaluates a corresponding whatever?() predicate in the expected object—the question mark is important, since that's the convention in Ruby of a boolean predicate method.

Every Ruby object responds to nil?, so any object in RSpec can be verified with the following:

```
expected.should be_nil
```

RSpec allows a couple of bits of grammatical syntactic sugar. You can add a or an to any matcher for readability, and RSpec will ignore it, so kind_of?() can be tested with the following:

```
expected.should be_a_kind_of(String)
```

Also, if the predicate method is in present tense, like matches?, you can write the expectation as should be_a_match. RSpec will try the method with an "s"—in this case, matches(). It does not find the method without the "s"—in this case, match(). The goal is to make your tests read as close to natural sentences as possible.

Similarly, if the predicate method starts with has, RSpec allows your matcher to start with have for readability so your tests don't look like they have been written by LOLCats:

```
expected.should have_key(:id)
```

You can also do this:

```
expected.should have(11).things
```

This passes if expected.things.size equals 11. The weird thing about this construct is if the expected object is actually a collection, you can use any symbol you want at the end and RSpec just ignores it:

```
[:a, :b].should have(2).items
[:a, :b].should have(2).gazorgenplatzes
```

You can pull the same trick with have_at_least() and have_at_most(). By the way, if you try to do should_not have_at_least, RSpec tells you the test is too confusing and to try should have_at_most instead.

You can define your own custom matchers, which we'll discuss later in this section, but in general, you're often better off just adding the predicate method to your class and letting the existing RSpec mechanisms work.

RSpec and Mocks

Mock objects are very important in RSpec—so important, in fact, that RSpec has its very own mock framework, subtly different from Flex-Mock, Mocha, or RR. In particular, RSpec users often strive to use mock objects to make each individual spec independent to other specs such that any individual flaw in the application breaks exactly one spec. Like many design goals, this one is probably honored more in the breach, but the basic idea of isolating a spec to a particular method, class, or layer is very important in using RSpec effectively. For a more general look at how to use mock objects, see Chapter 7, *Using Mock Objects*, on page 95.

If you don't like RSpec's own mock object framework, use your preferred mock framework by including a line like this in the file spec_helper.rb:

```
config.mock_with :mocha
```

RSpec helpfully includes those lines in comments, so all you need to do is adjust the commented lines to taste.

The RSpec native mock object package allows you to create bare mock objects with the method double(), as in:

```
mock_obj = double("an object")
```

Without any further description, the mock_obj class does not know about any methods and will return an expectation error if it is called. You can quickly get it to silently return null when called by calling the method as_null_object(). This is often done in the original declaration:

```
mock_obj = double("an object").as_null_object
```

You can stub any method on any object with the method stub().[6] This strategy works for ordinary objects as well as classes. Follow the stub() with and_return() to set the value that the stubbed method returns. As a shortcut, you can specify the method and the return value as a key/value pair when calling stub(). You can also chain stub() with and_raise(), allowing you to fake an exception being raised:

```
user.stub(:friend_count).and_return(12)
user.stub(:friend_count => 12)
User.stub(:total_friend_count).and_return(345)
User.stub(:find).and_raise(ActiveRecord::RecordNotFoundException)
```

If you want the return value of the stubbed method to be dynamic, pass a block to stub() that will be invoked with any arguments passed to the method:

```
user.stub(:find) do |arg|
  if arg == 1 User.me else User.you end
end
```

The and_return() method can take multiple arguments, in which case RSpec returns the arguments one at time on subsequent calls to the stubbed method. It will not cycle back to the first argument if more calls are made but returns the last value over and over again. You can also pass the block to and_return(), in the same way that you can pass it to stub().

You can set up a mock expectation on any method of any object by using the should_receive() method. As discussed in more detail in the Chapter 7, *Using Mock Objects*, on page 95, a mock differs from a stub in that it sets up an expectation that the specific method will be called and fails the test if that expectation is not met:

```
user.should_receive(:friend_count).and_return(12)
user.should_not_receive(:friend_count)
```

As with Mocha, you can filter the mock based on the calling arguments using the with() method. These arguments work for both stub() and should_receive():

```
user.should_receive(:is_a_friend?).with(:noel).and_return(true)
```

There are several matchers that can be used in place of an argument to with(). They are similar in scope to the Mocha versions, so I won't

---

6. This is as good a place as any to mention again that we're talking about RSpec 2; in RSpec 1, the method was called stub!(), although both RSpec versions alias the other call as a duplicate of the main one.

cover them in depth here. Check out the RSpec docs on expectations at http://rspec.info/documentation/mocks/message_expectations.html.

The default expectation for RSpec is that a mocked method will be called exactly once, an expectation you can make explicit by including the method once() in the mock method chain. Again, as with Mocha, other methods such as twice(), at_least(), at_most(), and exactly(x).times() can change the default behavior:

```
user.should_receive(:friend_count).exactly(3).times.and_return(7)
```

Let Subjects Be Subjects

RSpec has a number of ways to make tests more concise while still remaining clear. One common issue with test setup is that the before() blocks become cluttered with a number of different, unrelated setup items. In Test::Unit, you can have multiple setup methods to clean up things. In RSpec, you have the let() method:

```
Line 1  describe "user behavior"
     2    let(:me) { User.new(:name => "Noel") }
     3    let(:you) { User.new(:name => "Erin") }
     4
     5    it "should let users be friends" do
     6      me.add_friend(you)
     7      you.should have(1).friend
     8    end
```

Using let(), you can make a variable available within the current example group, without having to place it inside the before() block. Each let() method takes a symbol argument and a block. The symbol can then be called as if it was a local variable: the first call to the symbol invokes the block and caches the result; subsequent calls return the same result without reinvoking the block. In the previous example, invoking me on line 6 triggers the let() block on line 2, returning a user object name "Noel" that can subsequently be used in the example. The you object behaves similarly, but notice that the you block is triggered by the reference to you on line 6; when you is referenced in the next line, the cached object is used.

In essence, a let() call is syntactic sugar for defining a method and memoizing the result, like this:

```
def me
  @me ||= mock_model(User, :name => "Noel")
end
```

The main gotcha here is that the let block isn't executed unless it's invoked. That's often a good thing, since your test won't spend time creating unused objects. You can get in trouble sometimes if you expect that the object already exists. For a contrived problem case, note that this example will fail, since the two let() blocks are never invoked:

```
describe "user behavior"
  let(:me) { User.new(:name => "Noel") }
  let(:you) { User.new(:name => "Erin") }

  specify { User.count.should == 2 }
end
```

You can ensure that the block is invoked by using the method let!() instead of let().

I use let() frequently to clean up example setup and to reduce the need to create instance variables. When I really want to make my RSpec code concise, though, I use RSpec's *subject* functionality. RSpec uses subjects to reduce duplication in a series of tests that are all directed at the same object under test. Fair warning, though—there are definitely Ruby developers who think the subject stuff is too magical and that it's concise at the cost of being clear.[7]

Say we have a series of tests that look like this:

```
describe "a lot of tests" do
  let(:me) { User.new(:name => "Noel") }
  let(:you) { User.new(:name => "Erin") }

  before(:each) do
    me.add_friend(you)
  end
  specify { me.should have(1).friend }
  specify { me.should be_valid }
  specify { me.should be_friends_with(you) }
  specify { me.should_not be_friendless }
end
```

There's a duplication in those four assertions, namely, that they all start with me. In this particular case, that's more in the nature of a minor annoyance than a serious readability gap. However, you could easily see a series of tests that need to examine something like me. friends.first.addresses.first, which is a little annoying to type repeatedly.

---

7. For the record, I like using subjects, especially because they work nicely with a single-assertion style.

In RSpec, you can use the subject() method to specify a common receiver for all the specifications in an example group. The subject() takes a block and, like let, caches the result after the block is called the first time. Within the enclosing example group, any should() call without a receiver uses the defined subject as the receiver. So, the example can be rewritten as follows:

```
Line 1  describe "a lot of tests" do
    -     let(:me) { User.new(:name => "Noel") }
    -     let(:you) { User.new(:name => "Erin") }
    -
    5     before(:each) do
    -       me.add_friend(you)
    -     end
    -     subject { me }
    -     it { should have(1).friend }
   10     it { should be_valid }
    -     it { should be_friends_with(you) }
    -     it { should_not be_friendless }
    -   end
```

The subject() declaration in line 8 means that all the apparently bare should calls in the next four lines are directed to the subject. Whether this improves the readability of your tests is subjective—I think it does, as long as the specifications are short and reasonably close to the subject declaration. While the subject in this particular test is pretty simple, the block can be arbitrarily complex. (Also, notice that I've switched from specify() to it(), simply because one reads better than the other if you say the line out loud.)

One apparent limitation on the use of a subject is that you have to specify matchers against the subject itself, and not any attribute or subordinate method of the subject. In the previous code, for example, we can specify that the subject should be_valid, but we can't say anything about, say, the name of the subject. That's a constraint that could severely limit the usefulness of RSpec subjects, so it's not surprising that there's actually a way to do it:

```
Line 1  subject { me }
    2   its(:name) { should == "Noel" }
    3   its("friends.first.name") { should == "Erin" }
```

The its() method takes a symbol or string as an argument along with a block. If the argument is a symbol, the method of that name is called on the subject, and the resulting value is used as the receiver of the should() call in the block. In line 2 shown earlier, me.name is called, since me is the subject and :name is the argument to its(). So, the block is equivalent to me.name.should == "Noel".

If the argument is a string, RSpec assumes the string is a series of method names separated by dots. It applies the methods to the subject and uses the final result as the receiver of the should() in the block. In line 3, the block is effectively { me.friends.first.name.should == "Erin"}.[8] Granted, there is a certain fog-on-fog quality to this. However, since we're talking about an implicit receiver based on a previously defined subject, I find this style to be useful and a good way to briefly specify simple assertions on an object.

RSpec subjects have one more trick up their sleeve, and if you thought we were already a little too far into magic land, you might want to avert your eyes. If the argument to describe() is a class rather than a string, if that class has a initialize() method that can be called with no arguments, and if the describe block has no explicitly defined subject, then (and only then), a new instance of that class will be used as the implicit subject. You can use its() against the implicit subject:

```
describe User do
  it { should be_valid }
  it { should be_friendless }
  its(:name) { should be_nil }
end
```

In most cases, the implicit subject goes a little too far and can be too subtle to read. That said, it works very nicely with the Shoulda matchers, and it makes sense to use this sparingly in cases where the class under test already has a no-argument constructor and there are simple specifications of that default state.

12.3 RSpec and Rails

RSpec is not Rails-specific by itself. However, the rspec-rails plug-in provides several additions to the RSpec core, aimed at integrating RSpec with Rails. You will get the following:

- Rails generators to create skeleton RSpec files, instead of Test::Unit files. In Rails 3, these generators are automatically invoked by

---

8. Technically, RSpec evaluates the its() call as me.send(:friends).send(:first).send(:name), not as eval("me.friend.first.name"), in case there's ever a practical difference between the two.

Rails if RSpec is installed; in Rails 2, they are a separate set of generators that you need to use instead of the Rails defaults.

- Custom, Rails-specific example group classes that are automatically associated with the specific RSpec directory that the file is in. So, files in the spec/controllers directory automatically have RSpec controller functionality.

- Matchers for specific Rails features that are part of each example group. In most cases, these matchers are wrappers around Rails assertions.

In this code sample, I re-created the Huddle application using the steps from Appendix A, on page 323, up until the point where the appendix indicates you need to have RSpec installed. At that point, add the following to your bundler Gemfile—remember, we're using Rails 3 and RSpec 2:[9]

```
group :development, :test do
  gem 'rspec-rails', ">= 2.0.0"
end
```

RSpec needs to be in the test group because it's a test tool, and it needs to be in the development group so the generators it defines are accessible from the command line during development.

At this point, if you continue with the Devise setup, you'll see an RSpec-generated test file:

```
% rails generate devise:install
% rails generate devise User
      invoke  active_record
      create    app/models/user.rb
      invoke    rspec
      create      spec/models/user_spec.rb
      inject  app/models/user.rb
      create  db/migrate/20100822050454_devise_create_users.rb
       route  devise_for :users
```

There isn't much to that generated user_spec.rb file, but note that Rails automatically passes off to RSpec to create it. We can get a more interesting set of boilerplate tests by re-creating the Huddle resources (output edited to show only RSpec).

---

9. Instructions on installing RSpec with Rails 2 depend on exact versions and can be found at http://wiki.github.com/dchelimsky/rspec/rails.

```
% rails generate scaffold project name:string
invoke    rspec
     create      spec/controllers/projects_controller_spec.rb
     create      spec/views/projects/edit.html.erb_spec.rb
     create      spec/views/projects/index.html.erb_spec.rb
     create      spec/views/projects/new.html.erb_spec.rb
     create      spec/views/projects/show.html.erb_spec.rb
     invoke      helper
     create        spec/helpers/projects_helper_spec.rb
     create      spec/routing/projects_routing_spec.rb
     invoke      rspec
     create        spec/requests/projects_spec.rb
```

And similarly, for status reports:

```
% rails generate scaffold status_report project:references \
  user:references yesterday:text today:text status_date:date
  invoke    rspec
     create      spec/controllers/status_reports_controller_spec.rb
     create      spec/views/status_reports/edit.html.erb_spec.rb
     create      spec/views/status_reports/index.html.erb_spec.rb
     create      spec/views/status_reports/new.html.erb_spec.rb
     create      spec/views/status_reports/show.html.erb_spec.rb
     invoke      helper
     create        spec/helpers/status_reports_helper_spec.rb
     create      spec/routing/status_reports_routing_spec.rb
     invoke      rspec
     create        spec/requests/status_reports_spec.rb
```

RSpec's generated files are slightly different from Test::Unit's. Most notably, controller, view, and routing specs are all placed in separate files. Let's take a tour of RSpec's Rails features and walk through the boilerplate tests.

RSpec and Models

Let's start with the model tests, because models have the shortest generated file. Here's the file for Huddle's status reports:

huddle3_rspec2/spec/models/status_report_spec.rb

```ruby
require 'spec_helper'

describe StatusReport do
  pending "add some examples to (or delete) #{__FILE__}"
end
```

OK, that's very short. In fact, it doesn't do much at all.

RSpec provides three custom matchers for ActiveRecord: one for classes and two for instances. Qwik Qwiz! I'll run them here, and then we can all guess what they do:

```
StatusReport.should have(1).record
StatusReport.should have(5).records

a_report.should have(:no).errors_on(:yesterday)
a_report.should have(1).error_on(:today)

a_report.should be_a_new(StatusReport)
```

Time is up. The have(x).record construction tests how many rows are in the database table for that model; basically, it's StatusReport.all.size == x. The errors_on() matcher tests for ActiveRecord validation errors attached to the given attribute. The be_a_new() matcher returns true if the instance is an unsaved instance of the provided class. You might most commonly use that to determine whether a controller has correctly saved a model based on a user's create request.

RSpec also provides a shortcut for mocking an ActiveRecord model called, oddly enough, mock_model(). Ordinarily, you'd use this in a controller or view test to isolate the controller test from model implementation details so that the controller test is completely independent from the correctness or even the existence of the model code. Using mock models makes your controller tests run faster—no trips to the database—and makes them potentially more robust. Also, it explicitly places the burden of specifying model behavior in the RSpec model file, where it belongs. The usage pattern goes something like this:

```
mock_project = mock_model(Project, :name => "fred")
Project.stub(:find).and_return(mock_project)
```

The first argument to mock_model() is either a class that extends the Rails 3 ActiveModel::Naming module or a string. A string argument must evaluate to either a class that doesn't exist or a class that extends ActiveModel::Naming. In other words, you can't create a mock model of a non-ActiveRecord class. Any further arguments are key/value pairs for methods of the model that should be stubbed.[10]

Using mock_model() provides stubs to make the mock behave like a consistent ActiveRecord model. The mock_model() method generates an ID and stubs new_record() and persisted() to be consistent. This behavior can be overridden by passing as_new_record() to the mock, which causes it to behave as a new record, meaning no ID.

---

10. As always, using "model" and "module" in the same paragraph is grounds for confusion—or at least calls for some vocal warm-ups before I read it out loud.

The mocked model also stubs is_a?(), kind_of?(), intstance_of?(), and class(), to be consistent with the original first argument to the mock_model() call. If you override save() or update_attributes() to be false, the mocked model will consistently stub errors.empty?.

RSpec also provides a stub_model(), which is declared almost identically to mock_model(), with a couple of significant differences. The first argument to stub_model() must be an ActiveRecord class, though the following arguments are still key/value pairs. The stub_model() creates an actual ActiveRecord object, not a mock, and stubs the methods that are passed in the key/value pairs. The new ActiveRecord object also prevents the stubbed model from accessing the database by raising an exception if you try, which should make tests using this object faster.

RSpec and Controllers

In core Rails Test::Unit, both controllers and views are tested using Rails functional tests. RSpec splits the two apart, with files in the spec/controllers directory to specify controller behavior without calling the views (at least, not without explicitly being told to) and with separate files in the spec/views directory for view testing. Again, the idea here is to keep things as separate and independent as possible. The controller's job is to marshal together objects to pass to the view and that behavior can be specified independent of whether the view properly puts it on the screen. (Again, there's also a speed benefit in not running the display engine where it isn't needed.)

Let's talk about the controllers first. RSpec offers a few special matchers for use in controller testing (some of these are just normal RSpec magic given boolean methods in ActiveController):

```
response.should be_success
response.should be_redirect
response.should redirect_to(url or hash)
response.should render_template('app/views/projects/index')
response.should render_template(:partial => "show_form")
```

There is one RSpec 2 change to be aware of if you are familiar with older versions of RSpec. Although the controller spec does not render the view templates by default, unlike RSpec 1.*x*, the view template must actually exist in the project. This is because of internal changes in Rails 3. If, for some reason, you want to throw caution to the wind, override the RSpec default and integrate view testing with your controller testing. You can do so by placing the command render_views inside an RSpec example group. This is not recommended RSpec practice but might be the easiest way to validate a piece of view behavior too small to get a view test or a Cucumber test.

The assigns, flash, and session variables are available as hashes. If you want to test an assigned variable, use the form assigns(:variable).should == thing.

What do RSpec controller tests look like? Here's a representative sample from the generated file (the file is too long to include the entire thing):

huddle3_rspec2/spec/controllers/projects_controller_spec.rb

```ruby
require 'spec_helper'

describe ProjectsController do

  def mock_project(stubs={})
    @mock_project ||= mock_model(Project, stubs).as_null_object
  end

  describe "GET index" do
    it "assigns all projects as @projects" do
      Project.stub(:all) { [mock_project] }
      get :index
      assigns(:projects).should eq([mock_project])
    end
  end
end
```

Here are some things to note:

- The outermost describe() block contains the controller name as its description. This is not just a convention; RSpec uses that class to specify which controller to call for all the tests.

- Innermost describe blocks are split up by controller call and annotated with the controller action and HTML method being described. This is just a convention, but it's a useful one. If you look at the actual file, you'll see that some actions are further split: the create and edit actions are split into a test with valid data and a test with invalid data.

- The get() method and other methods that mimic accessing the controller via a browser action work in RSpec exactly the way they do in Test::Unit.

- The mock_project() stub is used to manage the result of the find(:all) call in the index method without actually having to create data, making the test super-fast.

RSpec View Specs

Since RSpec allows you to specify controllers independent of views, you might assume that you can also specify views independent of controllers. You'd be right.[11] The RSpec convention is to place view tests in the spec/views folder, with one spec file to a view file, so the view in app/views/projects/edit.html.erb is specified in spec/views/projects/edit.html.erb_spec.rb. Here's the scaffold file for the project controller's edit view:

```
huddle3_rspec2/spec/views/projects/edit.html.erb_spec.rb
require 'spec_helper'

describe "projects/edit.html.erb" do
  before(:each) do
    @project = assign(:project, stub_model(Project,
      :new_record? => false,
      :name => "MyString"
    ))
  end

  it "renders the edit project form" do
    render

    rendered.should have_selector("form", :action => project_path(@project),
        :method => "post") do |form|
      form.should have_selector("input#project_name", :name => "project[name]")
    end
  end
end
```

The basic drill here is simple: in your before() block, use the assign method to initialize any variables you expect the controller to set up. You can also tweak this in individual specs to try various logical branches. Then each actual spec renders the view file and validates the HTML output.

There's a couple of things to point out. The outermost describe() block has the actual path to the view file being rendered, relative to the app/views directory. This is not, strictly speaking, required. Just useful. In addition, the render() method, if called with no arguments, renders the view referenced in the outermost describe() block. (See, I said it was useful.) You can override that behavior by passing a filename as the first argument to render (again, the filename is relative to app/views). Any

---

11. In practice, most RSpec applications use Cucumber as their view testing layer these days.

other options passed to render() behave exactly as in ActionView::Base. After a call to render, the rendered() method contains the resulting text.

All the standard Rails helper modules are automatically loaded, but any of the application-specific helper modules that you plan on calling need to either be explicit, using something like include ProjectsHelper, or be added to the render() commands, as described in the previous section. All helper modules are available in the view spec.

For specifying the actual view contents, RSpec defaults to using have_selector(), which is actually part of Webrat.[12] The have_selector() method is similar to assert_select(), except it supports describing the HTML attributes as key/value pairs, as in have_selector("form", :method => "post""), as opposed to the assert_select() or CSS syntax form[method=post]. The Webrat version makes it easier to use dynamic values for the attributes. Like assert_select(), have_selector() takes count and content options to specify the number of times the selector is found or the content of the selector. As you can see from the example, have_selector() can be nested.

If you want a simpler test, use the contain matcher, which does a simple regular expression match, as follows:

```
rendered.should contain("Name")
```

Often, the view layer calls helper methods along the way. In keeping with best RSpec practice, the idea is to limit the interaction of different levels during testing. That would suggest that helper methods should be stubbed during view specs and only truly exercised in helper specs. If you choose to stub out a helper method in your view test, use the view() object to get the template that has access to the method, as in view.should_receive(:helper_method).and_return("result"). Section 12.3, *RSpec Helper Specs*, on the following page demonstrates how to specify the helper module in RSpec.

RSpec Routing Specs

Unlike Test::Unit, RSpec provides a separate file specifically for testing routes. You can test routes using core Rails test features; however, those tests would normally be combined with the regular controller tests.

---

12. Webrat is a runtime dependency of RSpec, which is why we didn't need to explicitly install it.

RSpec gives you a helper file for each controller, and the default contains a lot of examples that look like this:

`huddle3_rspec2/spec/routing/projects_routing_spec.rb`

```
it "recognizes and generates #index" do
  { :get => "/projects" }.should route_to(
        :controller => "projects", :action => "index")
end
```

The key matcher here is route_to(), which takes as its receiver a hash consisting of a key with an HTTP verb, and a value with a URL path string. As the argument, it contains the resulting Rails params hash. The actual route_to() matcher defers to the standard Rails assert_routing(), which tests the relationship in both directions—that the string routes to the hash and that the hash is routed to from the string.

RSpec also provides a be_routable() method, which is designed to be used in the negative to show that a specific path—like, say, the Rails default—is not recognized:

```
{ :get => "/projects/search/fred" }.should_not be_routable
```

RSpec Helper Specs

RSpec provides a spec/helpers directory to specify the behavior of helper modules, an innovation picked up by Rails core in the 2.2 timeframe.

There's not a lot of magic here; all the generated file does is show a sample of the kinds of tests you might write:

`huddle3_rspec2/spec/helpers/projects_helper_spec.rb`

```
require 'spec_helper'

# Specs in this file have access to a helper object that includes
# the ProjectsHelper. For example:
#
# describe ProjectsHelper do
#   describe "string concat" do
#     it "concats two strings with spaces" do
#       helper.concat_strings("this","that").should == "this that"
#     end
#   end
# end
describe ProjectsHelper do
  pending "add some examples to (or delete) #{__FILE__}"
end
```

If you'd like to take the time to specify helper methods—and I recommend it (otherwise, they tend to become the dark, scary attic of your application)—RSpec automatically includes all Rails core helper modules, plus the module specified in the outermost describe() block.

Since you don't have access to a controller or even a mock controller, as you might in a Rails core helper test, you might wonder how to test helpers that assume instance variables from the controller. You can specify those values into the assigns hash, as you might in a controller test, and then use the helper() method to call your actual helper method. Here's an example to illustrate:

Say we have a helper method that does this:

```ruby
def headline_project_name
  "<h1>#{@project.name.uppercase}</h1>"
end
```

Temporarily ignore that we should really be passing the project as an argument rather than assuming it's an instance variable.

In RSpec, we test that method as follows:

```ruby
describe ProjectsHelper do
  it "should headline a project " do
    assigns(:project) = mock_model(Project, :name => "Mock")
    helper.headline_project_name.should == "<h1>MOCK</h1>"
  end
end
```

In other words, prefixing the headline_project_name() with helper. gives us access to the pretend instance variables that we added to the assigns hash.

RSpec Request Specs

Request specs are the RSpec analog to Test::Unit integration specs. I'm guessing they don't get a whole lot of use, since most BDD adherents use Cucumber for integration testing.

Requests specs are broadly similar to Test::Unit specs, which means they are also similar to controller specs, except that we specify an entire path, as in get projects_path, rather than just the name of a method in the controller under test. For further specification of actions and output, Webrat or Capybara is strongly recommended.

12.4 Running RSpec

RSpec provides a couple of different options for running the spec suite. The simplest option is to use the rspec command, which can take either a directory or a specific file as its argument.

You also have a set of Rake tasks. The main one, rake spec, is the default task when RSpec is installed. It runs the entire contents of the spec directory. As you might expect, you can also limit the task to a specific subdirectory with spec:controllers, spec:helpers, spec:lib, spec:mailers, spec:models, spec:requests, and spec:routingspec/views. If you run via Rake, you can specify standard command-line options by placing them in the file .rspec. The default looks like this and specifies that RSpec's terminal output is in color:

```
--colour
```

The rspec --help command gives you a list of options that can be placed in the .rspec file.

12.5 RSpec in Practice

RSpec suggests a different way of writing tests than Test::Unit, in part because of its heavy use of mocks and a strong bias toward isolating tests and keeping controller and model tests separate. For example, the first test that I wrote in Section 3.1, *The First Test-First*, on page 35 looked like this in Test::Unit:

```
test "creation of status report with data" do
  assert_difference('StatusReport.count', 1) do
    post :create, :status_report => {
      :project_id => projects(:one).id,
      :user_id => users(:quentin).id,
      :yesterday => "I did stuff",
      :today => "I'll do stuff"}
  end
  actual = assigns(:status_report)
  assert_equal(projects(:one).id, actual.project.id)
  assert_equal(users(:quentin).id, actual.user.id)
  assert_equal(Date.today.to_s(:db), actual.status_date.to_s(:db))
  assert_redirected_to status_report_path(actual)
end
```

The translation to RSpec in a style where a mock object is used to cover the transition between the controller and model layer might look like:

```
huddle3_rspec2/spec/controllers/status_reports_controller_spec.rb
```
```
it "assigns a newly created status_report as @status_report" do
  StatusReport.stub(:new_from_params).with({'these' => 'params'}) {
      mock_status_report(:save => true) }
  post :create, :status_report => {'these' => 'params'}
  assigns(:status_report).should be(mock_status_report)
end
```

This is a very slight gloss on the boilerplate RSpec spec for creation in a controller. The strategy here is to set up a stub on the StatusReport class such that it responds to the method new_from_params() with a particular mock object. The spec, then, says that a particular method of the model is called, and the result is assigned to a particular instance variable of the controller. Unlike in the Test::Unit test, as far as RSpec is concerned, exactly what the new_with_params() method does—even whether the method exists—is the model's problem and should be dealt with in model specs.[13]

In a related story, if you go back to the original test in Section 3.1, *The First Test-First*, on page 35 test, the upshot of this particular test was not a change in the controller; the eventual result was a change in the model. That's not a coincidence—since there's no code change in the controller, when you isolate the controller from the model, there's nothing to test in the controller.

You'll sometimes hear people say that when done well RSpec testing is a lot like design—this is what they're talking about. The structure of a good RSpec test actually implies the structure of the resulting application. Specifically, RSpec's bias toward testing modules in isolation encourages you to place your test in the place where the code is actually changing, which in turn encourages you to write code where the modules interact as little as possible. From a code quality standpoint, less interaction is generally a good thing. However, because RSpec is so keen on isolating modules, it becomes very important to have an end-to-end test of some kind, such as an integration test or Cucumber test, to verify that the interface between each module works as you expect.

---

13. Of course, you can write mock style tests in Test::Unit. I didn't, in part because in the tutorial we are using only Rails core features.

12.6 Creating Your Own Matchers

RSpec's matchers are great, but eventually you'll come to a situation where you'd like a particular matcher syntax to make your tests read cleanly, and the matcher doesn't exist. You have a few different options in that case.

The first option is to just write a predicate method to cover the matcher you want and let RSpec's default be_whatever() functionality implicitly create the matcher. This is sometimes the best solution if you control the object being covered—you'll often wind up using the predicate in your main code. If the object you want to write the matcher on is a Rails or Ruby library object, it's more complicated. One possibility is to monkey-patch the class in your RSpec file. At one time, I recommended the following code in an RSpec model spec file:

```ruby
class String
  def parsing_to?(hash)
    expected = Ingredient.new(hash)
    actual = Ingredient.parse(self, Recipe.find(1), 1)
    actual == expected
  end
end
```

That led to the following RSpec code:

```ruby
it "should parse a basic string"
  "2 cups carrots, diced".should be_parsing_to(:amount => 2,
      :unit => "cups", :ingredient => "carrots",
      :instruction => "diced")
end
```

From a perspective of two years, I'm pretty sure that's not the best way to manage the custom matcher. On the other hand, every now and then I like to advocate for Ruby structures that would make a mainline Java programmer sputter, so we have that going for us, which is kind of nice.

The way you are *supposed* to do it is to use the Matchers DSL:

```ruby
RSpec::Matchers.define :parse_to do |hash|
  match do |string|
    expected = Ingredient.new(hash)
    actual = Ingredient.parse(string, Recipe.find(1), 1)
    actual == expected
  end
end
```

Which parts of the matcher call get translated to which arguments is critical here and slightly nonintuitive. The recipient of the should() method—the object being evaluated—is the block argument to the innermost call to match(). In the previous example, that would be the block argument string. The right side of the RSpec call, which in this case is the hash containing the expected value, becomes the argument to the outside method. In the previous snippet, that hash is the hash argument to the parse_to() method. The block can take a second argument, the matcher itself, which can be used to specify specific failure messages if desired. Call this like so:

```
it "should parse a basic string"
  "2 cups carrots, diced".should parse_to(:amount => 2,
    :unit => "cups", :ingredient => "carrots",
    :instruction => "diced")
end
```

And the string argument on the left of the matcher is the string argument to the match() block, while the hash is the argument to the define() block.

In addition to match(), there are other methods you can call in the define() block to refine the behavior of the matcher. All these methods take the same left side of the matcher as the argument to a block. The most commonly used would be failure_message_for_should(), which returns the string to use when reporting a positive failure. You also have failure_message_for_should_not(), which returns the message for negative failure, and descriptions(), which is used to generate the name of an example if the example doesn't have its own name—say when specify() is used without a string argument.

The most flexible matcher you can build is any arbitrary class that has a matches?() method and a failure_message_for_should() method, along with a separate method that returns an instance of that class. Again, the following snippet would be used the same as the previous two:

```
Class ParseTo
  def initialize(hash)
    @hash = hash
  end

  def matches?(string)
    expected = Ingredient.new(hash)
    actual = Ingredient.parse(string, Recipe.find(1), 1)
    actual == expected
  end
```

```
    def failure_message_for_should(string)
      "Bzzz! Wrong!"
    end
  end

def parse_to(hash)
  ParseTo.new(hash)
end
```

This should look very similar to the description of Shoulda matchers in Section 11.6, *Writing Your Own Shoulda Matcher*, on page 177, which is why Shoulda matchers can be dropped into RSpec as is. The failure_message_for_should_not() and description() methods can also be defined here, along with an optional does_not_match?() method, which, if defined, is used in the should_not() case.

12.7 Summarizing RSpec

I have what you might call a history with RSpec. There's a lot about it I've always liked. I love the matchers and the matching syntax and the string descriptions of tests (which was, of course, widely copied on the Test::Unit side). Plus, it's somewhat a purist's tool, and I'm enough of a purist to be attracted to it. My first serious incursion into RSpec was after I researched it for a previous book and decided that it was worth seriously trying on my next project.

I didn't last long with it. In retrospect, I realize I was Doing It Wrong: trying to write heavily mocked and brittle tests. That's the painful way to go about RSpec, and the mocks upon mocks can get frustrating.

Since then, single-assertion style has come to RSpec (or perhaps it was there all along; I just got to a place where I could see its value). In addition, I had the chance to work with it as my primary test tool for about eight months. And some recent innovations in Rails testing, such as Cucumber and Webrat, have tended to favor RSpec. As a result, I got much more comfortable with RSpec and much more attuned to its flexibility, and as I said, I've always liked the basic syntax.

Even if you don't like RSpec's syntax, there is still a lot to take away from the philosophy of testing that RSpec embodies. RSpec encourages the use of tests to create the public interface of your program and to design the interaction of objects. RSpec also encourages tests to be clear, concise, and independent of each other and independent of the parts of the program not under test. Using these ideas to guide your testing improves the quality and usefulness of your tests.

Part V

Testing Everything All Together

Chapter 13

Testing Workflow with Integration Tests

Integration tests seem to be used less frequently than other Rails built-in test types. Certainly there is much less online chatter about how and when to use the built-in integration tests, probably because integration tests don't quite map to the classic TDD/BDD process (and where they might fit in, they've been largely supplanted by Cucumber). On the one hand, this is a shame, because integration tests are a powerful and flexible way to do high-level testing on your application. Done right, they can even serve as acceptance tests. On the other hand, I'm as guilty as anybody of underusing them. For what it's worth, integration tests have been extremely handy when I've used them.

What's in a Name, Part Three

I like the name *integration tests*. So, I've got nothing here.

Well, I should point out the difference between an integration test and an acceptance test. An integration test is written by the developer for a developer audience, whereas an acceptance test is written by or in close consultation with the customer for a customer audience. Acceptance tests often have some kind of domain-specific language magic that allows for something readable by the customer to be automatically executed as a test; see Chapter 15, *Acceptance Testing with Cucumber*, on page 235 for details.

13.1   What to Test in an Integration Test

Integration tests are the tool of choice in Rails to test any process that spans one or more controller actions. Two common use cases are a multistep registration process and a purchase/checkout e-commerce function. In both cases, the entire user task flow has an integrity that can be completely tested only when all the steps can be executed together. As a rule of thumb, if one controller action is communicating with a future controller action via session state or other data-sharing method, you probably should have an integration or acceptance test covering the entire procedure.

Integration tests tend to be written separately from the normal tight loop of the test-driven development process. Often, a whole bunch of them are written up front to serve as requirements, a guide to development, or proof of completion. Sometimes they are written after primary development to ensure that pieces that have only been tested separately are in fact making the expected communications—for example, to catch a potential issue created when one method saves to the session with one key, while the later method looks for a different key in the session. Oops.

13.2   What's Available in an Integration Test?

Rails integration tests are similar to controller tests. They import the same assertion modules, so any assertion available in a controller test can also be called from an integration test. The same set of method names are available to simulate HTTP requests (get, post, put, delete, head, and xhr), although we'll see in a second that there are some minor differences from the controller versions of these methods.

The two biggest differences between integration tests and controller tests are as follows:

- Integration tests are not tied to a specific controller. This means the action argument to the HTTP request methods needs to be a an object that resolves to a known URL in the system. Most often, this is simply the URL string, such as get 'tasks/show'.

- Integration tests maintain one or more separate sessions that persist between the different simulated user requests—in a controller test, the session is a characteristic of the response and is not guaranteed to behave correctly if you simulate multiple calls.

With the HTTP simulation methods, you can use any object that Rails can convert into a URL by using the method url_for(). The argument could be a hash or a resource object, as in get url_for(tasks(:one)).

The second argument to all the HTTP request methods is a hash of parameters. Using the second argument is the preferred mechanism for adding parameters in an integration test, rather than building up a query string for the URL or using a complex url_for() call. The third argument (rarely used) contains any arbitrary HTTP headers that you want to set for the request. As with controller methods, the xhr() method takes a first argument specifying the HTTP verb and then includes the same arguments as the other request methods in order.

By default, integration test requests do not follow redirects. However, each method except xhr() has a via_redirect variant, such as post_via_redirect(), that performs the request and follows all redirects until it gets to a result that isn't a redirect. Any and all session changes it hits along the way will go into the session object, and the output to be tested will be the output of the final destination. If you want to control the redirect behavior less automatically from inside your test, the integration test method follow_redirect!() will, as you might expect, follow exactly one redirect, raising an exception if the last request did not end in a redirect. You can use the integration test method redirect?() to determine whether the last request was or was not a redirect.[1]

There are also two methods that allow you to change a setting for all future requests in a test. The https!() method will make all future requests behave as though they use HTTPS. Note that this won't actually encrypt anything, since there isn't a real server request being made, but any other controller-side logic that is dependent on the secure nature of the request will be appropriately tested. Switching back to non-HTTPS requests is done using https!(false). Similarly, a multihosted application can be tested using the host!() method. If your application has logic that depends on the subdomain, you can switch back and forth with lines like host!(blog.railsprescriptions.com).

Note that unlike controller tests, integration tests do not allow you to pass session values into the request methods. You can set the initial state of the session directly via the session() method, which returns a hash—so session[:user_id] = 3. You should use this mechanism only for

---

1. The implementation of redirect?() is status/100 == 3. I'm torn as to whether that is clever or not.

setting the initial state of the session data. During the actual test, you should let the session be implicitly set by the controller actions being tested.

13.3 Simulating Multipart Interaction

The general structure of an integration test is pretty simple: make a bunch of controller calls, and validate that everything has worked out as planned.

The key to successful integration testing is to realize that integration tests have a different purpose than the detailed tests that already exist (or will exist) in your controller and model tests. Integration tests are for verifying end-to-end behavior of the application as a whole, not for testing the inner workings of your code. Attempting to use integration tests to fill the role of unit tests is not only going to make it harder to write the integration tests, but it's also going to mean more test breakage when you make legitimate changes to the application.

The purpose of the integration test during development is to validate that data getting passed between the different parts of a larger whole is correctly being saved and correctly being used—you're trying to avoid test gaps. The point of using an integration test as an acceptance test is to perform a high-level verification of the application's behavior. In neither case do you need great levels of detail as to the specific HTML being output or the details of the model back end—that's a job for the actual functional or unit tests. You're trying to test the overall behavior of the system, without worrying about implementation details.

So, what should an integration test look like? Let's make up an example from the Huddle project, the daily scrum support tool from Chapter 3, *Writing Your First Tests*, on page 33. Let's assume that there are a number of pages from which a user can click a checkbox and add a user to a list of people to follow. At some point, the user can go to a page that lists all the people currently being followed, allowing the user to see their current status or send a message or something.

Create the integration test with the following command:

```
$ script/generate integration_test add_friends
```

Your skeleton test looks like this:

```ruby
require 'test_helper'

class AddFriendsTest < ActionController::IntegrationTest
  fixtures :all

  # Replace this with your real tests.
  test "the truth" do
    assert true
  end
end
```

Assuming that all these controller methods actually exist, a first pass at the integration test might look like this (note that none of the code that will make this pass actually exists in the project right now):

```ruby
test "add friends" do
  post "sessions/create", :login => "quentin", :password => "monkey"
  assert_equal(users(:quentin).id, session[:user_id])

  get "users/show", :id => users(:quentin).id
  xhr :post, "users/toggle_interest", :id => users(:aaron).id
  assert_equal [users(:aaron).id], session[:interest]

  get "users/show", :id => users(:old_password_holder).id
  xhr :post, "users/toggle_interest",
      :id => users(:old_password_holder).id
  assert_equal [users(:aaron).id, users(:old_password_holder).id].sort,
      session[:interest].sort

  #testing removal from the session
  xhr :post, "users/toggle_interest",
      :id => users(:old_password_holder).id
  assert_equal [users(:aaron).id], session[:interest]

  get "users/show", :id => users(:rover).id
  assert_select "div.interest" do
    assert_select div, :text => "Aaron", :count => 1
    assert_select div, :text => "Old", :count => 0
  end
end
```

The test is similar to controller tests, so the activity should be relatively clear; it's going through some site traversal, occasionally making the Ajax call back to the server to add or remove an interesting person and then checking that the session is as expected. At the end, we do just enough testing of the output to ensure that the values in the session are actually used.

In a real system, you might want to refactor this long test into some shorter methods that encapsulate a call and some of the assertions that go with it. Integration tests seem to encourage the creation of reasonably elaborate mechanisms for quickly defining complicated user behavior—which when taken to their logical conclusion result in Webrat or Capybara (see Chapter 14, *Write Better Integration Tests with Webrat and Capybara*, on page 223). Here is a sample method, which takes in a user and an expected list of users already in the session. The method simulates the Ajax toggle call and confirms that the session matches the expected list:

```
def toggle_user(user_symbol, initial_user_expectation)
  new_friend = users(user_symbol)
  xhr :post, "users/toggle_interest", :id => new_friend.id
  expected_users = initial_user_expectation.map { |sym| users(sym).id }
  assert_equal expected_users.sort, session[:interest].sort
end
```

The method would be called like this (note that the arguments are all symbol names from the fixture list that are converted to user instances in the method):

```
toggle_user(:aaron, [:aaron])
toggle_user(:old_password_holder, [:aaron, :old_password_holder])
```

Using this kind of common factoring makes a dramatic difference in how quickly you can write integration tests.

13.4 Simulating a Multiuser Interaction

Integration testing has one more trick up its sleeve. Each integration test gets an implicit session that backs all the controller calls. That's nice, but what if you want to test the integration of two or more consecutive or simultaneous sessions? This is a common issue in, say, a social-networking site where users might be communicating with each other.

Happily, it's possible to create an arbitrary number of different sessions and validate values against any of them. By calling the method open_session(), you get a separate session with its own set of instance variables that you can make requests and perform assertions on. A sample might look something like this:

```
test "user interaction" do
  aaron_session = open_session
  quentin_session = open_session
```

```
    quentin_session.post("sessions/create", :login => "quentin",
        :password => "monkey")
    quentin_session.post("messages/send", :to => users(:aaron))
    aaron_session.post("sessions/create", :login => "aaron",
        :password => "monkey")
    aaron_session.get("messages/show")
    assert_equal(1, aaron_session.assigns(:messages))
end
```

Each session is targeted by its own post() or get() messages and its own set of instance variables. In this case, we're testing that a message created by Quentin shows up in Aaron's message queue; in a real test, you might do some slightly more detailed testing, but again, the point here is making sure that the entire flow works—testing that the show controller action displays messages properly is the work of the controller and view tests.

You can also invoke open_session() with a block, in which case the session created is the argument to the block:

```
test "user interaction" do
  open_session do |quentin_session|
    quentin_session.post("sessions/create", :login => "quentin",
        :password => "monkey")
    quentin_session.post("messages/send", :to => users(:aaron))
  end
end
```

Note that the open_session() call still returns the session object after the block is evaluated, which means the session can be stored in a variable for further calls to be made on it even after the block has closed.

The obvious disadvantage of using the block style is that multiple sessions overlapping is awkward. If there's an obvious advantage, I haven't seen it yet.

Where this gets interesting is when you want to integrate those shorter helper methods with the session—it's obviously useful to have shortcuts for interactions that multiple session objects are going to need to perform. There are some different suggestions that use various metaprogramming contortions to inject helper methods into the session object. For instance, the Rails API docs place the open_session() call inside a login() method.

Helper methods defined in a separate module are injected into the session by starting the block with an extend call, something like the following:

```
module MyAssertionModule
  def message(to)
    post("messages/send", :to => to)
  end
end

def login(un, pw)
  open_session do |s|
    s.extend(MyAssertionModule)
    # more stuff, including actually making a login request
  end
end

test "trying logins"
  quentin_session = login("quentin", "monkey")
  aaron_session = login("aaron", "monkey")
  quentin_sesson.message(users(:aaron))
end
```

Since the open_session() returns the session and it's the last expression in the method, the login() method returns a session, fully logged in and ready to take more calls. What's nice about this mechanism is that the helper methods in the assertion module can use the session as the implicit self(), so calls within the helper methods can be of the form get "login" rather than session.get "login".

Still, as much as I generally love all things Ruby and metaprogrammy, this does feel a little awkward to me. I'm not going to complain if you want to do something a little more straightforward, like this:

```
def login_as(session, un, pw)
  session.post("session/new", :username => un, :password => pw)
end

def message_from(session, to)
  session.post("messages/send", :to => to)
end

test "trying logins" do
  quentin_session = open_session
  aaron_session = open_session
  login_as(quentin_session, "quentin", "monkey")
  login_as(aaron_session, "aaron", "monkey")
  message_from(quentin_session, aaron_session)
end
```

13.5 When to Use Integration Tests

The testing tools in this part of the book—Rails integration tests, Webrat, Capybara, and Cucumber—are designed to work at a level above a unit test. These tools work best when you use them to validate the interaction between components that are unit tested elsewhere. Cucumber, with its natural-language syntax, is ideal for cases in which a customer or other nondeveloper is creating or approving acceptance test scenarios. Integration tests tend to be of more use strictly as a developer tool, although Webrat and Capybara do make the syntax for specifying interactions much easier to write and read. All three of these testing tools are also useful as "black-box" tests, in which you interact with the application only via URL request and evaluate only the application response. Black-box testing can be helpful in testing legacy code, since the tests are not dependent on the actual structure of the code.

Integration or acceptance tests should be used to cover any process in your application that has multiple steps, is based on previously created session data, or otherwise crosses multiple user actions. The trick is integrating these tests into your TDD process. Often, integration tests at this level are either written first or last relative to the TDD tests for a feature. When written first, they can act as acceptance tests and can drive coding in a TDD fashion—a failing acceptance tests triggers a regular TDD process to make the acceptance tests past. When written last, integration tests tend not to drive new code, since they are validating the interaction between TDD-created components that should already work.

Rails integration tests offer by far the easiest way to test the behavior of your application across multiple user sessions—they offer the only easy way to simulate more than one user hitting the site in a test.

## Chapter 14

Write Better Integration Tests with Webrat and Capybara

Webrat, created by Seth Fitzimmons and maintained by Brian Helm-kamp, can be used to make acceptance tests—the ones that treat the application as a black box—easier to write and execute. By now, you know I can't resist a good naming story; the "RAT" in Webrat is an acronym for Ruby Acceptance Testing. When Jonas Nicklas created a library to augment Webrat as an acceptance tool, he continued the rodent theme and called his library *Capybara*.

Although frequently used in conjunction with Cucumber, Webrat and Capybara can support ordinary Rails integration tests and provide a more expressive, easy-to-read syntax. In addition, the same test can be run headless within a Rails environment and, by changing the driver, also run using a browser-based test environment such as Selenium. Capybara also allows you to use the Celerity and Culerity gems to test JavaScript scenarios without opening an actual browser window.

Webrat and Capybara are quite similar. In fact, if Internet scuttlebutt is to be believed (and really, when has the Internet ever lied?), the two are likely to merge into a single project by the time you read this. For the purposes of this chapter, I'm going to treat them as though they are more or less already merged and note differences between the two as they arise.

14.1 Installing Webrat and Capybara

Both Webrat and Capybara are test framework-agnostic and will work inside Rails for Test::Unit/Shoulda, RSpec, and Cucumber. (Outside Rails, they will also work with Merb and Sinatra, but that's not our focus right now.)

Install either as a gem:

```
$ sudo gem install webrat
$ sudo gem install capybara
```

Both tools have a dependency on the Nokogiri XML parser. If you are on Ubuntu Linux, you may need to run this command in order for Nokogiri to install properly. Installing Capybara on Mac OS X sometimes requires the use of a library called libffi, which can be installed using MacPorts with the command sudo port install libffi.[1]

```
$ sudo apt-get install libxslt1-dev libxml2-dev.
```

Once Webrat is installed, a bit of setup code needs to be placed in your test/test_helper.rb file if you are using Webrat outside of Cucumber:

```
require "webrat"

Webrat.configure do |config|
  config.mode = :rails
end
```

Note that this code goes *outside* the TestCase class structure.

Capybara's default setup is simpler. If you are using Capybara outside of Cucumber, you need the following:

```
require 'capybara'
require 'capybara/dsl'
```

And then inside the module or class using the Capybara commands, you need an include Capybara call.

Cucumber, for its part, automatically detects which of the two libraries is installed for the application and generates the appropriate installation and support code. You can also make that decision when generating Cucumber's initial support files.

---

1. Assuming, of course, that you have MacPorts installed. See http://www.macports.org.

14.2 Using the Acceptance Testing Rodents

Webrat and Capybara are relatively simple libraries with two main purposes: first, to provide a DSL for easily specifying form output and user interaction within an integration or acceptance test, and second, to provide a similarly uncomplicated way to specify the expected output of an interaction.

The signature element of the rodent libraries is their flexibility in how form and link elements are specified in the test; this flexibility is consistent across all of the core API methods listed in a moment. In a Webrat or Capybara API method, you identify the element to be acted on with a string. That string, which is called a *field identifier* or a *locator*, can match a DOM element in one of three ways:

- The text of the associated label (or, for anchor tags, the text inside the tag)
- The DOM ID
- The form field name (or, for anchor tags, the HTML title attribute)

If the field identifier is a regular expression, Webrat will correctly find a matching field based on the regular expression in any of these attributes except the form field name. Capybara, which is much more closely tied to XPath in implementation, does not take regular expressions. The XPath back end of Capybara also means that Capybara lookups are case-sensitive, whereas Webrat lookups are not.

The following HTML snippet would be accessible from Webrat or Capybara as "Phone Number", "phone", or "user[phone]".

```
<label for="phone">Phone Number</label>
<input id="phone" name="user[phone]" />
```

Another consistent element throughout these libraries is all methods that manipulate a form element via a field identifier also serve to verify the existence of the element—if the library can't find a matching form element, the test fails.

Most of your interaction with Webrat or Capybara occurs through the following nine methods:

- attach_file(field_locator, path, content_type = nil)

  Simulates a file attachment to a multipart form. The field_locator is the field getting the file, as specified previously. The path is the path to the local file, and the content_type is an optional MIME type. The Capybara version does not take a third argument.

- check(field_locator)

  Asserts that the field matching field_locator is a checkbox and changes the checkbox to its checked state.

- choose(field_locator)

  Similar to check() but for radio buttons. Any other radio buttons in the same group would then be unchosen.

- click_button(value = nil)

  Clicks a submit button; if the value is passed, then uses that as a field locator to find the button. In Webrat, if there is no value, then it will click the first button on the page. In Capybara, the locator value is required.

- click_link(text_or_title_or_id, options = {})

  Clicks an anchor link as specified by the first argument. The text_or_title_or_id argument is similar to a field locator, except it matches against the text of the anchor tag, as well as the DOM ID or HTML title attribute. One quirk is that for text or title, Webrat does a substring text match, but DOM IDs must match exactly. Webrat intelligently handles   in the text by treating it as a space and is also smart enough to follow the Rails JavaScript that fakes HTTP verbs (but not smart enough to follow Rails link_to_remote() calls). We'll talk more about Capybara and JavaScript in a moment.

  In Webrat, you can override the HTTP verb by passing a :method option, and you can disable the Rails HTTP checking by passing :javascript => false. The similar click_link_within() takes as arguments a CSS-style selector and the text or title, clicking a link only if there is a matching link within a DOM element matching the selector.

  Capybara has a different way to limit scope and takes no optional arguments. Capybara also does not perform any special treatment of   arguments.

- fill_in(field_locator, options = {})

  This method has one option, and it's used in every call, as in fill_in("Email", :with => "railsprescriptions@gmail.com"). It looks for an input field or text area that matches the field locator and sets that field's value to the :with option when the form is eventually submitted.

- save_and_open_page()

This is a wildly helpful method used to diagnose tests that aren't working as expected. It causes the current response to be saved to a file (including any DOM changes from other methods like fill_in) and then opened in your default browser.[2] This is helpful in Cucumber tests, too.

- select(option_text, options = {})

Also used with an option most of the time, select("Automotive", :from => "Industry"). This method causes an HTML option with the given display text to be the selected option in its select menu. If a :from option is specified, that is used as a field locator for the select box.

- select_date(date_to_select, options = {})

select_datetime(time_to_select, options = {})

select_time(time_to_select, options = {})

This trio of methods, which are only in Webrat, lets you specify an entire date/time series of pickers in one go, assuming that your form uses the Rails default date and time pickers. Most JavaScript pickers give you a text field that you can manipulate via fill_in(). The :from() option is used as in select(), and these methods all share an :id_prefix option that matches a prefix specified when the date fields are created.

- uncheck(field_locator)

The converse of check().

- visit(url = nil, http_method = :get, data = {})

Creates a browser request to the specified URL, using the specified HTTP verb and passing the key/value pairs in the data argument as parameters. Normally, you'd use this at the beginning of a test; later requests would be triggered by click_button() or click_link(). In Capybara, the method signature is visit(path, attributes = {}), and the HTTP verb is preset to GET.

---

2. The Webrat docs say the opening works only in Mac OS X, but the docs for the gem Webrat uses (Launchy) doesn't seem to make any similar claim. See http://ramblingsonrails. com/using-webrats-save_and_open_page-on-linux for Linux instructions.

14.3 A Brief Example

In Section 13.3, *Simulating Multipart Interaction*, on page 216, we saw an example of an integration test that used the Rails core integration test features to test adding a friend to Huddle. Let's take a look at what that test might look like in a more rodent-y style. Here's the test using Webrat. There are a couple of different ways this might go:

```
Line 1   test "add friends" do
           visit login_path
           fill_in :login, :with => "quentin"
           fill_in :password, :with => "monkey"
    5      click_button :login
           assert_equal(users(:quentin).id, session[:user_id])

           visit users_path(users(:quentin))
           click "toggle_for_aaron"
   10      assert_equal [users(:aaron).id], session[:interest]

           visit users_path(users(:old_password_holder))
           click "Toggle"
           assert_equal [users(:aaron).id, users(:old_password_holder).id].sort,
   15          session[:interest].sort

           visit users_path(users(:old_password_holder))
           click "Toggle"
           assert_equal [users(:aaron).id], session[:interest]
   20
           visit users_path(users(:rover))
           assert_select "div.interest" do
             assert_select div, :text => "Aaron", :count => 1
             assert_select div, :text => "Old", :count => 0
   25      end
         end
```

There are a few things that are interesting about this test relative to the basic integration test.

This test has much more of an acceptance test style than the original test. The language has changed, moving away from application-like language such as get "users/show", :id => users(:quentin).id to the somewhat more user-level language visit users_path(users(:quentin)) and click "Toggle".[3] Where the original integration test made server calls directly from code, this test infers server calls based on simulating form submits and user

---

3. I can't imagine it makes much difference, but you can assume that I mean the capitalized "Toggle" to be the text label, and the lowercase "toggle_for_aaron" to be a DOM ID.

clicks. In cases like the login on lines 2–5, this makes the code more verbose. However, it makes the test a more complete exercise of the entire stack from start to finish.

Almost. Because here's a critical point: compared to the original test, this test cheats. In the original plain integration test, the toggle calls were all xhr() calls triggering an Ajax response. Webrat, however, doesn't handle Ajax (unless, as we'll see in Section 14.4, *Webrat and Ajax*, on page 231, you configure it to run much slower Selenium tests). In this case, the Webrat test is assuming that the toggle method links will still return the same values if called from something other than an Ajax link.

Capybara and Webrat each have their own methods for asserting output in both Test::Unit and RSpec flavors. Webrat has the following for Test::Unit:

```
assert_contain("text")
assert_not_contain("text")
assert_have_selector("selector", :attribute => "something")
assert_have_no_selector("selector", :attribute => "something")
assert_have_xpath("xpath")
assert_have_no_xpath("xpath")
```

which look like this in RSpec:

```
response.should contain("text")
response.should_not contain("text")
response.should have_selector("selector", :attribute => "something")
response.should_not have_selector("selector", :attribute => "something")
response.should have_xpath("xpath")
response.should_not have_xpath("xpath")
```

The contain methods merely search for text within the output (the response body is the implicit source for output in all the Test::Unit methods). The selector methods are just like assert_select() with two differences. Instead of specifying content with the :text option, these methods use :content, and any HTML attribute does not need to be specified in the selector but can be specified as a key/value pair argument, as in assert_have_selector("a", :href => /solr/). The value part of the argument can be a string or a regex.

Capybara has a slightly different set of tools for specifying output. By default, these tools are XPath-based, but if you're like me and are more comfortable using CSS selectors, you can set CSS as the default by placing the line of code Capybara.default_selector = :css somewhere in your test, like in a setup block. The last couple of lines of the previous test might look like this in Capybara:

```
within("div.interest") do
  page.has_css?("div", :text => "Aaron", :count => 1)
  page.has_no_css?("div", :text => "Old")
end
```

The CSS default selector value applies only to the within() method. In this case, within() acts the same as the outer assert_select() block; namely, it checks for the existence of the selector and limits searches inside the block to the portion of the page inside that matching tag. In Capybara, a within() is not limited to being used with the query methods but can be placed around the interaction methods to limit their searches to a particular part of the page.

Capybara's overall query methods are a little different. The generic one is also named has_selector?(). This method takes either a CSS selector or an XPath expression but does not take arbitrary HTML attributes as options the way the Webrat method does. It does take :count and :text options for the basics and also takes a :visible option, which can be set to true or false and filters based on display status. Capybara also defines has_css?() and has_xpath?(), which both just delegate back to has_selector?(). Capybara has a has_content?(); like the Webrat method, it searches for text within the page.

All of these methods have associated negative versions, such as has_no_selector(). Because these methods are defined on the page object and are booleans with a question mark, RSpec's normal magic renaming allows them to be used as RSpec matchers, like so:

```
within("div.interest") do
  page.should have_css("div", :text => "Aaron", :count => 1)
  page.should_not have_css?("div", :text => "Old")
end
```

Capybara also defines a bunch of specific matcher methods aimed at specific elements. All of these take a string argument, which is a Capybara locator, so matches the DOM ID or element text, and all have associated negative methods.

```
has_button?
has_checked_field?
has_content?
has_field?
has_link?
has_select?
has_table?
has_unchecked_field?
```

14.4 Webrat and Ajax

Webrat has a significant Achilles' heel when run from within Rails. It does not have its own JavaScript interpreter, so any JavaScript in the page you are loading, the link you are clicking, or the form you are filling will be quietly ignored. This is a limitation when trying to test an application with any kind of significant Ajax or JavaScript component.

As a partial workaround, Webrat can be used to drive tests with in-browser verification using Selenium or Watir. You must have the tool you want to use installed, and you need a Rails environment set up for type selenium, meaning a database.yml listing and a file in config/environments. Somewhere in that environment or the test file, you need the following configuration code:

```
Webrat.configure do |config|
  config.mode = :selenium
end
```

You can set the port that Selenium listens on inside that same configure block with the method config.application_port; avoid Selenium's default port, which is 4444.

In this configuration, Webrat will run a Mongrel server and simulate browser interactions via Selenium, which allows you to test your Java-Script.[4]

14.5 Capybara and Ajax

Capybara has a slightly more advanced approach to Ajax testing. Although it still doesn't support Ajax through the Rails default stack, it does provide drivers for two tools that can run JavaScript without requiring a browser window. Capybara can take advantage of Celerity, which is a headless browser simulator running under JRuby (see http://celerity.rubyforge.org/), or, in the very likely event you aren't using JRuby, there is Culerity (see http://github.com/langalex/culerity for information and installation details), which is designed to run in your regular test stack and spawn a JRuby/Celerity process for your JavaScript requests.

---

4. (Thanks to the Webrat wiki at http://wiki.github.com/brynary/webrat/selenium for these instructions.)

You can change the default driver in Capybara with the line Capybara.default_driver = :culerity, where the valid drivers are :celerity, :culerity, :rack_test, and :selenium. The RackTest driver is used for any Rack application that the Capybara tests are being run within, including Rails. You can override the driver for a single test by using a line such as Capybara.current_driver = :selenium and then return to the default with Capybara.use_default_driver. This allows you to only specify the slow JavaScript drivers for those tests that actually require them. In Chapter 15, *Acceptance Testing with Cucumber*, on page 235, we'll see that Capybara also allows you to manage the drivers on a test-by-test basis in Cucumber.

Capybara has one additional trick for managing Ajax. By definition, an Ajax call is, well, asynchronous. That's great in a web page, since it means the entire page doesn't hang while waiting for the result. But it's a problem for a test, since the test doesn't wait for the result. Because the test normally wouldn't wait, assertions that might depend on the Ajax call having finished might fail because the test goes faster than the Ajax call.

Capybara gets around this by inserting wait periods into the test. In essence, any Capybara query call such as has_css?() continues to check the page until the expected DOM elements show up or until two seconds have passed—at which point the test will throw up its virtual hands in exasperation and fail. If you have particularly slow Ajax elements and you can't speed them up for some reason, you can change the wait time with Capybara.default_wait_time = 3; the right-hand side is the timeout in seconds.

This causes a weird gotcha when testing for the removal of text. As we saw in Section 14.3, *A Brief Example*, on page 228, Capybara provides explicit negative methods, like has_no_css?(). You should always use the negative method, as opposed to something like !has_css?.[5] The reason for this is Capybara's wait behavior. Let's say you are testing that an Ajax call removes a DOM element from the page. When the negative method has_no_css?() is called and the Ajax method hasn't returned, the element may still be there, but the negative method knows to wait and check again for the removal of the element. If you erroneously use the positive method has_css?(), the method will see that the element in question is there and immediately stop waiting, since the positive

---

5. In RSpec, you should avoid should_not have_css.

method's purpose in life is to wait until something shows up. Then the bang operator would cause the entire assertion to fail. The lesson is that Capybara provides negative methods for a reason, and you should use them.

There's one other minor gotcha when using Rails as a driver: Capybara doesn't like an anchor tag with just a hash href, as in <a href="#">, so you'll need to avoid that in your Rails code.

14.6 Why Use the Rodents?

In some sense, it's difficult to provide stand-alone examples of Webrat and Capybara, because both tools have seen most of their usage inside Cucumber tests. Used with the core Rails tools, though, they can make the Rails integration tests behave more like acceptance tests. If Cucumber is not an option for practical or aesthetic reasons, adding either of these libraries can give you some of the acceptance test benefit.

At the moment, I tend to start a new project with Capybara, but there isn't enough difference between the two right now that I'd feel the need to convert already existing Webrat code. Of course, by the time you read this, the tools might have merged, in which case you should definitely use the one left standing.

Having looked at what core Rails offers for acceptance and integration testing, it's time to move on to a library that is specifically designed for acceptance testing, namely, Cucumber.

Acceptance Testing with Cucumber

Cucumber is a tool for writing acceptance tests in plain language (I almost said in plain English, but that's too limiting—Cucumber speaks a lot of different languages, including LOLcat). It can be a great way to do acceptance testing simply and clearly, especially when you want a nontechnical client to sign off on your acceptance tests. On the other hand, Cucumber can also be a tempting way to spin your wheels while feeling like you are accomplishing something. There's a sweet spot, and we'll take a look at where that is in this chapter.

15.1 Getting Started with Cucumber

Cucumber is distributed as a gem. As I write this, the stable gem is 0.9.2. You also want to install either Webrat or Capybara, which Cucumber will use to define common web-browser simulation tasks (see Chapter 14, *Write Better Integration Tests with Webrat and Capybara*, on page 223). Like RSpec, Cucumber has both a core gem and a separate gem for the Rails-specific parts.

If you're using Rails 3 and Bundler, the Cucumber gems go in your Gemfile like this—you can substitute Webrat for Capybara if you'd like. The cucumber-rails gem will automatically bring in the core cucumber gem.

```
group :test do
  gem 'capybara'
  gem 'database_cleaner'
  gem 'cucumber-rails'
end
```

In Rails 2.3.*x*, the Cucumber gem can be specified in your environment.rb file or the test.rb-specific environment file. Then a rake gems:install and a rake gems:unpack:dependencies put Cucumber in the vendor/gems directory.

In either case, expect Cucumber to bring in a number of other gem dependencies. The GitHub wiki page for Cucumber at http://wiki.github.com/aslakhellesoy/cucumber is the best source for complete documentation and project status.

To start using Cucumber for Rails testing, you need to generate some files. Run the following command from the root directory of your application. In Rails 2.3.*x*, the command looks like this:

```
$ script/generate cucumber --testunit --capybara
      create   config/cucumber.yml
      create   config/environments/cucumber.rb
      create   script/cucumber
      exists   features/step_definitions
      create   features/step_definitions/web_steps.rb
      exists   features/support
      create   features/support/paths.rb
      create   features/support/env.rb
      exists   lib/tasks
      create   lib/tasks/cucumber.rake
```

In Rails 3, that first command is as follows:

```
script/rails generate cucumber:install --testunit --capybara
```

The options after the word cucumber allow Cucumber to generate support files based on the other tools you are using. I've decided to use the Test::Unit version of the Huddle code and also chosen Capybara. Unsurprisingly, the other supported options are --rspec and --webrat. However, the choice of tools should not affect the Cucumber experience overall. (Capybara, though, has a greater ability to test JavaScript actions through Cucumber.)

The generator creates a features directory, into which your actual Cucumber features go, as well as two subdirectories. One of the subdirectories contains some setup code; the other will be where you put your Cucumber step definitions, which we'll learn more about in a moment. You also get a Rake file and a cucumber script, which lets you run Cucumber features from the command line and can be used to run just one Cucumber feature file, among other tricks. If you look at the database.yml file, you'll see that it has been augmented with a Cucumber environment entry, making it at least theoretically possible to run your Cucumber features simultaneously with other tests and not have the two tests trip over each other. By default, Cucumber features run in the "test" environment, but you can change this by editing the features/support/env.rb file line whose default is ENV["RAILS_ENV"] ||= "test".[1] The cucumber.yml file contains some setup settings that need not concern us at the moment.

15.2 Writing Cucumber Features

Cucumber allows you to write acceptance tests for new features in a lightly structured natural-language format and then convert those tests into executable Ruby code that can be evaluated for correctness. We'll talk more about how this might affect your workflow in a little bit. First, let's go through an example.

Right now, the Huddle application doesn't have much of a user interface. There's no way to associate a user or a user's status reports with a project, for example. So, let's create one. From the Huddle root directory, run the following command:

```
$ script/rails generate cucumber:feature users_and_projects
    exist  features/step_definitions
    create features/manage_users_and_projects.feature
    create features/step_definitions/users_and_projects_steps.rb
    gsub   features/support/paths.rb
```

In Rails 2.x, the initial command is script/generate feature.

The Cucumber generator gives you a feature file where you put the actual Cucumber code[2] and a Ruby file where you put the step definitions that bridge the gap between Cucumber and your actual Rails application. There's also some boilerplate code, which is useful if you are trying to do acceptance test for basic CRUD functionality. (We are not, so I'm deleting it all.) There's related boilerplate in the step definition file that's going away as well.

---

1. If you follow Cucumber development, you may have some whiplash here, because Cucumber did have a default "cucumber" Rails environment for a while, but it was removed as the default in the 0.9.x line.
2. Technically, Cucumber is the entire system. The feature language is called Gherkin (an outstandingly fun word to say over and over again).

Instead, I'm going to describe the feature I do want. A Cucumber feature starts with a header:

huddle3/features/manage_users_and_projects.feature

```
Feature: Add users to project
  In order to make this program even minimally useable
  Pretty much everybody on the planet
  wants to be able to add users to a project
```

This is strictly for humans. The only Cucumber requirement in version 0.7 and up is that the first real line of the file ("real" line means not a comment and not a tag) must start off with the keyword Feature. Earlier versions of Cucumber have no constraints on the header.

After the header, there's an optional background section.

huddle3/features/manage_users_and_projects.feature

```
Background:
  Given a project named "Conquer The World"
  And the following users
    | login| email              | password| password_confirmation|
    | alpha| alpha@example.com| alpha1  | alpha1                |
    | beta | beta@example.com | beta12  | beta12                |
```

The Background line is indented in-line with the In order to lines, meaning that it's two spaces in from the left side. Statements within the background are indented a further two spaces—Cucumber uses the indentation to infer structure, similar to Python or YAML. The Background statements are analogous to a startup block and are evaluated before each scenario is run. We'll walk through the details of the statements in the background in just a moment.

An individual unit of a Cucumber feature is called a *scenario*. I've defined two. The first goes to the edit page display for a project:

huddle3/features/manage_users_and_projects.feature

```
Scenario: See user display on edit page
  Given that user "alpha" is a member of the project
  When I visit the edit page for the project
  Then I should see 2 checkboxes
  And the "alpha" checkbox should be checked
  And the "beta" checkbox should not be checked
```

And the second goes to what happens when the edit form is actually submitted:

```
Scenario: See users in project edit
  Given I am on the edit page for "Conquer The World"
  When I check "alpha"
  And I press "Update"
  Then I am taken to the show page for "Conquer The World"
  And I should see "alpha@example.com"
  And I should not see "beta@example.com"
```

A Cucumber scenario has a basic structure with three parts: Given, which indicates a precondition to the action; When, indicating a user action that changes the state of the application; and Then, verifying the result of the state change. A line beginning with And belongs to its most immediate predecessor clause. For the most part, though, the distinction between Given, When, and Then is for the humans; Cucumber does not require the steps to be in a particular order, nor is the Given/When/Then header used to determine which step definition is matched.

Obviously, the items in the Background clause are all expected to be Given. As for the rest of each clause, that's pretty much free-form; it's the step definitions that give those structure. Oh—the thing that looks like a table in the Background clause. Guess what? It's a table, and that's the preferred method of defining a set of data for a Cucumber feature, rather than using fixtures or factories.

As it happens, this feature can be executed right now, using the command rake cucumber. At the moment, however, we must comment out the before_filter :require_user line in app/controllers/application_controller.rb. (We'll see how to handle logins from Cucumber in Section 15.6, *Login and Session Issues with Cucumber*, on page 251.) Running the features is not going to do much yet.

Each scenario gets run step-by-step; if your terminal accepts it, the results are color-coded for success, failure, skipped due to an earlier failure, and undefined. Here is enough of the output to get the gist:

```
$ rake cucumber
UUUUUUU--UU---U--

2 scenarios (2 undefined)
15 steps (7 skipped, 8 undefined)
0m0.022s
```

At the end, you get a summary. The "15 steps" is a count of the steps in the background section as part of each test: the two scenarios define eleven steps, then the two background steps are run twice, giving a total of fifteen steps. After that, you get some handy boilerplate descriptions of the steps that are undefined, suitable for pasting directly into your step definition page.

```
You can implement step definitions for undefined steps
with these snippets:

Given /^a project named "([^\"]*)"$/ do |arg1|
  pending # express the regexp above with the code you wish you had
end

Given /^the following users$/ do |table|
  # table is a Cucumber::Ast::Table
  pending # express the regexp above with the code you wish you had
end


«many other undefined steps»
```

At this point, it's time to tell Cucumber what each of these steps should actually do.

15.3 Writing Cucumber Step Definitions

Step definitions need to be created for each undefined step. Cucumber does its level best to create useful step definition shells for undefined steps when run. We can paste these shells directly into the features/step_definitions/users_and_projects_steps.rb file, at least as a start.

As you can see from the sample, each step definition starts with a regular expression that defines what steps match it. When a matching step is found, the block attached to that step definition is executed. Groups in the regular expression that are, as always, marked by parentheses, are passed as arguments to the block, which enables a single step definition to match many different steps. Since we want this step to actually create a project, we need to tell Cucumber how to accomplish that creation:

```
huddle3/features/step_definitions/users_and_projects_steps.rb
Given /^a project named "(.*)"$/ do |project_name|
  @project = Project.create!(:name => project_name)
end
```

Running Cucumber

The cucumber-rails gem provides three separate Rake tasks to run Cucumber; rake cucumber (also aliased as rake cucumber:ok) is the default. This will run all features that are not tagged as @wip, or "work in progress." See Section 15.7, *Annotating Cucumber Features with Tags*, on page 252.

Alternately, you can run only in-progress features with the command rake cucumber:wip, which runs all scenarios tagged with @wip. The cucumber:wip task also has the same behavior as a Cucumber command-line option also called wip, namely, that it expects all the tests to fail—otherwise they wouldn't be "work in progress." The cucumber:wip task also fails if there are more than three scenarios tagged as wip, although you can change this parameter by editing the default options in the config/cucumber.yml file.

You can run both in-progress and not-in-progress tasks with the rake cucumber:all task, which will run all scenarios. Alternately, you can run rake cucumber:rerun, which when first called will run the entire suite and make a note of which scenarios failed. If there are known failing scenarios, subsequent runs of rake cucumber:rerun will automatically be limited to the failing scenarios until they pass.

You can also use the cucumber command-line script directly for more options, including the ability to specify tagged scenarios to run. There's more on that in Section 15.7, *Annotating Cucumber Features with Tags*, on page 252. Further behavior of the Rake tasks can be tweaked by changing parameters that are stored in the file config/cucumber.yml.

This step definition matches the step Given a project named "Conquer The World". The regular expression group notation causes Conquer The World to be the argument to the block and, eventually, the name of a new project added to the database. Assigning that project to @project allows the project to be accessed from other steps, though you do need to be careful with instance variables. Creating too many instance variables makes steps more interdependent, and as a result, it's more challenging to reuse steps in multiple scenarios.

The way I like to work when using Cucumber is to go one step at a time. Define the step, and then add any regular tests and code needed to make the step pass. (At least, that's how I like to work with Cucumber this week. It's very flexible, and my workflow changes.) In other words, a failing line in a Cucumber scenario triggers a regular Rails test in the same way that a failing Rails test triggers application code. Sometimes this means going back to Cucumber and changing the scenarios around some, especially when setting up the available data.

This step already passes. Let's move on. The next step is And the following users. The step definition is as follows:

`huddle3/features/step_definitions/users_and_projects_steps.rb`

```
Given /^the following users$/ do |user_data|
  User.create!(user_data.hashes)
end
```

Starting with maybe the most obvious point, even though the step is actually introduced in the scenario with And since it's actually part of the Given clause, we describe it with a Given step definition.

The body of this definition shows how to use the table data. The data comes in as a custom Cucumber object; calling hashes() on the object converts the object to an array of hashes, with keys corresponding to the first row of the table and the values corresponding to each remaining row in turn. With the table that was written in the feature, this means that two users are created with the logins alpha and beta. This step passes already as well.

Moving on to the actual scenario, we start with one more given: Given that user "alpha" is a member of the project. This is another relatively easy one that passes without much further work:

`huddle3/features/step_definitions/users_and_projects_steps.rb`

```
Given /^that user "(.*)" is a member of the project$/ do |login|
  User.find_by_login(login).projects << @project
end
```

To make this work, we need to add has_and_belongs_to_many() lines to both Project and User. In app/models/project.rb, do this:

```
class Project < ActiveRecord::Base

  has_many :status_reports
  has_and_belongs_to_many :users
```

And in app/models/user.rb, do this:

```
class User < ActiveRecord::Base
  has_and_belongs_to_many :projects
```

OK, we have one more that will pass before we get to the hard stuff:

huddle3/features/step_definitions/users_and_projects_steps.rb

```
When /^I visit the edit page for the project$/ do
  visit("/projects/#{@project.id}/edit")
end
```

In this case, I'm using the visit() method, provided by Capybara to simulate a browser call to the given URL. You can read more about Capybara in Chapter 14, *Write Better Integration Tests with Webrat and Capybara*, on page 223; for the moment, all we need to know is that Cucumber lets us call Capybara functions to simulate user actions. This step also passes as is.

If you are at all inclined to be skeptical about Cucumber's general awesomeness, right about now you may be wondering "What's the point of all this silliness?" So far, we've written some formal-sounding natural language stuff and some Ruby that has served merely to confirm things about our application that we already know, at the cost of something like a page of code.

True, so far—although to some extent this is a side effect of the fact that we're adding Cucumber tests to an application that already exists. In much the same way that adding tests to an existing legacy application has some cost, adding the first Cucumber tests to an existing non-Cucumber'd program has some cost. In essence, we're paying off some of the technical debt accrued by Huddle for not having acceptance tests. However, it is easier to add Cucumber tests to an existing program than unit tests—since Cucumber works only at the level of user input and output, any crazy or messed-up code structures in the application code don't really affect it.

As for the eventual benefit, bear with me for a little bit. I'll make that case after we complete the successful scenarios.

15.4 Making Step Definitions Pass

We're going to write the next three step definitions together and then make them all pass. The first step definition to write is for the step Then I should see 2 checkboxes. The definition of the step looks for checkboxes in the HTML using Capybara's page.has_css?() method, which is, for our purposes, effectively equivalent to assert_select():

```
huddle3/features/step_definitions/users_and_projects_steps.rb
```
```
Then /^I should see (.*) checkboxes$/ do |checkbox_count|
  page.has_css?("input[type = checkbox][id *= user]",
      :count => checkbox_count.to_i)
end
```

The next step definition to write is for the step Then the "alpha" checkbox should be checked. As it happens, this step is already defined by Cucumber as part of the web_steps.rb file:

```
huddle3/features/step_definitions/web_steps.rb
```
```
Then /^the "([^"]*)" checkbox should be checked$/ do |label, selector|
  with_scope(selector) do
    field_checked = find_field(label)['checked']
    if field_checked.respond_to? :should
      field_checked.should be_true
    else
      assert field_checked
    end
  end
end
```

After that comes the step Then the "beta" checkbox should not be checked. That one is also defined by Cucumber.

```
huddle3/features/step_definitions/web_steps.rb
```
```
Then /^the "([^"]*)" checkbox should not be checked$/ do |label, selector|
  with_scope(selector) do
    field_checked = find_field(label)['checked']
    if field_checked.respond_to? :should
      field_checked.should be_false
    else
      assert !field_checked
    end
  end
end
```

Both of these steps are defined similarly, using Capybara to find the desired checkbox in the DOM and then using either RSpec matchers or Test::Unit assertions to verify that the checkbox is or is not checked.

Does Cucumber Replace Tests?

There's an ongoing debate among Rails testing people over whether Cucumber is best used in addition to the TDD/BDD tests you would already be writing or whether Cucumber should be used to replace some of those tests, particularly the controller and view tests. One side says that the Cucumber test already covers the code added by a controller test. The other side says that although the same code is touched by each test, the tests have different purposes and are both useful. In essence, the question is whether writing unit or functional tests has value beyond merely verifying correctness, since the Cucumber test already verifies that. Cucumber's value in end-to-end testing and keeping development focused does not replace the exploration, design, or code-quality benefits of a regular TDD process.

The goal of Cucumber is to test end-to-end from a user perspective. As such, Cucumber is not the place to test internals of the program that only tangentially show up to users. Internal logic of models should be tested in unit tests. Best practice suggests that controllers shouldn't have much logic of their own, which means you might not need many controller tests—not because the Cucumber tests replace them but because there isn't much controller logic to test.

That said, I do often find Cucumber to be an easier way to specify view tests than the view test facilities provided by Test::Unit or RSpec. As a result, I find myself basically moving the view tests I would normally have written to Cucumber.

The answer to whether Cucumber replaces regular tests is, sometimes. Cucumber does not eliminate the need for the benefits of TDD in regular testing. However, Cucumber can be used as an easy way to write TDD tests for user-facing code. The point of Cucumber is decidedly not to get bogged down in whether you need extra tests. The goal of Cucumber is to write better code and focus your development efforts. Try using Cucumber a few different ways and see what works best for you.

With the step definitions for our scenario complete and two of them not passing, we finally have a direction for our code. We need to add the checkboxes to the edit view for the project.

Adding the checkboxes to the edit screen probably does not require me to change the controller code. What with this being the Cucumber chapter and all, I'm feeling bold, so let's go to directly to the view.

I inserted this right below the name field in the file app/views/project/ edit.html.erb. I am under no illusion that this view code will scale beyond about ten users.

huddle3/app/views/projects/edit.html.erb

```
<h2>Users In Project</h2>
<table>
  <% User.all.each do |user| %>
    <tr>
      <td>
        <%= check_box_tag "users_in_project[]", user.id,
              user.projects.exists?(@project.id),
              :id => dom_id(user, :checkbox) %>
      </td>
      <td>
        <label for="<%= dom_id(user, :checkbox) %>">
          <%= user.login %>
        </label>
      </td>
    </tr>

  <% end %>
</table>
```

So, for each user in the database, we add a table row with a checkbox and username. The label tag is important here, because that's what the Cucumber/Capybara steps are looking for.

At this point, the scenario passes. Yay, us! Now let's get to work on the next one.

15.5 The Edit Scenario: Specifying Paths

Since it's been pages and pages since we've seen the second scenario, I'll rerun it here:

huddle3/features/manage_users_and_projects.feature

```
Scenario: See users in project edit
  Given I am on the edit page for "Conquer The World"
  When I check "alpha"
```

```
And I press "Update"
Then I am taken to the show page for "Conquer The World"
And I should see "alpha@example.com"
And I should not see "beta@example.com"
```

This scenario currently fails right off the bat with Given I am on the edit page for "Conquer The World". Hmm. Given I am on is a preexisting web step, but the rest of step assumes something that can be converted to a URL.

Let's try this:

```
Given /I am on the edit page for "(.*)"/ do |project_name|
  @project = Project.find_by_name(project_name)
  visit("/projects/#{@project.id}/edit")
end
```

Seems reasonable, if very similar to the When statement I wrote a couple of paragraphs back. The problem, though, is that Cucumber doesn't like it:

```
Ambiguous match of "I am on the edit page for "Conquer The World"":

    features/step_definitions/web_steps.rb:18:in `/^I am on (.+)$/'
    features/step_definitions/users_and_projects_steps.rb:15:
        in `/I am on the edit page for "(.*)"/'
```

And that answers the question of what Cucumber does if there's a step that matches two definitions.

There's another way to specify the path. The definition for the default Cucumber step /I am on (.*)/ defers to a method called path_to(), which is passed the regular expression group as an argument. That method is defined in the file features/support/paths.rb as follows:

```
def path_to(page_name)
  case page_name

  when /the home\s?page/
    '/'

  # Add more mappings here.
  # Here is an example that pulls values out of the Regexp:
  #
  #   when /^(.*)'s profile page$/i
  #     user_profile_path(User.find_by_login($1))

  else
    begin
      page_name =~ /the (.*) page/
      path_components = $1.split(/\s+/)
```

```
      self.send(path_components.push('path').join('_').to_sym)
    rescue Object => e
      raise "Can't find mapping from \"#{page_name}\" to a path.\n" +
        "Now, go and add a mapping in #{__FILE__}"
    end
  end
end
```

See that part where it helpfully says "add a mapping"? What we want to do here is add more where clauses that return some kind of Rails URL-like object. So, delete the Given clause we just wrote, and add the following When clause to the path_to() method in features/support/paths.rb:

`huddle3/features/support/paths.rb`

```
when /edit page for "(.*)"/
  @project = Project.find_by_name($1)
  edit_project_path(@project)
```

I want to walk through this step-by-step:

1. Cucumber sees the step Given I am on the edit page for "Conquer The World".

2. The step is matched to the existing web step Given /^I am on (.+)$/.

3. The web step takes as an argument the grouped text, the edit page for "Conquer The World", and passes it to the path_to() method.

4. The path_to() method matches the regular expression we have just added, /edit page for "(.*)"/.

5. The grouped text in this regex is used to convert that expression to the RESTful edit path for the associated project. The $1 is a Ruby global for the first match group of the most recently matched regular expression. Although that's a Perlism that I don't normally use in my Ruby code, it's the easiest way to get at the regular expression match data that's in the when clause.

There are two ways of looking at this mechanism. On the plus side, it's a very flexible way to allow a path to be specified in a meaningful plain-language way. On the other hand, it has a certain fog-on-fog quality, and there's a lot of indirection.

At this point, the step should pass, and the next two steps, When I check "alpha" and And I press "Update", should also pass because they are web steps that are dependent only on the existence of the form elements we created for the first scenario. They have the effect of mimicking the user actions of checking a checkbox and submitting the edit form with one user checked.

Route Support

One problem with the path_to() method is that it requires you to separately enter paths before they can be used by Cucumber. This feels like duplication. To prevent unnecessary duplication, Cucumber recently added the snippet in the else clause, originally posted by Solomon White. It infers a RESTful route from the text. This code replaces the else clause of the path_to() method:

Using this snippet, something like "the story page" would convert to story_path, while "the edit user page" would send the route edit_user_path.

The fourth step, Then I am taken to the show page for "Conquer The World", needs to be defined. The intent of this step is to validate that the form submission takes the user to the page intended. The step definition looks like this:

`huddle3/features/step_definitions/users_and_projects_steps.rb`

```
Then /^I am taken to (.*)$/ do |path|
  assert(current_url.ends_with?(path_to(path)))
end
```

This definition is dependent on another clause in the path_to() method, very similar to the last one:

`huddle3/features/support/paths.rb`

```
when /show page for "(.*)"/
  @project = Project.find_by_name($1)
  project_path(@project)
```

The step definition is comparing the URL for the current page, which will be http://www.example.com/projects/1 to the URL path output from path_1, which will be projects/1.

Now we're at the meat of the scenario. The last two steps, And I should see "alpha@example.com" and And I should not see "beta@example.com", are web steps that search for specific text in the body output. In this case, we're assuming that the eventual project show page will include the emails of the users on the project—and not include the emails of users who aren't in the project.

You have to be careful here: the Cucumber test is explicitly not testing that the user has actually been added to the project in the database.

You could write such a test, but it is considered better practice to manage that at the controller and model test levels and keep Cucumber at the level of user interaction. That's fine, but it's also true that we could make the Cucumber test pass by just including the text string in the output. Or, more insidiously, by just passing the form submission data to the view without saving it.

My point here is not that Cucumber is bad—it's not. It's more to say that Cucumber is only part of your nutritious testing breakfast. In this case, we are going to change the controller, so we should step down to controller tests. Put this controller test in test/functional/projects_controller_test.rb:

```
huddle3/test/functional/projects_controller_test.rb
test "should update with users" do
  set_current_project(:huddle)
  put :update, :id => projects(:huddle).id,
      :users_in_project => [users(:quentin).id]
  huddle = Project.find_by_name("Huddle")
  assert_equal [users(:quentin).id], huddle.user_ids
end
```

This confirms that sending user IDs to the update will be converted to users in the actual project. The case where there are no users being passed is actually being taken care of by the already existing update test. To pass the controller test, the following goes into update() in app/controllers/projects_controller.rb:

```
huddle3/app/controllers/projects_controller.rb
def update
  @project = Project.find(params[:id])
  @users = begin User.find(params[:users_in_project]) rescue [] end
  @project.users = @users
  respond_to do |format|
    if @project.update_attributes(params[:project])
      flash[:notice] = 'Project was successfully updated.'
      format.html { redirect_to(@project) }
      format.xml  { head :ok }
    else
      format.html { render :action => "edit" }
      format.xml  { render :xml => @project.errors,
          :status => :unprocessable_entity }
    end
  end
end
```

That passes the controller test and puts the data in the database. But to pass the Cucumber test, the data needs to get into the view. Please add the following to the beginning of the app/views/projects/show.html.erb file:

`huddle3/app/views/projects/show.html.erb`

```
<h2>Users for <%= @project.name %></h2>

<table border="0" width="">
  <% @project.users.each do |user| %>
    <tr>
      <td><%= user.login %></td>
      <td><%= user.email %></td>
    </tr>
  <% end %>
</table>
```

I will grant that the previous is not anything like a beautiful design. But Cucumber doesn't care and happily passes. All green; the feature is complete, for some definition of complete.

15.6 Login and Session Issues with Cucumber

There's a big issue that we've kind of glossed over so far: authentication. In a real application, we'd probably need to be logged in to view and edit projects. From a controller test, simulating a login is easy—we have direct access to the controller and session, so we can add the fake user directly to the fake session.

From Cucumber, we don't have access to the controller or the session, so we need to log in by simulating user actions. Something like this works if we are using Devise:

```
Given /^the user successfully logs into Huddle$/ do
  @user = User.create!(:email => "email@email.com",
      :password => "password",
      :password_confirmation => "password")
  visit "login"
  fill_in("user_email", :with => @user.email)
  fill_in("user_password", :with => "password")
  click_button("Sign In")
end
```

This step definition creates a user as an instance variable and then travels to the Devise login screen and simulates filling in and submitting the login form with Webrat or Capybara. If we wanted a specific username, it'd be easy enough to change the step definition to take one in. On the plus side, this is largely boilerplate and can be applied to most projects with little or no modification.

Anything session-based will have a similar issue and needs to be generated by simulating user actions. Again, this indicates that Cucumber isn't going to solve all your testing problems—just some of them.

15.7 Annotating Cucumber Features with Tags

Cucumber test suites, especially on large sites, tend to be slow. Even with the recent speed improvements in parsing the feature files, the end-to-end testing is still slow relative to unit tests. To speed up the development test/code loop, it's handy to be able to run a limited subset of the Cucumber features so that you can focus on the scenarios that are actually under development.

In Cucumber, you can separate scenarios or features into groups by using *tags*. To define a tag, put the tag in the line before the scenario declaration, preceded by the @ symbol:

```
@userpage
Scenario: See user display on edit page
  Given that user "alpha" is a member of the project
  When I visit the edit page for the project
  Then I should see 2 checkboxes
```

If you want to have multiple tags apply to the same scenario, the tags all go on the same line with a space between them. You can then use the tags by specifying them from the Cucumber command line. For example, to only run scenarios with the userpage tag, use this command:

```
cucumber --tags @userpage
```

You can run all the scenarios that *don't* have a particular tag by prefacing the tag with a tilde:

```
cucumber --tags ~@userpage
```

If you want to make things more complicated, you can logically combine tags. If you include multiple --tags options, they act as a logical and. To run scenarios that are both @userpage and @complete, use this command:

```
cucumber --tags @userpage --tags @complete
```

For logical or behavior, include multiple tags in the same option, separated by commas. To run @userpage or @reporting scenarios, you'd do this:

```
cucumber --tags @userpage,@reporting
```

Also, you can specify a limit to the number of scenarios that can be run with a given tag. Running Cucumber will fail if the number of tagged tests exceeds the limit:

```
cucumber --tags @userpage:3
```

This behavior is used by the default cucumber:wip task, but I'm not sure how useful it is in general.

Cucumber gives privileged status to the @wip tag, which stands for "work in progress." The @wip tag is special because Cucumber gives you the default Rake task rake cucumber:wip, which runs only those scenarios that have @wip tags.

If you are using Capybara, then the Capybara/Cucumber combination uses the special tag @javascript to indicate a scenario that should be run using Capybara's JavaScript driver, which is usually Selenium or Culerity. The JavaScript driver is used instead of the default headless stack. This behavior is not dependent on the command-line options; the JavaScript driver will be applied to all appropriately tagged scenarios. Naturally, you'd expect those scenarios to run more slowly.

15.8 Implicit vs. Explicit Cucumber Tests

After writing Cucumber tests for a while, issues of style and structure start to show. One of the first questions is whether to put specific details of the scenario in the Cucumber feature or in the step definition.

For example, a scenario that requires differentiating a newly created user from an experienced user could be written in any of the following ways (and others, but these are enough to make the point):

```
Given a user named "Noel Rappin" who joined the site 2 years ago
Given a pre-existing user named "Noel Rappin"
Given a pre-existing user
```

The topmost version is the most explicit; the step definition would take the data in the Cucumber step and use that directly. The bottom-most version is completely implicit; the step definition will need to create a user and creation time on its own. The middle one, obviously, is in the middle.

Toward Cucumber Style

The key to whether you have a good or bad experience with Cucumber is how well you write the step definitions. Here are some guidelines that I've found useful:

- Let the scenario have the natural language that feels right for your context, and smooth things out in the step definition.

- Try not to include code in your feature descriptions. This includes CSS selectors.

- Where possible, keep the step definitions simple; they absolutely need to be 100 percent accurate.

- I find it better to have multiple simple steps than to have one step that performs tricky regular expression acrobatics.

- Keep the When and Then steps at the level of the user, rather than the database.

- As with other tests, verifying what isn't there is as important as verifying what is.

- Cucumber is not the place to sweat implementation details; save that for the regular tests.

- Avoid tautological tests—it's pretty easy for the indirections of the step definitions to mask an always-passing step.

There are advantages to each way. The implicit view leads to simpler, more natural-sounding Cucumber scenarios and is generally going to be easier for a nontechnical client to use. However, the step definitions are more complex and need to manage more implicit data, leading to a greater possibility of error in the step definitions. It's also less likely that you'll be able to reuse implicit definitions. An explicit Cucumber step leads to simpler step definitions, but it can be hard to distinguish the salient details of the Cucumber step. For example, a client who saw a line of code similar to the explicit line here wondered what was special about "two years ago."

There isn't a particular right answer here; it's something to keep in mind as you write your Cucumber tests.

15.9 Is Cucumber Good for You?

For a long time, Cucumber and its predecessor StoryRunner were on my list of interesting projects to get around to someday, but it didn't seem tremendously practical. One of the things that made me turn the corner and start using it was the realization that a lot of my objections to Cucumber—writing extra code, the fact that the tests might not always be accurate, that kind of thing—were similar to the kinds of objections I'm always hearing about Test-Driven Development in general. That gave me pause, and I decided to make a concerted effort to try to figure out Cucumber.

It turned out that the analogy to regular TDD continued to hold as I used Cucumber. The startup costs turned out to generally be less than I feared, but the benefit of specifying end-to-end behavior of the application turned out to be high. Somewhat surprisingly, I found that my coding sessions were more focused when I used Cucumber, and I had a much better sense of what needed to be completed and what needed to be done next.

What I ended up with was a double loop, where a failing Cucumber test triggers a regular unit test and a failing unit test triggers code. It's not a perfect analogy—unit tests have design value and can cover areas of the program that are difficult to reach from Cucumber—but it's a good way to think of Cucumber's place.

If you are dealing with a client or nonprogramming customer, the value of an acceptance test that is both natural language and executable is outstanding. My only caution at the moment would be that even though there isn't much structure in Cucumber tests, there still is some. We tend to use the Given/When/Then structure for user stories even without Cucumber, but my first attempts at executing some of them in Cucumber still required some translation. For example, the story definitions tended to do too much in one scenario. Be prepared to go back and forth and rewrite your Cucumber steps a little bit over time, for clarity and as new features become apparent. Also, try to keep your step namespace clean; on large projects, finding the steps can become a problem.

Where is the sweet spot for using Cucumber? Cucumber's strengths are in its ability to easily specify and document the end-to-end behavior of your application. It makes an excellent blueprint, both in the sense of describing what needs to be done and in the sense of allowing you to plan the direction of development. It makes an excellent complement to a typical TDD/BDD process, taking a big-picture role that smaller unit tests can't really play. Where you can get in trouble with Cucumber is by trying to move it to areas where it's not really strong, such as attempting to manage model or implementation details. Keep Cucumber in its appropriate place. If you make sure you aren't forever fiddling with the details of the steps and use it to drive your regular tests the same way you use tests to drive code, Cucumber will improve your code.

Part VI

Testing Your Tests

## Chapter 16

Using Rcov
to Measure Test Coverage

Test coverage is the most commonly used numerical metric for evaluating the quality of tests. Coverage measures the amount of application code that is actually executed over the course of running a test suite. At the end of the day, this is usually expressed as a percentage, as in, "My project has 85 percent test coverage" or, in other words, "85 percent of my application code is actually touched when the tests run."

In the right circumstances, you can get into a nice little argument about how meaningful test coverage is, but most people agree on the following points:

- The absence of code coverage indicates a potential problem—a part of your code is not being tested at all. How big a problem that is depends on the context.

- The existence of code coverage, in and of itself, means very little. The coverage metric says nothing about whether the application code being executed is actually being verified at all, let alone being verified completely.

- That said, in conjunction with good testing practices, a coverage run might say something useful about your test suite and its reach. To put it another way, if you are using good TDD practices, you probably are getting good test coverage, but coverage by itself doesn't indicate that you are using good TDD practices.

16.1 85 Percent of What?

Did you see where I tried to put one by you right there in the first paragraph of this chapter? When I referred to a project having "85 percent" test coverage. Leading to the natural follow-up question, "85 percent of what, exactly?" Good question. While the idea of code coverage may seem intuitively clear, nothing is simple once the computer scientists get done with it.

Wikipedia currently lists no less than seven different ways to measure coverage, ranging from the theoretically useful to the downright goofy. But really, there are only two measures that are both easy enough to calculate and useful enough to have any currency at all. *Line coverage* is a measure of the percentage of actual, textual lines of code in your application that are executed by your test suite. The alternative, *branch coverage*, attempts to measure each branch of your code and counts each branch equally. (Spoiler alert: Rcov measures line coverage.) For example, say you have a method like the following:

```
def code_coverage_example_silly_method
  if something_good
    tell_all_my_friends
  else
    ignore_it
    run_in_circles
    scream_and_shout
    jump_up_and_down
    run_in_circles_some_more
    whine_all_day
  end
end
```

If you only had a test for the case where something_good == true—and don't we all wish that was the only case we ever had to test—then a line coverage estimate would say you had covered four of the twelve lines, for 33 percent coverage. Specifically, the tests would cover the def itself, the if statement, the tell_all_my_friends, and the end at the end of the method. A branch coverage estimate, on the other hand, would determine that this method has two branches (the if clause and the else clause) and one of them is covered, for 50 percent branch coverage.

In theory, branch coverage provides a "truthier" picture of your coverage. In the previous method, all six lines in the else clause are essentially one unit; they are either all tested or all not. It makes very little sense for the length of each branch to have an effect on how that branch is weighted for calculating code coverage. On the other hand, the practical difference between the two measures is usually not all that great on real code, and line coverage is about a jillion times easier to calculate. Also, 100 percent is 100 percent either way. I submit that if you are deeply concerned about the difference between branch and code coverage in your app, you have bigger problems than your code coverage.

Still, there are some odd artifacts from Rcov's use of line coverage. The most potentially annoying is for fans of single-line if statements or post-statement if clauses, as follows:

```
return nil if x
if x then 3 else 2 end
```

Rcov will happily mark the entire line as covered, whether or not the if statement is actually tested in both true and false states. Again, this is more an annoyance than a life-or-death concern, and I absolutely would not recommend adjusting your code style to accommodate Rcov, but it is something to keep an eye on.

16.2   Installing Rcov

Like so many things in life, installing Rcov is at least 10 percent more complicated than it should be. You download the gem normally but then need to install a native extension that allows Rcov to run quickly. Without the extension, Rcov pretty much runs in geologic time: instrumenting for code coverage is a slow process.

As I write this, the current, live official version of the Rcov gem is a fork of the original gem maintained by Relevance, a leading Rails consulting shop. As far as http://www.rubygems.org is concerned, the Relevance version is now the canonical version of Rcov. To install the gem, do this:

```
$ sudo gem install rcov
```

If you have not been able to download a binary, once Rcov has been installed as a gem, you must compile the native binary that allows Rcov to run quickly enough to actually be useful. Those of you who are not Windows users need to navigate in the command terminal to the Rcov gem directory (the exact directory will depend on your system; for a native Mac OS X installation, it's /Library/Ruby/Gems/1.8/gems/rcov-VERSION) and run the following:

```
$ sudo ruby setup.rb
```

Windows users aren't officially supported (at least as of the note that I see dated February 28, 2010); however, you should be able to install Rcov via the Windows development kit at http://www.rubyinstaller.org. Note that Ruby 1.9.*x* is not supported yet but is in progress.

Windows users can still create a binary from the original prerelevance version of Rcov by downloading the binary file rcovert.so from http://eigenclass.org/static/rcov/binary-win32/rcovrt.so and placing the file in the Ruby extension directory, which if you used the standard one-click installer, is probably c:\ruby\lib\ruby\site_ruby\1.8\i386-mswin32\.

At this point, you might want to try a simple command like rcov --version to make sure that everything is installed correctly.

16.3 Rcov and Rails

Don't worry, installation fans, we're not done yet. There's still a separate plugin for integrating Rcov with Rails. Luckily, this one is pretty easy:

```
$ ./script/plugin install http://svn.codahale.com/rails_rcov
```

In Test::Unit, this gives you a series of Rake tasks; we'll talk about RSpec in Section 16.6, *Rcov and RSpec and Cucumber*, on page 268. Specifically, each rake:test task you have defined gets a rake test:rcov and a rake test:clobber_rcov, such as rake test:functionals:rcov and rake test:functionals:clobber_rcov. The global test task is test:test:rcov. The Rcov task runs the associated tests using Rcov, resulting in an Rcov report. This report is placed in a coverage directory at the top level of your Rails app. The clobber task clears out the report data from that directory. You can also run coverage on a specific test file by including the file as the TEST option, as follows:

```
$ rake rcov TEST=file_to_test.rb
```

There are some things to be aware of. First, you really don't want those coverage files in your source control, so be sure to use the appropriate ignore mechanism to keep that coverage directory out of the source control tree. Second, the rails_rcov plugin depends on the existence of Rcov. This means your staging and production environments either need to have Rcov installed or need to have the plugin removed, which you can do as part of your Capistrano deploy script, perhaps.

Finally and most importantly, Rcov completely ignores view files that aren't "real" Ruby, such as ERb and Haml. While I suppose in the abstract I'd kind of like to see my view coverage, I have to admit that

> **The Invisible Class Gotcha**
>
> Since the Rcov output contains only files that are touched by the test suite, a file that is completely untouched will not show up with 0 percent coverage—it just won't show up, period. As a result, your coverage score will be artificially high, and you may not see the problem. What with Rails making it pretty easy to get every file in your app at least minimally touched by a test, it's rare to get bitten by this problem. But it does happen—well, it's happened to me—so I thought I'd mention it.

in practice my attitude is more along the lines of "one less thing to worry about today." Ideally, you'll be putting any complicated logic in the model or helper, where it can be tested and the test coverage can be measured.

16.4 Rcov Output

When you run Rcov from one of the Rails Rake tasks, you get output in your console, as well as a full HTML output report. (In the next section, we'll talk about how to tweak that output.)

The console output is simply a list of touched files and will show up after the normal Test::Unit output. Here's an edited look at the text:

```
+-------------------------------------------------+-------+-------+--------
|                      File                       | Lines |  LOC  |  COV  |
+-------------------------------------------- ----+-------+-------+-------+
|app/controllers/application_controller.rb        |    75 |    50 |  86.0% |
|app/controllers/projects_controller.rb           |    87 |    61 |  80.3% |
|app/controllers/status_reports_controller.rb     |    91 |    65 |  80.0% |
|app/controllers/user_sessions_controller.rb      |    25 |    20 |  60.0% |
|app/helpers/application_helper.rb                 |     3 |     2 | 100.0% |
+-------------------------------------------------+-------+-------+--------+
|Total                                            | 78429 | 41952 |  51.2% |
+-------------------------------------------------+-------+-------+--------+
```

The columns are filename, total lines of text in the file, actual lines of code in the file (meaning, lines that are not blank and are not comments), and percentage of lines of code that are covered. The last line of the output is a sum for the project as a whole.

Huddle C0 Coverage Information - RCov

File Filter: [app/ ⬍] Code Coverage Threshold: [Show All ⬍]

NAME	TOTAL LINES	LINES OF CODE	TOTAL COVERAGE		CODE COVERAGE	
app/controllers/application_controller.rb	75	50	90.67%		86.00%	
app/controllers/projects_controller.rb	87	61	86.21%		80.33%	
app/controllers/status_reports_controller.rb	91	65	85.71%		80.00%	
app/controllers/user_sessions_controller.rb	25	20	68.00%		60.00%	
app/helpers/application_helper.rb	3	2	100.00%		100.00%	
app/helpers/projects_helper.rb	2	2	100.00%		100.00%	
app/helpers/status_reports_helper.rb	2	2	100.00%		100.00%	
app/helpers/user_sessions_helper.rb	2	2	100.00%		100.00%	
app/models/project.rb	12	6	100.00%		100.00%	
app/models/status_report.rb	26	17	88.46%		82.35%	
app/models/user.rb	3	3	100.00%		100.00%	
app/models/user_session.rb	2	2	100.00%		100.00%	
TOTAL	**78429**	**41952**	**70.84%**		**51.21%**	

Generated on Sat Jun 19 17:34:06 -0500 2010 with rcov 0.9.8

Figure 16.1: RCOV INDEX PAGE

You'll note, especially if you have an unusual Ruby installation, that the default Rake task will include seemingly zillions of gem, plugin, and library files that you don't really care about, which are also getting included in the total, making it less useful than it might be. The next section discusses how to get those lines out of your reports to make them more meaningful.

Inside the coverage directory, Rcov has created an entire directory for your coverage report. If you open the index.html file in that directory, you will see something like Figure 16.1—I've filtered it to the app directory to make the output more meaningful. Depending on your setup, you might need to limit yourself to just one of the Rcov tests, such as rake test:units:rcov, in order to get a meaningful index file.

At the top of the page, you'll see pull-downs that do some JavaScript filtering of the code based on a top-level directory or a threshold value for coverage, showing only those files below a specified value. Both of these filters are new in the Relevance Rcov and are greatly welcome. The columns here are the same as the console output with the addition of Total Coverage, which is the percentage of lines covered, counting both code and noncode lines of text.

What does it mean to cover a comment, blank line, or other nonexecutable line? Rcov claims to infer coverage of nonexecuted lines by attaching them to the lines nearest them, so an end is considered to

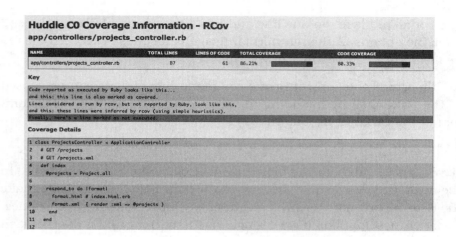

Figure 16.2: RCOV FILE PAGE

have been executed if its associated block or if statement is covered, and a comment is generally attached to the first executable line of code after the comment. In practice, the code percentage in the last column is going to be the most useful.

Clicking any of the filenames takes you to an individual report for that file, as shown Figure 16.2.

By default, the individual report shows various shades of green for covered code (a different green for nonexecutable lines that have been inferred by Rcov) and various shades of red for uncovered lines—these are the ones that might need more testing.

16.5 Command-Line Rcov

You can run Rcov directly from the command line without Rake. By way of comparison, the system command generated by the default Rake Rcov task looks like this:

```
$ rcov -o "/Users/noel/Projects/tasker/coverage/test" -T
-x "rubygems/*,rcov*" --rails  -I"lib:test"
"/Library/Ruby/Gems/1.8/gems/rake-0.8.7/lib/rake/rake_test_loader.rb"
test_file_1.rb test_file_2.rb
```

The command is all on one line and has a list of actual files at the end after the options. Although normal usage is for those executed files to be tests, they can be any Ruby script.

An important note: any of Rcov's command-line options can be passed to the Rake task by including them as a string in an RCOVOPTS command-line variable, as follows:

```
$ rake rcov RCOVOPTS="--only-uncovered --sort coverage"
```

Here's a brief guide to the most useful Rcov command-line options. In the next section, I'll show you how to roll your own Rake tasks to make the Rcov report more useful. As with most Unix command-line utilities, many of these options have a single-dash shortcut and a double-dash full name. This is not a complete list.

--aggregate FILE
> Aggregate the current data with existing data from a previous run that is in the associated Rcov data file.

--annotate -a
> Generate annotated source code.

--comments
> Mark all comments as covered (the default is the opposite, --no-comments).

--exclude PATTERNS --x
> Do not generate coverage information for files matching the list of comma-separated regular expression patterns.

--html
> Generate HTML output. The opposite is --no-html.

--include DIR:DIR -I DIR:DIR
> A colon-separated list of paths to be included in the load path.

--include-file PATTERNS -i PATTERNS
> Only generate coverage information for files matching the given set of comma-separate regular expression patterns. The inverse of --exclude.

--no-color -n
> Generates output that is colorblind-safe.

--only-uncovered
> A synonym for threshold 100.

--output DIR -o DIR

> The directory to which the HTML output reports will be saved.

--rails

> Equivalent to -x config/,environment/,vendor/.

--save FILE

> Saves raw coverage info to a file. Use with --text-coverage-diff.

--sort OPTION

> Sorts files in the output by the option. The option is name, loc, or coverage.

--sort-reverse

> Reverses the list of sorted files.

--spec-only

> Only count code that is covered from within an RSpec spec. In normal RSpec usage, this is redundant.

--text-coverage-diff FILE -D FILE

> Compares this coverage run with a previous run that was saved using --save.

--test-unit-only

> Only count code is covered from within a Test::Unit test. In normal Rails usage, this is redundant.

--text-report -T

> Place a detailed report in standard output (default).

--text-summary -t

> Place a summary in standard output.

--threshold VALUE

> Outputs data only for files with coverage below the value, as in --threshold 95.

--xrefs

> Generates a cross-referenced report showing where methods are called from.

If you need to pass options to the program being run by Rcov, not just Rcov itself, you do that by placing those options after a double-dash in the output, as follows:

```
$ rcov --only-uncovered script.rb -- --opt-to-script
```

16.6 Rcov and RSpec and Cucumber

RSpec and Cucumber use a similar mechanism for integrating with Rcov. In both cases, the recommended way to run coverage of your Cucumber feature set is by also by creating a new Cucumber Rake task in the Rake file created by the tool. For RSpec, that's lib/tasks/rspec.rake; for Cucumber, it's lib/tasks/cucumber.rake. In RSpec 1.3.x and 2.x, a spec:rcov task is predefined, but you can add Rcov support to any custom RSpec Rake task. The key is to set a task variable rcov to true inside the task you create. For RSpec, you get something like this:

```
RSpec::Core::RakeTask.new(:rcov => "db:test:prepare") do |t|
  t.pattern = "./spec/**/*_spec.rb"
  t.rcov = true
end
```

In Cucumber, the task looks like this one, which uses other options from the default Cucumber rake:ok task:

```
Cucumber::Rake::Task.new({:coverage => 'db:test:prepare'}) do |t|
  t.binary = vendored_cucumber_bin
  t.fork = true
  t.rcov = true
  t.rcov_opts = %w(--rails --exclude \/Library\/Ruby\/)
end
```

The rcov_opts variable, which works in both RSpec and Cucumber, takes command-line options that would be sent to Rcov. The options are expected to be in an array. If no options are set, the Cucumber default is %w{—rails —exclude osx\/objc,gems\/}. To my knowledge, RSpec does not have a default.

If those options are good for you, you can just append to the list using something like t.rcov_opts << %w(aggregate data\/coverage.data). In RSpec 1.3.x, Rcov options can be placed in spec/rcov.opts, one option to a line, similar to the way that spec.opts works.

16.7 Rcov Tricks

Personally, I find the default Rcov tasks kind of inflexible and irritating, which is why I wrote my own. The main goal of this was to provide two different views of my test coverage, the first being just the model and helper tests against the model and helper code only and the second aggregating that report with the result of the controller test against the entire app directory. I also wanted some better control over the output.

The simpler part of this is just a Rake task to delete the last round of data, to be invoked as rake test:coverage:clean. I'm hoping you are basically familiar with writing Rake tasks, because explaining all of Rake is way out of scope. (See http://rake.rubyforge.org for full Rake docs or http://jasonseifer.com/2010/04/06/rake-tutorial for a good tutorial by Jason Seifer.)

```ruby
namespace :test do
  namespace :coverage do
    desc "Delete aggregate coverage data."
    task :clean do
      rm_rf "tmp/functional"
      rm_rf "tmp/unit"
      rm_f "tmp/coverage.data"
    end
  end
end
```

That done, it's time to define the actual rake test:coverage task. What I'm doing here is defining a blank task that is dependent on the cleanup task and then defining two tasks, one for each coverage run. Each of these tasks is dynamically made an antecedent of the main rake test:coverage task. I'm helped greatly here by the Rcov::RcovTask class defined by Rcov. Here's the code (this is not the only or even necessarily the best way to write this task):

```ruby
namespace :test
  task :coverage => "test:coverage:clean"
  %w(unit functional).each do |target|
    namespace :coverage do
      Rcov::RcovTask.new("cov_#{target}") do |t|
        t.libs << "test"
        t.test_files = FileList["test/#{target}/**/*_test.rb"]
        t.verbose = true
        t.rcov_opts << '--rails --aggregate data/coverage.data'
        t.rcov_opts << '--exclude app/controllers/' if target == "unit"
        t.rcov_opts << '--exclude db/'
        t.rcov_opts << '--exclude lib/authenticated'
        t.rcov_opts << '--exclude vendor/plugins'
        t.rcov_opts << '--exclude /Library/Ruby/'
        t.output_dir = "data/#{target}"
      end
    end
    task :coverage => "test:coverage:cov_#{target}"
  end
end
```

The Rcov::RcovTask.new() method takes an initializing block; in that block, we set up any options to the task that we want. The class defines a number of attributes to help. Just in this example, you can see libs, which contains directories to be added to the load path; test_files, which takes the list of test files to be run; verbose, which specifies output verbosity; output_dir, which is the directory where Rcov writes to; and then rcov_opts, which takes any other arguments you want.

Note that the two tasks differ only in their test directories and in that the unit test task excludes the controller directory. Rcov options being used include the --aggregate option, which allows the data from the unit test to be rolled into the controller run to create a combined coverage report the second time through.

This is what I use to measure coverage on my projects. Season to taste, and try it on your own.

16.8 How Much Coverage Is Enough?

How valuable is code coverage? The inimitable Jay Fields, who has probably forgotten more about testing than I ever knew, compares code coverage to money—in that having a lot of it doesn't necessarily mean you are happy, but having none pretty much sucks.

It's not hard for a Rails project to run at 100 percent coverage, but there's having coverage for the purpose of getting the magic 100 number, and there's having coverage as a result of an actual test-driven development project, plus some occasional corner filling. The magic number on its own is probably useless; however, going through the process is quite valuable.

If you are executing the process correctly, your coverage should be 100 percent or pretty close as a natural side effect. If you find yourself writing an awful lot of tests after the fact just to get the number up, it's a hint that you could stand to improve your TDD process.

## Chapter 17

Beyond Coverage: What Makes Good Tests?

One of the great things about the Ruby and Rails community is the extent to which they have accepted the idea that Test-Driven Design is a good process for developing software. That's a huge accomplishment and a genuine difference between the Rails community and other programming groups that I have been part of. We've spent a lot of time in this book on the mechanics of Ruby on Rails testing, how the tools work, how to get them running, and how to manage the basic TDD process. In other words, we've been talking about the craft of testing. Now, I'd like to talk about the art of testing: what makes a good test, how to balance testing priorities, how to troubleshoot, and, in the next chapter, how to test when you already have a pile of bad code.

I'd like to see the discussion of testing in the Ruby community move to the next step, which is how to improve the quality of the tests you write. I see two modes of debate about testing in the community, both of which are interesting at times, but neither of which is the discussion I want to have at the moment.

- *TDD/BDD naming debate.* I've been testing for long enough that I still need to catch myself from calling it *Test-First Programming.* So, I don't have a lot of patience when I refer to TDD, only to be greeted with an eye-roll and "Don't you mean BDD?" response. We probably all have better things to do then argue over Scrabble tiles.

- *Tools you should never use.* There have been a lot of posts over the last few months—some insightful, some less so—on the general theme of "Why You Should [Never/Always] Use Cucumber." Tool choice is a useful discussion, but almost any of the popular tools in Rails can be used effectively, so this debate doesn't necessarily give much guidance as to how to test well.

There's a more fundamental debate lurking behind both of these discussions: a debate over what makes a test or a suite of tests effective and useful over the life of your application. To date, there's really only one commonly accepted objective metric of test quality—coverage. As we saw in Chapter 16, *Using Rcov to Measure Test Coverage*, on page 259, though, coverage is a flawed measure of test quality.

For the purposes of this discussion, we'll use a more subjective metric: that a good test saves time and effort over the long term, while a poor test costs time and effort. Using my own test experiences, I've focused on five qualities that tend to make a test successful by this metric. The absence of these qualities, on the other hand, is often a sign that the test could be a problem in the future.

17.1 The Five Habits of Highly Successful Tests

The best, if most general, piece of advice I can give about the style and structure of automated tests is this: *remember your tests are also code.* Also, remember your tests are code that don't have tests. Your code is verified by your tests, but your tests are verified by nothing. So, having your tests be as clear and manageable as possible is the only way to keep your tests honest and keep them going.[1]

A successful test has the following five features:

- Independence

- Repeatability

- Clarity

- Conciseness

- Robustness

---

1. That said, in practice I'm slightly more willing to allow duplication in tests in the name of readability. But only slightly.

Independence

A test is *independent* if the test does not depend on any external tests or data to run. An independent test suite gives the same results no matter what order the tests are run and also tends to limit the scope of test failures to only those tests that cover the buggy method. In contrast, a change in one part of an application with a very dependent test suite could trigger failures throughout your tests. A clear sign that your tests are not independent is if you have test failures that happen only when the test suite is run in a particular order—in fully independent tests, the order in which they are run should not matter.

The biggest impediment to independence in the test suite itself is the use of *global data*. If the application is poorly designed, it may be difficult or impossible to make the tests fully independent of one another, but that's not exactly our lookout at the moment. Rails fixtures are not the only possible cause of global data in a Rails test suite, but they are a really common cause. Somewhat less common in a Rails context is using a tool or third-party library in a setup and not tearing it down. For example, the FlexMock mock object tool needs to be explicitly torn down between tests, as does the Timecop time-freezing gem.

Other than the use of fixtures, most Rails developers know to steer clear of global data in general, not just in a test suite and for the same reason—code that has strange, hard-to-trace dependencies. One reason factory tools are preferable to fixtures is that they result in tests that have better independence.

Repeatability

A test is *repeatable* if running the same test multiple times gives the same result. That is to say, a test is repeatable if running the same test multiple times gives the same result.[2] The hallmark of a test suite that lacks repeatability is intermittent test failure.

Two classic causes of repeatability problems are time and date testing and random numbers. In both cases, the issue is that your test data changes from test to test. The date and time have a nasty habit of continuing to get higher, while random data tends to stubbornly insist on being random.

---

2. Sorry, couldn't resist. If it's any consolation, the joke also didn't get a laugh when I did it as part of an actual talk.

The problems with the two types of data are slightly different. Dates and times tend to lead to intermittent failures when certain magic time boundaries are crossed. Random numbers, in contrast, make it somewhat difficult to test both the randomness of the number and that the randomly generated number is used properly in whatever calculation requires it.

The basic order of attack is similar for both cases and applies to any constantly changing dataset. The goal is a combination of encapsulation and mocking. Encapsulation generally involves creating a service object that wraps the changing functionality. By wrapping the functionality, you make it easier to stub or mock the output values, providing the consistency you need for testing. You might, for example, create a RandomService class that wraps Ruby's rand() method and, critically, provides a way for you to preset a stream of output values either by using an existing mock package or by giving the service object a way to use a predefined value stream. Once you have verified that the random service class is random with its own unit tests, the service class can be stubbed in any other test to provide oxymoronic consistent random behavior.

The exact mix of encapsulation and mocking varies. Timecop, for example, stubs the time and date classes with no encapsulation. That said, nearly every time I talk about Timecop in a public forum, some audience member is sure to point out that creating a time service is a superior solution.

Clarity

A test is *clear* if its purpose is immediately understandable. Clarity in testing has two components. The first is the standard sort of readability that applies to tests as it applies to any code. The second is the kind of clarity that describes how the test fits into the larger test suite. Every test should have a point, meaning it should test something different from the other tests, and that purpose should be easy to discern from reading the test.

Fixtures are a test-specific issue that can lead to poor clarity, specifically, the way fixtures tend to create to "magic" results. To wit:

```
test "the sum should be 37" do
  assert_equal(37, User.all_total_points)
end
```

Where does the 37 come from? Well, if you were to peek into the user fixture file of this fake example, you'd see that somehow the totals of the total points of all the users in that file add up to 37. The test passes. Yay?

The two most relevant problems for the current discussion are the magic literal, 37, which comes from nowhere, and the fact that the name of the test is utterly opaque about whether this is a test for the main-line case, a test for a common error condition, or a test that exists only because the coder was bored and thought it would be fun. Combine these problems, and it quickly becomes next to impossible to fix the test a few months later when a change to the User class or the fixture file breaks it.

Naming obviously helps with the latter problem. Factory tools have their place solving clarity issues, as well. Since the defaults for a factory definition are preset, the definition of an object created in the test can be limited to only the attributes that are actually important to test behaving as expected. Showing those attributes in the test is an important clue toward the programmer intent. Rewriting the test with a little more clarity might result in this:

```
test "total points should round to the nearest integer" do
  User.make(:points => 32.1)
  User.make(:points => 5.3)
  assert_equal(37, User.all_total_points)
end
```

It's not poetry, but at the very least, an interested reader now knows where that pesky 37 comes from and where the test fits in the grand scheme of things. The reader might then have a better chance of fixing the test if something breaks. The test is also more independent, since it no longer relies on global fixtures—making it less likely to break.

We'll talk more about long tests in the next section, but as far as clarity goes, long tests tend to muddy the water and make it hard to identify the critical parts of the test. Basically, the guideline is that tests are code, and for the most part, the same principles that would guide refactoring and cleaning up code apply. This is especially true of the rule that states "A method should only do one thing," which here means splitting up test setups into semantically meaningful parts, as well as keeping each test focused on one particular goal.

On the other hand, if you can't write clean tests, consider the possibility that it is the code's fault, and you need to do some redesign. If it's hard to set up a clean test, that often indicates the code has too many internal dependencies.

There's an old programming aphorism that since debugging is more complicated than coding, if you've written code that is as complicated as you can make it, then you are by definition not skilled enough to debug it. Because tests don't have their own tests and need to be correct, this aphorism suggests that you should keep your tests simple, so as to give yourself some cognitive room to understand them. In particular, this guideline argues against clever tricks to reduce duplication among multiple tests that share a similar structure. If you find yourself starting to metaprogram to generate multiple tests in your suite, you're probably going to find that complexity working against you at some point. You never want to be in a position to have to decide whether a bug is in your test or in the code. Well, you'll be in that position at some point, but it's an easier place to be if the test side is relatively simple.

Conciseness

A test is *concise* if it uses the minimum amount of code and objects to achieve its goal. Concise and clear are sometimes in conflict, as in the previous example, where the clear version is a couple of lines longer than the original version. Most of the time, I'd say clear beats concise— we're not playing code golf here. Conciseness is useful only to the extent that it makes writing and maintaining the test suite easier.

Conciseness often involves writing the minimal amount of tests or creating the minimal amount of objects to test a feature. In addition to being clearer, concise tests will run faster, which is a big deal when you are running your test suite dozens of times a day. A slow test suite is a pain in the neck in all kinds of ways, obvious and subtle, and one of the best ways to prevent a slow suite is not to write slow tests.

To put this another way, how many objects do you need to create to test a sort? A simple sort can be tested with two objects, though I often use three because the difference between the initial input and the sorted input is easier to see in the test. (As an aside, if you are testing a sort, be sure to declare the items in a different order than the eventual sort; otherwise, it's hard to trigger a failure from the test.) Creating any more objects is unnecessary and makes the test slower to write and run.

To look at the issue of conciseness in another way, let's say you have a feature in which a user is given a different title based on some kind of point count; a user with less than 500 points is a novice, 501–1000 is an apprentice, 1001–2000 is a journeyman, 2001–5000 is a guru, and 5001 and up is a super Jedi rock star. How many assertions do you need to test that functionality?

In this case, there's a legitimate possibility of difference of opinion. I'd test the following cases—setup obviously is being handwaved here, and in practice I'd probably do separate single assertion tests. Also, in practice I'd be writing code after each new assertion.

```
def assert_user_level(points, level)
  User.make(:points => points)
  assert_equal(level, user.level)
end

def test_user_point_level
  assert_user_level(1, "novice")
  assert_user_level(501, "apprentice")
  assert_user_level(1001, "journeyman")
  assert_user_level(2001, "guru")
  assert_user_level(5001, "super jedi rock star")
  assert_user_level(0, "novice")
  assert_user_level(500, "novice")
  assert_user_level(nil, "novice")
end
```

That works out to one assertion for the start of each new level, plus an assertion for the special cases 0 and nil, and an assertion at the end of a level to assure that I don't have an off-by-one bug. That's a total of eight assertions. Given the way this code would probably be implemented, as a case statement with the while clauses using ranges, I don't feel the need to test the end condition of more than one field, nor do I feel the need to test every point value in a range. (Don't laugh, I've seen tests that would have effectively looped over every integer in the range and tested all of them. Unsurprisingly, that was on a Java project.)

Robustness

A test is *robust* if it actually tests the logic as intended. That is, the test passes when the underlying code is correct and fails when the underlying code is wrong. It seems simple enough, but we've already seen cases in this book of tests that miss the mark.

A frequent cause of brittle tests is targeting the assertions of the test at surface features that might change even if the underlying logic stays the same. The classic example along these lines is view testing, in which you base the assertion on the actual creative text on the page that will frequently change, even though the basic logic stays the same.

Like so:

```
test "the view should show the project section" do
  get :dashboard
  assert_select("h2", :text => "My Projects")
end
```

It seems a perfectly valid test (or, if you are using Cucumber for integration testing, a perfectly valid Cucumber step definition)—right up until somebody decides that "My Projects" is a lame header and decides to go with "My Happy Fun-Time Projects." And breaks your test. You are often better served by testing something that slightly insulated from surface changes, like a DOM ID.

```
test "the view should show the project section" do
  get :dashboard
  assert_select("h2#projects")
end
```

The basic issue here is not limited to view testing. There are areas of model testing in which testing to a surface feature might be brittle in the face of trivial changes to the model (as opposed to tests that are brittle in the face of changes to the test data itself, which we've already discussed). For example, the test in the previous section with the novice levels is actually dependent on the specific values of the level boundaries. You might want to make the test more robust with something like this:

```
def assert_user_level(points, level)
  User.make(:points => points)
  assert_equal(level, user.level)
end
```

```
def test_user_point_level
  assert_user_level(User::NOVICE_BOUND + 1, "novice")
  assert_user_level(User::APPRENTICE_BOUND + 1, "apprentice")
  # And so on...
end
```

You must be cautious at this point, because the other side of robustness is not just a test that brittlely fails when the logic is good but a test that stubbornly passes even if the underlying code is bad—a tautology, in other words. The previous test isn't a tautology, but you can see how it might easily get there.

Speaking of tautologies, mock objects have their own special robustness issues. As discussed in Chapter 7, *Using Mock Objects*, on page 95, it's easy to create a tautology by using a mock object. It's also easy to create a brittle test by virtue of the fact that a mock object often creates a hard expectation of exactly what methods will be called on the mock object. If you add an unexpected method call to the code being tested, then you can get mock object failures simply because an unexpected method has been called. I've had changes to a login filter cause hundreds of test failures because mock users going through the login filter bounced off the new call. One workaround, depending on your mock package, is to use something like Mocha's mock_everything() method, which automatically returns nil for any unexpected method call without triggering an error.

17.2 Troubleshooting

Dot, dot, dot, dot, dot—tests are passing, looks like it's time for lunch—dot, dot, dot, dot, F. F? F? But the code works. I know it does. I think it does. Why is my test failing?

One of the most frustrating moments in the life of a TDD developer is when a test is failing and it's not clear why, as opposed to the more normal case in which the test fails as expected. Here's a grab bag of tips, tricks, hints, and thoughts to get us all through that difficult time.

Look for What Changed

This may be the most obvious piece of advice in the history of ever, but it's worth repeating, mantra-like, when confronted with a bad bug:

When a formerly passing test fails, it means something changed.

It may be in the code, the system, or the test. But it's probably not sunspots, and it's probably not evil spirits possessing your MacBook.[3]

Looking through recent changes can help you figure out what the cause of the failure is. Git's bisect tool does this automatically; or you can just look through recent changes in your source control viewer of choice. If the test was passing at one time, there's a good chance the answer is in there somewhere.

This is a great argument in favor of committing to your source control very, very frequently (especially when you are using Git and can do local commits) so that your changes are very granular.

---

3. Unless you are living in a Charles Stross novel. Or programming in Perl.

Remember, a change to a fixture file can cause test failures all over the place—removing a model without deleting the fixture file will create errors in every test. Also, if you have a database migration, rake will automatically load the new structure to the test database, but the spec, cucumber, and autotest commands do not do so by default.

Isolate the Failure

When looking at a small number of failing tests, it's helpful to be able to run just those tests. Autotest is outstanding for this, since it runs the failing tests over and over until they pass. Cucumber's default behavior also reruns failing tests. This is especially helpful if you have a number of failing tests that are not in the same test class.

The little code and terminal snippet at http://gist.github.com/101130 is very helpful for quickly running one class at a time, which is almost like isolating a failing test, or at least close enough to be useful. Depending on your IDE and test framework of choice, you may also be able to run individual tests from the IDE.

Isolating tests makes the tests run faster when you are focused on just a few tests and also makes any diagnostics you insert easier to interpret.

Here are two valuable tips that I've learned from listening to and reading Kent Beck:

- Back out your entire most recent change since your last passing test and start over. This works best if you work in very small increments, but it gets you out of the "I know I typed something wrong, but I just can't see it" nightmare.

- Replace all the expressions in the method under test with literals—if that passes, put the expressions back one by one until you find the culprit.

Diagnostics

I'm not a big fan of using stop-and-step debuggers, graphical or command line. I've used them when I've been in an IDE, but I've never really used the Rails command-line debugger. I haven't found that to be a great experience compared to having tests in which I can make assertions.

Normally, to diagnose what's going on in a test, I either add additional assertions in the test or have the code print information to the console or log. If I diagnose via assertions, generally I'm able to test the values of variables in more detail.

For some reason, I see a lot of people using Ruby's puts() method to write to the console—I recommend p(), which calls inspect() on the object before printing and generally results in more informative output. As a matter of course, I put require pp in my test_helper.rb file, which allows me to use pp() to get pretty-printed output, which is nice for nested data structures. Also, y() gives a YAML representation of the output—very readable for ActiveRecord objects. The gem awesome_print provides the ap method for an extremely readable output of complex data structures.

```
>> x = {1 => ['a', 'b'], 2 => 'c'}
>> puts x
1ab2c

>> p x
{1=>["a", "b"], 2=>"c"}

>> pp x
{1=>["a", "b"], 2=>"c"}

>> y x
---
1:
- a
- b
2: c

>> require 'ap'
=> true
>> ap x
{
    1 => [
        [0] "a",
        [1] "b"
    ],
    2 => "c"
}
```

I've been known to bury print statements all over the place—controllers, Rails itself (often educational). This is especially true if I have Autotest limiting the test-run to the one failing test. Just remember to take the print statements out when you are done. Adding additional assertions to the test can also act as a substitute for print statements.

If you need to get to the log, most frequently because you are running Passenger and trying to get output from the actual running app, you can write to the log from anywhere in your Rails app using Rails.logger. error(). You can substitute any of the other log levels for error, but why bother?

If you are using Cucumber or Webrat/Capybara, Webrat and Capybara have the save_and_open_page() method, which is outstandingly helpful. It takes the current Webrat DOM, including any changes you've made using Webrat form methods, saves the page to a temp file, and opens it in your default browser. The resulting page may be missing some images, and you can't really follow links, but you can see what page you got, and it's much easier to inspect the source in the browser using Firebug or the WebKit web inspector and then from print response.body.

Clear Your Head

Take a walk. Force your pair to solve the problem. Get a cup of coffee (actually, I hate coffee; get a Diet Coke). Take a nap. All these clear-your-head steps really do work. Try to explain the problem to somebody else—often, the act of explaining the issue helps identify something you overlooked.

It's tempting to comment-out the offending test; then your suite passes, and all seems well. That's generally a bad idea, although sometimes a major refactoring can genuinely make tests obsolete.

17.3 From Greenfield to Legacy

All of these style issues are helpful in planning and executing your tests. Like most testing advice, though, they have one thing in common: they are much easier to apply to a new application than to a pile of untested code that already exists. In the next chapter, we'll explore the special challenges that come from trying to add TDD to a project that has gone without for far too long.

## Chapter 18

Testing a Legacy Application

You've been asked to take over coding on an existing project. Theoretically, you just need to add a few new features to the existing code base, which is working fine. Well, there's the odd bug—weird stuff the original coders never could track down. Also, the new features to be added involve changes to nearly every model in the application. Oh, and the previous coders didn't pay much attention to testing. There's a test here or there, but overall, not much. The actual code has more spaghetti than a pasta factory, and you have no idea what some of those "tricky" code snippets do, and...

It wasn't all that long ago that there were no Rails legacy projects, but there are many these days. And so we have come upon a new situation: all the advice in this book so far is well and good, but what if you're not starting your TDD experience with a new application? What if you are starting with an existing code base?

Entire books have been written on working with legacy code bases. In this chapter, we're going to focus on techniques for getting legacy code under test. There are many other issues that you'll need to deal with in a legacy code base. Getting the legacy system up and running can be a chore, and there are a variety of techniques for safely adding features to or refactoring existing code. We will only discuss those topics here as they intersect with testing. For a more detailed look at managing a legacy project, check out Michael Feathers's *Working Effectively with Legacy Code* [Fea04]. For more Rails-specific advice, look at Mike Gunderloy's self-published *Rails Rescue Handbook*, available at http://www.railsrescuebook.com.

18.1 Accept That You're Powerless in the Face of a Higher Power

Namely, the previous coders' stupidity, a truly awesome resource.[1] You aren't going to convert this beast of an old project into a marvel of elegant, test-driven code with nearly full coverage overnight. It's just not going to happen.

Shake your fists, and curse the previous programmer's name if it makes you feel better.[2] Get it all out of your system, and then move on and start working with the code base.

There are two reasons it's a bad idea to do nothing but add test coverage to a legacy project first thing. From a purely logistical standpoint, when you take over a legacy project, you are often expected to do something with it, and going off in the corner and doing nothing but writing tests for weeks at a time may not be perceived as forward motion by your new client. Obviously, every situation is different, but it's rare to find a client that considers test coverage a "quick win."

The second reason that starting out by adding only test coverage does not work has to do the often-noted paradox of legacy development. Legacy code, by its nature, is often too interdependent to make it easy to unit test without substantial refactoring. However, substantial refactoring without unit tests is a great way to introduce bugs into the code base—especially when working with new code that you may not yet fully understand. This is also unlikely to be considered a "quick win."

What will work is to proceed in an agile fashion, making small steps that you can verify. You need to tweak the existing code as little as possible to get it to a state you can live with. Then you can ensure that the new code you write is as good, and as tested, as possible.

18.2 Basic Setup

When you are presented with a new code base for the first time, your first job is figuring out exactly what the heck is going on. Toward that end, there are three things you should do immediately. The next three sections define the foundation steps in converting a legacy project into a project that can proceed with a solid Agile and TDD work cycle.

---

1. This is doubly true if you are the previous coder and coming back to fix bad code you wrote in the past.
2. Again, doubly true if the previous programmer was you.

Get the Project Under Source Control

It probably is under source control, but you can't be too careful. While starting on a new legacy code base is not the time to get fancy with new tools, you will be much better served by using Git or some other source control system that lets you easily create and manipulate branches. This will enable you to easily explore changes to the code base using branches as scratch pads that can be kept or discarded as needed.

Get It Running

If the legacy project was conceived without much knowledge of Rails community practices (evidenced by the lack of tests), it won't be a surprise if the production environment is also a little sketchy. Conventional wisdom suggests that your development, staging, and production environments should be as similar as possible to prevent environment-specific errors. And although this is true in general, if your legacy project is being run by some random goofy server setup, it may be difficult or impossible to replicate that setup on your staging server, let alone your development machine.

If the exact production environment isn't an option, the staging and development environments should be as generic as possible. If possible, push to migrate the production environment to a less fragile and more standard environment as soon as possible.

Get the Test Suite Running

At first glance this may strike you as a totally useless piece of advice. If the legacy team has been ignoring tests, nothing is there, right? Of course everything will run.

Well, not necessarily. There are at least two things you need to look out for. Even if the previous coders totally ignored tests, Rails still probably autogenerated test code. The most likely problem you'll run into is that fixtures, generated when the initial model was created, have moved out of date. If columns were deleted or renamed, the fixtures won't load, and you'll get errors galore. It's only slightly less likely that the generated controller tests for a generated scaffold have drifted out of date with the code; if authentication and roles were added later, for example, you will need to match that authentication in the tests.

In some ways, your job is harder if the previous coder flirted with writing tests and then gave it up because he had not yet read this book. (I'm assuming.) In that case, you're likely to have all kinds of tests that may or may not have passed at one point and have since been broken by later code, combined with inattention. You have to assume for the moment that the code is right and the tests are wrong—the exact opposite of a standard TDD scenario. Take this opportunity to learn how the legacy code works, but do not change the code to match the tests at this point. If you can't figure out how to make a test pass, comment it out or delete it, add a note, and come back to it when you have a more thorough test scaffold in place. As we've discussed, test coverage is not the priority at this stage.

18.3 Test-Driven Exploration

Testing a legacy code base starts in earnest when there is a change to make. Often the first order of business on a new project is dealing with a critical bug left by the previous team—something that must be accomplished while preserving existing behavior and does not demand a dramatic refactoring of the application.

In this case, there are two goals to getting the code under test. You want to be able to tell when the bug has been fixed; this step involves a more or less standard TDD bug-fixing session with one or more failing tests isolating the bug, which pass when the bug is fixed. Also, you must confirm that any existing correct behavior hasn't been compromised. In a project that was TDD from the beginning, you'd already have this ability, but in a test-less legacy project, you need to build up that coverage.

Generally speaking, tests against an existing system come in two flavors: *black-box* and *white-box testing*—the phrases far predate software testing and apply to any kind of test process. A black-box test is so called because it ignores the internal structure of the application and tests only top-level input into the system and the output that is returned. Conversely, a white-box test uses knowledge about system internals to explicitly test specific paths through the code.

Black-Box Testing with Cucumber

We've already seen black-box testing of Rails applications in this book, although we didn't call it that. According to our definition, a black-box test of a Rails application works only at the level of user input and system output, typically HTML. Sounds a lot like a Cucumber test, right? Or any kind of integration test, but since Cucumber is outside the normal Rails code, it's ideal for interaction with legacy code. The main benefit of using Cucumber against a legacy database is its black-box nature. The acceptance tests interact with the system basically as a user would. Since there is no interaction with the internal structure of the code, it's possible to write acceptance tests no matter how gunky the code is.

Cucumber can be useful in a bug situation because bugs are often specified in terms of the users' actions and responses. These actions and responses are reasonably straightforward to translate to Cucumber, and it's easy to recognize if you've changed the behavior. In addition, it's not unheard of for a code base with few tests also to lack written requirements; the acceptance tests act as baseline requirements as you move forward.

It's not all sweet Cucumber salad, though. Acceptance-level tests are relatively easy to write for a legacy application but have somewhat limited utility. A Cucumber test won't tell you where in the application you need to make the change that fixes the bug or adds the feature. Also, Cucumber tests tend to run slowly, so you don't want them to be the only part of your test arsenal.

White-Box Testing

Eventually, there's no way around writing real unit tests. There are two distinct kinds of user tests that are helpful when dealing with legacy applications. We'll talk about the standard TDD tests in a moment; first, let's examine the unit test equivalent of the Cucumber tests discussed in the previous section. These tests are used to figure out what is actually going on in the application—a process we might call Test-Driven Exploration, if we didn't have enough three-letter acronyms already.

The basic process is straightforward: the difficulty of implementation depends on just how tangled the code is. First, select a method to test. Ideally, the method should be related to a change you are planning to make in the app, although this process also works for "what is going on here" exploration.

Let's write a test for this method that we know will fail. We don't need to go deep into the internals for this. What we are doing is basically sonar—sending a test into the depths of the code and hoping to get a signal back.

Luckily, even the most test-ignored Rails app probably still has the test directory, so we can write the first test without too much trouble:

```
test "calculation of sales tax" do
  user = User.create(:state => :il)
  order = user.orders.create
  order.line_items.create(:price => 250)
  order.line_items.create(:price => 300)
  assert_in_delta(order.sales_tax, -300000)
end
```

What we have here is a simple, straightforward test, right up until the last line (insert cheesy DJ scratch-record sound effect). We don't really expect the sales tax to be –300,000. But we don't want to guess what it is: we'll let the app tell us.

Run the test. At this point, one of two things will happen.[3] Most of the time the test will error out because there is some object dependency we didn't know about, some value is not as expected, or we have otherwise disturbed the delicate balance that our legacy app needs in order to function. We'll need to figure out how to smooth things over. Often, we'll have to create more objects. In this example, we might explicitly create Product objects. The object chain can get unwieldy, which is OK at this point: the goal is to understand what's happening. If the code itself is unwieldy, let the test stand as a monument to things that need to be changed.

Eventually, we run out of errors, the application spits out the sales tax, and the test has a normal validation failure—since, again, the answer probably isn't –300,000. At this point, we insert the actual value into the test and declare victory. We have some test coverage and a greater understanding of how the application fits together. It's time to move on to the next test, most likely trying the existing method in some other test case, such as a case designed to trigger a bad response.

We don't care if the value for the sales tax is actually correct. Well, we care in the sense that calculating sales tax is important from a business perspective; however, from a test perspective, we must assume that the code is correct so we have a stable base when we start making changes because of all the bugs.

---

3. Well, three things, if we include the very small chance that the sales tax really is –300,000.

> ## What Tools Should I Use? (Legacy Edition)
>
> Taking over a legacy code base has the side effect of clarifying tool decisions we might otherwise agonize over. To wit, if the previous coder used a tool and there's anything at all salvageable, use that tool. We don't want to be in the position of adding code coverage while juggling our RSpec tests with a batch of existing Shoulda/Test::Unit tests. I recommend adding a factory tool if there isn't one already in the mix. It's likely that writing tests for the legacy app will require creating complete chains of related objects. Setting up a factory tool to create the associations all at once saves a lot of time.
>
> There are, of course, exceptions to this rule. Two that spring to mind are when the original developer has chosen a tool that's just unsuitable to support the kind of testing weight we want to put on it. More often, the existing tests are useless, and it's best to delete them quickly and start over, at which point we can pick whatever tools we want.*
>
> ---
>
> *.   Mike Gunderloy presents a simple rule for initial triage of legacy tests in the *Rails Rescue Handbook*: if you can't figure out what a test is doing in five minutes, delete it.

The Rails console is our friend and ally during this exploration process. The console is a great way to try some of these object interactions quickly. Once we figure things out in the console, we transfer the commands to the test so they can be run repeatedly.

18.4   Dependency Removal

Dependencies are the single most challenging issue in legacy testing. Perhaps the greatest virtue of well-done TDD code is that the tests force individual pieces of the code to be maximally independent of each other. Without tests, legacy code has a tendency to be highly interdependent. This makes adding tests difficult in several ways: multiple objects might need to be created to test a single method; or it might be hard to limit a test to a true functional unit, if that unit is hard to reach or encased in some massive 300-line method. There are ways, though, to have the code we need to test be codependent no more and separate enough to enable the tests we must write.

Keep It Separate, Stranger

Maybe the easiest way to keep our new code from being dependent on legacy code is to separate it ourselves. Where possible, write new code in new methods or new classes, and merely call them from the existing legacy mess. In theory, this leaves our new code unencumbered enough to be written via TDD.

Let's try a brief example. Consider a possible and kind of messy method from a social networking site called Flitter:

```
class Flit
  def process_flit
    if text =~ /##/
      flit.text = "testing: remove this code after 3/10/08"
    end
    if text.ends_with?("%fb%")
      send_to_facebook
    else if user.flits_in_last_day > 423
      return
    end
    flit_server.check_for_mentions(self)
    flit_server.follower_list(user)
    user.update_attributes(:flit_count => user.flit_count + 1)
    # and so it goes...
  end
end
```

Within this tangled mess, we must add a new feature: if a flit contains text of the form $username, the user in question must be informed of the message. We could just add another if statement in the long line of if statements already in the method, but then it's very hard to test the new behavior without testing all the process_flit() apparatus, which brings in all kinds of other stuff. (In real life, this method could be 300 lines, and for all we know it could invoke PayPal.) Instead, we add the line check_for_dollar_sign to the method in the appropriate place and write the new method using regular TDD. If we're feeling adventurous and it seems plausible, a mock test to confirm that process_flit() calls check_for_dollar_sign() might also be appropriate.

If we are adding or extracting a lot of functionality, we might consider creating our own separate class, rather than just a method. One sign that a new class is warranted is if it passes the same set of instance variables to multiple methods. I'm a big fan of classes that represent processes and replace long complex methods. For testing purposes, moving new code to a new class can make testing the new code easier, because the new code is less dependent on the existing application.

Legacy Databases, Testing, and You

If our legacy application has only a nodding relationship with Rails common standards, chances are the database is also a mess. Many issues that plague a legacy database can be frustrating (such as odd naming conventions or unusual use of ActiveRecord features), but they don't affect our ability to test the features.

We do need to be careful if the database has added constraints that are not evident in the code. Typically, this involves column constraints that go beyond any validations specified in the ActiveRecord model or foreign key constraints that are not specified anywhere in the Rails code. Foreign key constraints are hardest to deal with. Rails has no native mechanism for specifying foreign constraints, but they are beloved by database admins the world over.

From a testing perspective, the problem is twofold. First, there is business logic outside the Rails code and in the database where it is hard to find, test, and change. Even worse, foreign key constraints add dependencies that require certain objects to be created together. In a test environment, that kind of dependency leads to mysterious bugs: the database doesn't let you create test data, and there are objects that need to be created that have nothing to do with the test but are only there to make the database happy. It's something to keep a close eye on in a legacy application created by a database-heavy development team that didn't trust ActiveRecord.

Although this technique helps us make a clean break from the legacy code, it has the short-term effect of making the code more opaque. In the words of Michael Feathers, "When you break dependencies in legacy code, you often have to suspend your sense of aesthetics a bit" (From *Working Effectively with Legacy Code* [Fea04]). To put it another way, you know when you're cleaning off your desk, you have an intermediate stage in which the room is covered in piles of paper, and it looks like an even bigger mess? Or is that just me? In any case, we're in an intermediate state here, between the undifferentiated mass of the original to the nicely factored and organized new version. Building up the test suite one broken dependency at a time moves us steadily toward cleaner code.

Using Mock Objects to Remove Dependencies

If you don't want to start off at 20,000-feet with acceptance tests, mock object testing is another way to get tests started without disrupting the untested code.

In a legacy context, the advantage to using mock objects is their ability to isolate a single class and method from the rest of the application by creating a mock or stub for any other method called from the method being tested. When working with a legacy application, this allows us to temporarily put aside the issue of how shaky the rest of the application may be and focus on the single part we are trying to figure out at that very moment. Similarly, factory objects make it easy to specify data as needed to easily isolate a legacy method.

In practice, this is very similar to the mock-heavy test practice associated with RSpec—only the code already exists, so it's not test-first or behavior-first. Here's what we do for a legacy method we need to put under test. First, we take the following legacy method (which we can assume is part of some kind of nebulous order model):

```ruby
def calculate_order_status
  self.total = 0
  line_items.each do |item|
    if item.quantity.blank?
      LineItem.delete(item.id)
      next
    end
    if item.cost.nil? then item.cost = 0 end
    if credit_card_is_valid? && item.ready_to_ship?
      self.total += item.cost * item.quantity
    end
  end
  self.to_be_paid = self.total - self.amount_paid
  if self.to_be_paid == 0
    self.paid_in_full = true
  end
end
```

This code is a bit of a mess. It's doing things that should be part of the LineItem class, and it probably could stand to be split. Of course, this example barely scratches the surface of how tangled a poorly written legacy system might be.[4]

---

4. You really want to beware the ones with 300+ line controller methods.

This code calls a number of things that are probably attributes that could be set with data, such as amount_paid or item.quantity, but it also calls a few things that could be complex methods in their own right, such as credit_card_is_valid?() or item.ready_to_ship().

A possible test for this code would mock those methods and might look like this (assume we're using factory_girl and have blueprints set):

```
test "calculating order status" do
    order = Factory(:order, :amount_paid => 2.50)
    order.expects(:credit_card_is_valid?).at_least_once.returns(true)
    item1 = Factory(:line_item, :quantity => 1, :cost => 3.50)
    item1.expects(:ready_to_ship?).returns(true)
    item2 = Factory(:line_item, :quantity => 2, :cost => 5)
    item2.expects(:ready_to_ship?).returns(false)
    order << item1
    order << item2
    order.calculate_order_status
    assert_equal 3.50, order.total
    assert !order.paid_in_full
end
```

Lines 2 and 3 set up the order and a mock for the credit_card_is_valid?() method. Lines 4–9 set up the items, with the actual test action taking place in line 10 and the last lines performing the validation. In a full test suite, we'd test a couple of other combinations of values, so some of the mock setup would probably be extracted to a repeatable method— either an explicit setup block or a method that is called by each test.

The strength of this process is that it allows us to unit test without further tangling the existing code logic: it's possible that credit_card_is_valid?() depends on another three different attributes of the order, the user, or the payment system, and that's a mess that we don't want to get into at this particular moment. The mock test lets us isolate logic issues. An additional strength of this style of mock object testing is that it limits test coverage to the method under test, making the coverage report more accurate.

However, there are some problems to watch out for. It can become time-consuming to set up the external mocks for a complex method, and we run the same risk as with any mock object testing, namely, that our test becomes a tautology because it's just parroting the input to the mock objects. We have to keep the mock data to the external methods and classes in order to avoid that problem.

Find the Seam

Mock objects are a specific version of a more general technique for working with legacy code, which involves finding *seams* in the code and exploiting them to make testing the legacy functionality possible.

A seam is a place where we can change the behavior of our application without changing the actual code. A mock object package acts as a seam because adding the mock object, which happens in the test, changes the behavior of the code by mandating a specific response to a method call without actually executing the method. Again, the behavior of the method under test changes in the test environment without affecting behavior in the production and without changing the existing development code.

It sounds magical, but the basic idea is simple, and Ruby makes it easy to execute. Essentially, redirect a method call from its intended target to some other code that we want to run during tests. A mock object does this by replacing the entire method call with a return value, but the generic form lets us do anything we want instead of the method call. We might do this if we wanted a side effect that a mock package wouldn't normally provide, such as diagnostic logging. Alternately, we might want a more elaborate processing of arguments or state than a mock can easily provide, to re-create the output of a web service our application depends on, for example.[5]

Let's take some sample Ruby code that we want to test. In this sample, flit_server is an object in our system representing an internal server, and those innocent-looking calls are actually genuine external service calls to a real server that exists in production but not in the test:

```ruby
def process_flit
  # a bunch of messy stuff
  flit_server.check_for_mentions(self)
  # more messy stuff
  flit_server.follower_list(user)
  # more messy stuff
end
```

---

5. Some mock packages do let us pass an arbitrary block as the result of the stubbed call, but if the result we need is complicated, it's often more readable to create our own object.

Now we need to get the process_flit() method under test. The test might look like this:

```
test "a flit is processed correctly if it has followers" do
  user = User.create(:screen_name => "zot")
  follower = user.followers.create(:screen_name => "jennyw")
  flit = Flit.new(user, "Hello to $jennyw, How are things on earth?")
  flit.process_flit
  assert_equal(1, follower.timeline.size)
end
```

For this test to work, we need to prevent the flit_server object in the original code from actually calling the production server that will not exist in the test environment. For the sake of argument, we'll assume there's a compelling reason a normal mock package can't be used here—possibly because the flit_server object is too tightly intertwined with the rest of the code. We have two problems to solve. We need to create a flit_server object that will perform test-safe activities when called, and we need to inject that object into the test so it is the object used when the method is run under test.

Luckily for us, Ruby is extremely flexible when it comes to redirecting code execution.[6] In a compiled object-oriented language, we might have to create a new subclass of the expected object and override the methods in question. We can do that in Ruby, too:

```
class TestFlitServer < FlitServer
  def check_for_mentions(flit)
    # test code
  end

  def follower_list(user)
    # test code
  end
end
```

Depending on the details of the FlitServer class, there may be other methods that we must override, such as the constructor.

There are a couple of other Ruby ways to do something similar. Rather than create a subclass, we can create an instance for testing and add overriding methods to that instance's singleton class.

---

6. Of course, this is exactly the kind of flexibility that drives security-minded programmers from other languages crazy. But here we're using for it good, not evil.

That class might be defined like this:

```ruby
test_server = FlitServer.new
class << test_server
  def check_for_mentions(flit)
    # test code
  end

  def follower_list(user)
    # test code
  end
end
```

Alternately, we could create a complete dummy class that covers the calls made by our method under test. Since Ruby doesn't do any type checking beyond seeing whether the object responds to methods, that's perfectly fine:

```ruby
class FakeServer
  def check_for_mentions(flit)
    # test code
  end

  def follower_list(user)
    # test code
  end
end
```

Now we need to inject our new object into the test code. In some sense, what we're doing here is reimplementing what a mock object package would be doing. We can try to inject in the test itself by doing the same thing to the flit object that we did for the flit_server object. Here's an example:

```ruby
Class TestFlit < Flit
  def flit_server
    TestFlitServer.new
  end
end

test "a flit is processed correctly if it has followers" do
  user = User.create(:screen_name => "zot")
  follower = user.followers.create(:screen_name => "jennyw")
  flit = TestFlit.new(user, "Hello to $jennyw, How are things on earth?")
  flit.process_flit
  assert_equal(1, follower.timeline.size)
end
```

In this case, we're mimicking the first option by subclassing Flit. The other two options shown earlier also have analogous usages inside the test.

If we are willing to allow a little bit of manipulation of the original code, we can use Ruby's default arguments to get an almost-seam:

```
def process_flit(flit_server = nil)
  flit_server ||= self.flit_server
  # a bunch of messy stuff
  flit_server.check_for_mentions(self)
  # more messy stuff
  flit_server.follower_list(user)
  # more messy stuff
end
```

In the new method, flit_server is a local, which, if not passed as an argument, is given the value of the object's instance method. Thanks to the magic of Ruby's ||= operator, if the argument is passed a value, the passed value is used for the rest of the method. The existing legacy code, which does not use this argument, behaves as is, but it gives us a lever to insert our own server in the test by calling process_flit with the test server as an argument:

```
test "a flit is processed correctly if it has followers" do
  user = User.create(:screen_name => "zot")
  follower = user.followers.create(:screen_name => "jennyw")
  flit = Flit.new(user, "Hello to $jennyw, How are things on earth?")
  flit.process_flit(TestFlitServer.new)
  assert_equal(1, follower.timeline.size)
end
```

Although this mechanism is slightly intrusive to the original code, you'll probably find you use this pattern often, not just for testing code but also as you add new features to existing code. The default argument lets new code have new behavior, while leaving old code behavior untouched.

Each legacy program you work on is going to have its own quirks and require its own kind of creativity using these methods or others to bring the code the kind of test coverage needed to confidently move forward with bug fixes and new features. As you tackle new problems, remember that reducing dependencies makes it easier to test your code, makes the code cleaner, and makes future work that much easier.

18.5 Don't Look Back

It's almost certainly not worth your time and effort to cover an entire complex legacy application before writing any code. I love tests, but the risks involved in doing that much coverage work at once are high, especially if the customer is expecting you to start working on new functionality.

You draw a line in the sand and start working in a test-driven mode moving forward. One critical element of moving forward is to ensure that every bug fix starts by writing a failing test somewhere—whether unit, functional, or integration. This is a good way to ramp up tests on your project and allows you to organically build test coverage over time with relatively small risk to your deadlines or chance of breaking existing functionality.

Similarly, new features must be added using a TDD process. In the beginning, this often requires the heightened use of mock objects, but over time, the code base and the test coverage both improve.

If you are like me, the temptation to clean up the entire code base at once can be almost overwhelming. In this situation, lie down until the feeling passes or you are so close to your deadline that fixing everything is no longer a viable option.

Do one thing at a time, to the extent possible. Don't extend test coverage while you are adding new functionality. Do not try to clean the code up while you are extending test coverage (occasionally this will be unavoidable, but keep it to a minimum). The fewer things you have moving at any one time, the easier it will be to identify the culprit when things go wrong.

## Chapter 19

Performance Testing and Performance Improvement

Talking about "performance" in your tests usually refers to two separate tasks. The first is performance testing, or using your test suite to automate testing of the actual performance of your application. The second is test performance, or trying to get your test suite itself to run as quickly as possible.

The tools Rails provides to set up and evaluate the results of performance testing are relatively simple to use, at least compared to the convoluted setups required before performance tests were added to core Rails. The results of these tools can be used to compare application performance over time, as well as track down the exact location of performance bottlenecks.

The tools to improve how fast your test suite runs are largely outside the test framework. Generally, test performance comes in three flavors. You can write tests that take fewer system resources to run, choose an alternate test runner that better takes advantage of available CPU time, or modify your environment to allow common test activities to run faster. The last option is mostly applicable to something like a dedicated continuous integration server, which does little or nothing besides run tests.

Effective TDD depends on a tight loop between writing a small amount of test code and writing a small amount of application code, and so on, back and forth. The implicit assumption is that you can run the relevant tests quickly enough to enable you to bounce back and forth between tests and code. However, as your application grows, your test suite takes longer to run. A slow test suite saps your productivity steadily and consistently. The slower it takes to run the suite, the more true TDD becomes painful, and the less often the test suite is run. All of this discourages the constant feedback that TDD—and agile coding in general—depend on.

Efforts to speed up your test suite tend to fall into one of the following categories:

- Focusing test execution so you only run tests most directly connected to the code you are writing. This isn't exactly a performance fix, but it has a similar, practical effect.

- Making performance improvements in your actual application. I trust it's clear why that would speed up your tests and why we aren't going to spend much time on it in this particular book.

- Improving the performance of your tests themselves, typically by reducing the amount of time spent setting up tests.

- Using a faster test runner. We will talk about two kinds here: test servers that stay loaded in the background and reduce the need to continually restart the Rails environment, and networked servers that try to find unused processors on your network and use them to run tests in parallel.

19.1 Performance and Benchmark Testing

Like the criminal justice system in the *Law & Order* opening narration, Rails performance tests have two separate but equal parts. In a *benchmark* test, a block of code, usually containing one or more page hits, is run multiple times. The benchmark test simply measures how long the test code takes to run. The data is then stored, allowing you to compare the current performance of the code with past performance. The goal of a benchmark suite is as a first hint that something has actually caused your code to slow down. Alternately, benchmarks can be used as a before-and-after when you plan on making a major performance change, as proof that the change has value.

In a *profile* test, the goal is to dissect a particular part of your application to determine exactly what pieces of that code are causing performance problems. In a profile test, you typically target a smallish piece of code: a single controller or model call, for example. The profiler keeps track of the amount of time your application spends in each separate method that is touched during execution. At the end, you get a rather complicated report that might be able to tell you what parts of your code it's worth your time to optimize.

You need to have the ruby-prof gem in your project in order to run performance tests. There's some additional magic you can add to your Ruby if you want to test object creation, rather than just CPU time, but we'll get to that in a moment.

```
gem "ruby-prof"
```

Create a new performance test in Rails by using a generator:[1]

```
% rails generate performance_test huddle_performance
      invoke  test_unit
      create    test/performance/huddle_performance_test.rb
```

Exciting. The last argument of the command is the name of the test and is completely arbitrary. You get a short piece of Rails code:

```
require 'test_helper'
require 'rails/performance_test_help'

class HuddlePerformanceTest < ActionDispatch::PerformanceTest
  # Replace this with your real tests.
  def test_homepage
    get '/'
  end
end
```

This should look something like an integration test without assertions, largely because it is basically an integration test without assertions. (The class ActionDispatch::PerformanceTest is a subclass of ActionDispatch:: IntegrationTest.) All the integration test syntax for accessing the application and managing sessions will work inside a performance test. Although strictly speaking the performance test is not limited to full-stack testing, you could have a test that exercises some random model call. Mostly, though, the full-stack measures are going to be most interesting to benchmark.

Your suite of tests, then, consists of a series of page views you consider important for getting an overall sense of how your application responds. Typically, that includes the home page, any other very popular page,

---

1. Rails applications do generate one for you at test/performance/browsing_test.rb, although it's not clear exactly why or why the initial test is ever-so-slightly different from the ones created by the generator.

and possibly any page load you might consider a potential problem. For the Huddle app we've been intermittently using as an example, a possible suite might look like this:

`huddle3/test/performance/huddle_performance_test.rb`

```
test "projects page" do
  get projects_path
end

test "show a project" do
  get projects_path(:id => 1)
end

test "status reports page" do
  get status_reports_path
end
```

There are two very important things that I'm hand waving at the moment: the process of logging in a user and the necessity of having data in the database during the production test. Hold that thought.

While you are holding, run the test using the rake test:benchmark command:

```
% rake test:benchmark
«»
BrowsingTest#test_homepage (92 ms warmup)
          wall_time: 2 ms
             memory: 0.00 KB
            objects: 0
            gc_runs: 0
            gc_time: 0 ms
```

That's only part of the output; you'll get one listing for each test in the class. The benchmark test runner runs each test four times and presents the average. The wall_time is the actual amount of real time that passes during that test. Any other applications running on your machine will affect this metric—turning your Handbrake video transcoding off is probably a good idea.

There are four other metrics: memory allocated during the test, objects allocated during the test, number of times the Ruby garbage collector is invoked, and amount of time spent in the Ruby garbage collector. All those numbers are zero right now. Unfortunately, that's not because we've created the perfect memory usage application but rather because the version of Ruby we are using is not instrumented to count these metrics.

To get these metrics, you have to patch your Ruby 1.8 and recompile. Full instructions are available at the Rails Guides site at http://guides. rubyonrails.org/performance_testing.html#installing-gc-patched-ruby.[2]

In addition to the console display, the benchmark results are also stored in a series of CSV files that go in tmp/performance—an unfortunate choice, since the CSV files are actually not temporary. You get one file per individual test metric or five files per individual test method in your performance test suite (for gc runs, gc time, memory, objects, and wall time). Each file has the measured data included with the time of the test run, the application name, the version of Rails, and the version of Ruby, like so:[3]

```
measurement,created_at,app,rails,ruby,platform
0.00452983379364014,2010-09-16T18:36:46Z,,3.0.0.beta4,ruby-1.8.7.174,
universal-darwin10.0
```

What's nice about this is when you run the suite again, Rails just appends the new line to the end of the same file, which is why they aren't really temporary files. The CSV data makes graphing the data a snap and makes it very easy to show performance trends over time.

Of course, in order to track trends over time, you need to actually run the tests over time, which takes some planning and foresight. One possibility is to place the benchmark tests on your continuous integration server and run the benchmark every night or so. The daily data can be very useful in detecting when part of your application's performance is slowly getting worse. (If you are really brave, you don't allow any check-ins that slow the benchmarks; I think WebKit had that rule for some time.) However, even one benchmark before a major change and one benchmark after can give you some confidence that application performance is heading in the right direction.

One of the problems in fixing a performance problem is that it is not always clear exactly which part of the application is causing the bottleneck. That's where a profile test comes in. The profile test traces the executing code and marks how much time is spent in each method. It's up to you to figure out how to interpret this information.

---

2. The instructions assume you are using the standard MRI Ruby interpreter. If you are using RVM, you can install the gc-patch as a patch; see http://blog.ninjahideout.com/posts/ruby-summer-of-code-wrap-up for suggestions.

3. Hmm...neither Rails 3.0.0.beta4 nor Ruby 1.8.7 patch level 174 is current as I write this; I think I need to update the Huddle code again.

Running a profile test is easy; just use the rake command:

```
% rake test:profile
(in /Users/noel/Dropbox/pragprog/nrtest/Book/code/huddle3)
Loaded suite /Library/Ruby/Gems/1.8/gems/rake-0.8.7/lib/rake/rake_test_loader
Started
BrowsingTest#test_homepage (97 ms warmup)
        process_time: 4 ms
              memory: unsupported
             objects: unsupported
```

The output continues, with one heading for each test in your performance suite. Notice the profile test is much, much slower than the benchmark test—the bookkeeping for the profile data adds a considerable amount of overhead. That's one reason the profile test runs the suite only once, rather than the four times that the benchmark test runs.

The profile test drops three files into test/performance for each individual test method. One of them, which ends in _tree.txt, is aimed at being consumed by a separate graphical analyzer called kcachegrind. If that name is meaningful to you, have at it—the rest of us will move on to the human-readable files.

The easier of the two remaining files to interpret is the flat text file, which looks roughly like this (only the beginning of the file, edited a bit):

```
Thread ID: 2148237740
Total: 0.019577

 %self    total    self    wait    child    calls  name
  3.91     0.00    0.00    0.00     0.00      367  Hash#[]
  3.39     0.00    0.00    0.00     0.00       54  Array#each
  1.72     0.00    0.00    0.00     0.00       69  Class#new
```

Each row of the table has six columns. This is a slightly weird data set, since it's based on the Huddle app that basically does nothing; in a real application, there'd be numbers in most of those columns. The rightmost column is the name of a method in the format Class#method. The leftmost column is the percentage of program execution time actually spent in the method. Often, that's the most important number. The next four columns are all based on clock time—that's actual CPU time, not the benchmark metric of "wall time" that passes while the computer is doing something else.

The total column is the total amount of clock time spent in that method or any methods called from that method. The self column is the amount

%self						calls	method	line
		0.00	0.00	0.00	0.00	1/18	Rack::Test::Session#env_for	164
		0.00	0.00	0.00	0.00	1/18	#<Module:0x103594e90>#hash_for_status_reports_path	148
		0.00	0.00	0.00	0.00	2/18	Rack::Mount::GeneratableRegexp::InstanceMethods#generate	53
		0.00	0.00	0.00	0.00	2/18	ActionDispatch::Routing::UrlFor#url_for	131
		0.00	0.00	0.00	0.00	2/18	ActionDispatch::Routing::RouteSet#url_for	425
		0.00	0.00	0.00	0.00	4/18	Rack::Mount::RouteSet#generate	217
0.94%	0.51%	0.00	0.00	0.00	0.00	18	**Hash#merge**	
		0.00	0.00	0.00	0.00	18/61	<Class::Hash>#allocate	
		0.00	0.00	0.00	0.00	18/50	Hash#initialize_copy	
		0.00	0.00	0.00	0.00	1/3	ActionDispatch::Http::Parameters#symbolized_path_parameters	21
		0.00	0.00	0.00	0.00	2/3	ActionDispatch::Routing::UrlFor#url_for	131
0.91%	0.10%	0.00	0.00	0.00	0.00	3	**Hash#symbolize_keys**	17
		0.00	0.00	0.00	0.00	3/5	Hash#symbolize_keys!	18
		0.00	0.00	0.00	0.00	3/41	Kernel#dup	18
		0.00	0.00	0.00	0.00	1/1	Devise::Strategies::Authenticatable#params_authenticatable?	46
0.91%	0.05%	0.00	0.00	0.00	0.00	1	**Devise::Models::Authenticatable::ClassMethods#params_authenticatable?**	72
		0.00	0.00	0.00	0.00	2/2	Devise::Models::Authenticatable::ClassMethods#params_authenticatable	73
		0.00	0.00	0.00	0.00	1/68	Kernel#is_a?	73

Figure 19.1: PERFORMANCE TEST GRAPH

of CPU time spent just in the method itself. The self column is the basis for the percentage in the leftmost %self column. The wait column is time spent doing nothing—honestly, I have no idea what triggers that column, unless maybe it's garbage collection. And the final floating-point column, child, is time spent in the method calls that come from the method. So, total is equal to self plus wait plus child. The calls column is the integer count of the number of times the method is called.

The other file, which ends in graph.html, presents basically the same information but breaks down where method calls come from and go to. You can see a sample in Figure 19.1.

In each table row, the bold method name is the central point of interest. The methods above call the bolded method, and the ones below are methods that are called by the bold method. The column headers are the same as in the flat file, with a couple of exceptions. The leftmost column is total%, analogous to self%, but for the total time spent in the method and all called methods. You will only see total% and self% for the bold method in each row. For the nonbold methods, the CPU time columns are only for those calls that are related to the bold method. The call row is interpreted slightly differently for nonbold methods in each row. For calling methods, you have two numbers: the number of calls that come from that method and the total number of calls made to the bold method. For called methods, it's the same idea, but you'll see the total number of calls that come from the bold method against the total number of calls to that method in the program as a whole. The last column only shows for calling methods and is the line number where the actual method call to the bold method takes place. If your system is in a known configuration, both the method name and the line number are clickable and will open your text editor to the appropriate file and location.

What you do with all this information is something of a dark art. Mostly, you're looking for outliers and surprises.[4] Focus on the methods that have the most time and/or calls. Keep the balance of time and calls clear when you look for a fix, because the remedy for a method that takes up 20 percent of your runtime is different if the method is called twice or 2,000 times. In the former case, you look for ways to speed up the method; in the latter, you look for ways to call the method less frequently.

One issue you may have noticed with these examples is that performance testing is more meaningful the closer you can get to replicating the production environment. Replicating the server settings of production is difficult in a development environment; if you have the resources to create a staging server suitable for performance testing, that's great. Database performance is particularly sensitive to the amount and distribution of data, and you can often get a reasonable facsimile of production data available to you in development.[5]

Once you have a reasonable amount of data, the problem is getting Rails to use that database. By default, Rails runs performance testing in the test environment, which means the database is shared with all your other tests and cleared before each test run—neither of which is particularly useful for performance testing.

This leaves you with two options. One is to load your production data into the test environment before the tests run. Although you can do this in the setup to your test, it's probably better to create a separate Rake task or script that loads the data and then invokes the rake test:benchmark or rake test:profile task, as desired. On Stack Overflow, somebody going by the name of Chang notes that if you are using SQLite3, this is as simple as cp db/production.sqlite3 db/test.sqlite3, which

---

4. There are other ways to access performance data about your Rails app, including log analyzers and external monitors such as NewRelic. I'm deliberately limiting the focus here to the methods available from the Rails test suite.

5. Obviously, this is impossible if you are on the order of Twitter or Facebook, or something like that, but most production apps with performance problems aren't at that scale. Anyway, you don't have to be perfect: any step closer to real data makes performance testing that much more meaningful.

shows a certain flavor of nuts-and-bolts genius, I think. In MySQL, you could do something similar with a database dump file, but it would be kind of slow for a larger dataset.

The other option is to create a full performance entry in database.yml and point it to a database instance with your performance data. Then you need to get Rails to run your tests in a performance environment. This takes some sneakiness, because Rails will abort a test run if it determines the environment is not test.

Still, it can be done.[6] Create a copy of your test_helper.rb file, and call it performance_test_helper.rb. Change the very beginning of the file to read like this:

`huddle3/test/performance_test_helper.rb`

```
ENV["RAILS_ENV"] = "test"
require File.expand_path('../../config/environment', __FILE__)
require 'rails/test_help'
Rails.env = "performance"
ActiveRecord::Base.establish_connection
```

The rest of the file you can take or leave—you may not need all the junk in your regular test_helper.rb to support performance testing. What we're doing is loading Rails in a test environment and then switching to a performance environment and reconnecting to the database, which points you at the database specified for the performance entry you put in the database.yml. This works, but with the downside that it loads application configuration based on the config/environments/test.rb settings, since Rails needs to boot in the test environment. In most cases, this shouldn't be a problem. You also need to change the line in all your performance tests from require 'test_helper' to require 'peformance_test_helper'.

19.2 Focusing Test Execution

I admit it, being able to run only one of your tests at a time is "speeding up" your test suite in much the same way that pushing everything to the back of your desk drawer is an organization plan—it kind of helps for a while, but eventually you have to deal with the mess. On the other hand, speaking, you know, purely hypothetically, you may someday

---

6. Credit to Rails Core contributor Pratik Naik, who did this in the Rails 2.2 time-frame at http://m.onkey.org/2009/7/29/running-rails-performance-tests-on-real-data. The version here works in Rails 3.

find yourself dropped into a project where the entire test suite takes twenty agonizing minutes to run, and being able to run a limited set of tests is the difference between finishing the feature today or sometime just after the heat death of the universe.

Test::Unit, RSpec, and Cucumber all have different mechanisms for allowing small groups of tests to be run. We've discussed some of these methods in other chapters, but I want to bring them all together in one place.

In Test::Unit, in addition to being able to break the tests down by type, you have the following options:

- Any Test::Unit file (technically, any file that requires test/unit) can be run on its own by invoking it as a Ruby script, as in ruby -Itest test/unit/my_test.rb. This allows you to run the test from the Rails root directory.

- Rails offers the rake test:recent task, which looks at any file that has been touched in the last ten minutes and attempts to run its associated test file.

- Rails offers the rake test:uncommitted task, which looks at all un-committed files and attempts to run the associated test files.

In RSpec, most of your support for minimal test runs comes from using the rspec command,[7] rather than a Rake task. You can give the rspec command a series of arguments that are RSpec files or directories containing RSpec files. You can filter further with command-line options:

- The -e or --example option takes text such as -e project, converts it to a Ruby regular expression, and runs any spec whose full description—the spec name and any descriptions it is nested in—matches the regular expression.

- The -l or --line_number option assumes the command is targeted at a single file, the argument is a number, and the spec at that line number is executed.

In RSpec 2.0, individual specs can be decorated with metadata, which, if you are determined enough, can be used to limit the scope of a test run. Basically, any spec or description definition takes an optional,

---

7. In RSpec 1.x, it's the spec command, which has slightly different command-line arguments.

completely arbitrary hash argument as the last argument. For example, a spec definition might read like this:

```
it "does something cool", :cool => true do
  «Your Spec Here»
end
```

In RSpec 2.0, there's no way to use these properties from the command line—the feature is planned for a later release, after some feedback in how people might use the metadata has been received. However, you can go in to the spec.helper method and filter a test run based on this data. Inside the RSpec.configure block, you need a line like one of these two:

```
c.filter_run :cool => true
c.filter_run_excluding :cool => true
```

Using filter_run() causes only specs or contexts with metadata matching the key/value argument to run. Conversely, filter_run_excluding() runs all the specs except those that match the key/value argument. The value argument of the key/value pair can be a lambda instead of a static value, which allows you to filter based on runtime environment information.[8]

Although the lack of command-line support makes this feature a little awkward to use, there are two things you can do to help. One is the run_all_when_everything_filtered_attribute, which, like it says on the label, changes RSpec's behavior so that if the described filter blocks every test, RSpec will run all the tests instead. In other words, you could do something like this:

```
c.filter_run :in_progress => true
c.run_all_when_everything_filtered = true
```

Now, if there are specs tagged as in_progress, those specs will be run. But if there are no such tags, all specs are filtered, and per the second line, RSpec then runs all the tests. This keeps you from having to continuously change the RSpec config just to have some focused testing.

You can also simulate command-line support by making the filter use the value of an environment variable that you might set at the command line.

---

8. Thanks to David Chelimsky (http://blog.davidchelimsky.net/2010/06/14/filtering-examples-in-rspec-2/) and Nathan Van der Auwera (http://www.dixis.com/?p=283) for blog discussions of this feature.

```
if ENV['FOCUS_TESTS']
  c.filter_run :in_progress => true
end
```

That can then be invoked from the command line like this:

```
spec FOCUS_TESTS=true
```

Cucumber also has command-line mechanisms for limiting the features executed in a Cucumber run. The cucumber command takes a file or a directory as its main argument. This can be augmented.

- If you follow the filename with a colon and a line number, then only the feature at that line is run. You can use multiple line numbers, as in cucumber login.feature:12:35.

- Cucumber allows you to annotate tests with tags, as described earlier in Section 15.7, *Annotating Cucumber Features with Tags*, on page 252. That section also shows how to invoke tags from the command line and the special status of the @wip tag.

- You can instruct Cucumber to make a list of failing specs for the purpose of only rerunning those specs the next time around. The command-line magic for this is a little arcane, since the output of failing tests needed to manage this feature is considered a formatter. So, the command is cucumber --format rerun --out rerun.txt, but the filename at the end is arbitrary. After that test runs, you can use cucumber @rerun.txt to pick up the failed test information and run only those tests. The Rake task rake cucumber:rerun is a shortcut for this behavior.

19.3 Using Autotest

Autotest is a very simple tool that will, if you are like me, quickly become indispensable. It's something of a bridge between the focused setups discussed earlier and the alternate test background runners discussed next. When you run autotest, it will execute all your tests. After that, it runs in the background. When you save a file, the tests associated with that file are rerun. If you have a failing test or tests, those tests will be rerun first, and when the failing tests pass, the entire test suite will be reexecuted to confirm that all your tests pass again.

In Rails 3, Autotest goes in the test group of your Bundler gem file:

```
gem 'autotest'
```

If you are not using RSpec, you may also need the autotest-rails gem in your bundler file. Whether you are running Test::Unit or RSpec, start it off by running autotest from the command line in the root directory of your Rails application.[9] Autotest will run all your tests from your test or spec directory. At one point, Autotest ran the tests in a random order by default, but that does not seem to be the default behavior anymore.

After the tests run, Autotest waits. When you save a file, if Autotest can determine which tests are associated with the file, Autotest will run those tests. For a controller, it runs the associated functional test; for a model, it runs the associated unit test. A change to a test file runs that test. A change to a fixture file will also trigger the associated test file for that model. Edits in the config or test_helper.rb files trigger the entire suite, and a change to the application helper also generally triggers a lot of tests. Edits elsewhere in the system, such as helper files or files in odd directories, may be ignored, but you can configure Autotest to map arbitrary files to tests—more on that in a moment.

If you have a failing test, Autotest's behavior changes slightly. The failure message and stack trace of all failing tests appears at the end of the Autotest run. After that, if you change any of the files associated with the failing tests, Autotest runs the failing tests first. If the tests still fail, Autotest stops. If you change files not associated with a failing test, Autotest runs the test associated with the change and then tries the failing tests again. Any newly failing tests are added to the list of failing tests. In any case, if a run makes all previously failing tests pass, Autotest automatically runs the entire test suite to ensure that there have been no regressions, although this behavior can be turned off by starting Autotest with the option -c.

At any time, you can hit Ctrl-C to cause Autotest to reset the list of currently failing tests and rerun the entire test suite from scratch. Hitting Ctrl-C twice in succession quits Autotest.

Here's where Autotest excels. If you are running something like a regular TDD, you'll write a new test that will fail, and Autotest will continually rerun that test every time you save until the test passes. At the simplest level, this removes the need to continually invoke the tests in your IDE or command line. More helpfully, limiting the test suite to the few failing tests leads to faster test runs and quicker feedback to your actual code.

---

9. In RSpec 1.x, the command is autospec.

Autotest on the Mac

Autotest does its magic by polling the operating system for file changes. The downside is that it can be somewhat processor-intensive, even when idling. If you are using Mac OS X 10.5 or newer, you can use the OS X FSEvent library to allow Autotest to receive notifications of file changes rather than polling. Naturally, this is much less processor-intensive. To use this, you need to install the autotest-fsevent gem. Then, in your .autotest file, add the line require 'autotest/fsevent'. The fsevent line must be last in the file.

A little more subtly, it makes it easier to inspect what's happening in the code. I'm not really one for the Rails debugger, preferring the humble print statement for determining what's happening. The huge advantage of running only one or two tests when in failure mode is that you can throw your print statements anywhere in the app with impunity, knowing that you'll see the relevant output only. I've been known to add a print statement deep in Rails core when I need to find out what's going on, and it all works pretty darn smoothly with Autotest (you can get the same effect in other IDEs, but Autotest works nicely).

There are a number of plugins and hooks that you can use to customize Autotest's behavior. Autotest looks for a file named .autotest either in your user home directory or in your project's root directory.

If you'd like Autotest to exhibit some custom behavior, add your own event-handling blocks. The basic form is this:

```
Autotest.add_hook :waiting do
  puts
  puts "# Waiting since #{Time.now.strftime "%Y-%m-%d %H:%M:%S"}"
  puts
end
```

The previous is actually the autotest/timestamp.rb plugin, which you can find in the ZenTest directory in your very own Ruby Gems directory. The symbol :waiting in line 1 is the actual hook, and the block is run at a time indicated by the hook. In this case, when Autotest goes into waiting mode, it adds a timestamp to your console output, which is helpful in telling you that Autotest is actually done for the moment.

The available hooks are :all_good, :initialize, :interrupt, :quit, :ran_command, :reset, :run_command, and :waiting.[10] Most of these are self-explanatory. You get :run_command at the beginning of an Autotest test cycle and :ran_command at the end. The :all_good hook runs after :ran_command after Autotest runs a complete, clean test suite.

Often, what you want to do is create a mapping so that Autotest associates a file with a specific test or set of tests. Here's an example from the auotest-rails plugin, which is automatically invoked if Autotest detects that it is being started from a Rails application:

```
add_mapping %r%^app/models/(.*)\.rb$% do |_, m|
  "test/unit/#{m[1]}_test.rb"
end
```

The add_mapping() command takes a regular expression—the one here uses a custom delimiter to avoid having to escape all the slashes in the path name—and a block. The block should itself take two arguments: the filename matched and the actual regular expression match object. The result of the block is a filename or a list of filenames. You can obtain a list of files that match a given regular expression by using the method files_matching() inside the block with a regular expression as the argument. When Autotest is running and detects a newly saved file, it searches for the mappings created by add_mapping() calls. If the file matches the regular expression argument to add_mapping(), the block is invoked, and the test file or list of test files returned by that block is added to the list of test files to run.

You can also specify that a file should not trigger tests by calling add_exception() with a regular expression argument. Any file matching that regex will not trigger tests, even if it matches other mappings.

Autotest comes with several plugins that can be included in your local Autotest run by requiring the module in your .autotest file. The following is a partial list of available plugins (we have already covered autotest/timestamp).

autotest/autoupdate allows you to run an arbitrary command after Autotest has been sleeping for a while, which you can manage by setting Autotest::Autoupdate.update_cmd = whatever in your .autotest file. The default command is svn up—this is designed as a way to ensure your code is always up-to-date with the repository.

---

10. That list is from the code itself; oddly, as I write this, the documentation has a different list.

A number of plugins allow various notifications. On Mac OS X, the autotest/growl plugin uses the popular Growl notification utility. The autotest/jabber plugin can be configured to send an IM message via Jabber. Similarly, autotest/blame, which can be configured to use Adium or iChat in an OS X envrionment, sends out a status message with your code-to-test ratio. If you are on a Linux/KDE environment, the autotest/kdenotify plugin uses knotify. If you are on Linux/GTK, use autotest/notify. On Windows, the notification application is Snarl, and the plugin is autotest/snarl.

The autotest/email_notify plugin lets you send an email when Autotest completes a run, which seems like it would have a high chance of getting annoying but might be the guts of a continuous integration environment.

The autotest/heckle plugin lets you specify classes to be run through the Heckle mutation tester after a clean Autotest run. You can automatically run an rcov report after a clean run by using the autotest/rcov plugin.

Several plugins allow for different output. The autotest/html_console plugin drops an HTML file in a directory of your choosing. Using autotest/pretty on OS X gives you a small window that displays a history of your Autotest run, with red squares representing failures and green squares representing success. The autotest/redgreen plugin colors the output of the Autotest report based on success or failure.

The autotest/menu plugin gives a menu of options rather than the more opaque Ctrl-C mechanism.

The autotest/migrate plugin fixes a minor Rails pain by automatically running Rails database migrations when autotest starts. Otherwise, you need to update the test database using the normal Rake commands.

19.4 Making Your Tests Faster

The steps you can take to improving your test performance are divided into things that are almost always a good idea and things that speed the test up at the cost of other positive features—usually independence or clarity—and should be done only when there seems to be a significant test performance issue separate from the performance of the application in general.

RSpec offers you the ability to identify your slowest tests, a handy piece of information when you are trying to speed up your test suite. In RSpec 2.0, the command for is rspec -f p, and in RSpec 1.3, the command is spec -f o.

The first general principle of speeding up your tests is to remember that Cucumber and integration tests are generally slower than controller tests because they hit the entire Rails stack, and controller tests are slower than model tests because they hit part of the Rails stack. So, oversimplifying, a fast test suite has a lot of model tests, a few controller tests, and relatively few integration tests.

If you are practicing good Rails thin-controller design, you probably won't have many controller tests, and the ones you do will frequently interact with mock objects rather than actual ActiveRecord objects. However, if you are using Cucumber in an acceptance test–driven process, you will probably wind up with a lot of relatively slow Cucumber tests. This is especially true given that you can go pretty far in a Rails application without a lot of model logic and therefore without a lot of model tests.

Within model and controller tests, you can keep speed under control by limiting the amount that each test does. In particular, you want to minimize contact with the database. In a controller test, this means mocked method calls, which is fine, since most of what we need to test at the controller level is just that specific model methods are called. In a model test, this means creating the minimum number of objects required for a test and not using model objects without saving them to the database where required. ActiveRecord makes this a challenge sometimes because associations depend on IDs that are assigned automatically only when an object is saved.

In desperate circumstances, you can fake a saved object by explicitly assigning it an ID, though I don't recommend making a habit of it, because it's dangerous. If you have an existing test that saves a lot of objects to the database and isn't amenable to either creating fewer objects or mocking the objects out, you can interrupt normal database interactions by overriding or monkey-patching the method ActiveRecord::Base#columns().

One key thing to do is limit the number of objects you create for each test. Ideally, a true unit test can be performed on a single object, with any other references being managed via mocking. That's not always desirable—too many mocks in a single test runs the risk of making a brittle test. However, too many mocks in a single test should also be taken to suggest that your code is trying to tell you that there are too many internal dependencies, and it is time to factor.

And now we have arrived at fixtures and factories. As great as factory tools are for creating a single focused object, because Rails loads fixtures only once, factories are much slower for creating a lot of objects than fixtures are. When factory tools first came out, it was a common pattern to migrate fixture tests to factories by creating a great blob of factory objects to match the fixtures. Naturally, this turned out to be kind of slow—factories are intended to guide you toward more focused unit tests.

That said, fixtures have a useful role in a Rails test structure. You may have a lot of classes that are background data, in which the database is a nearly static list of items. The first general example that comes to mind is a list of countries, but your application may have other kinds of list data that is, for one reason or another, stored in the database. In that case, it can be helpful to load up all these background objects in fixtures, especially for integration testing, where your application may expect all this data to be in place.[11]

Another, fairly quick way to speed up a test has to do with contexts and single-assertion testing. Aesthetically, I love single assertion testing, but there's no denying that it can slow down a test suite. More accurately, it can exacerbate the effect of a badly structured test by running the setup multiple times. If you have a series of single assertion tests that have some setup behind them, you'll get some speedup just by rolling them back together into a single test with a setup block that is executed only once.

In RSpec, you need to do that by hand, but if you are using Test::Unit and Shoulda contexts, you can use the fast_context gem. With that gem installed, you can replace any call to the Should context() method with the method call fast_context(), and the gem will automatically roll together all the tests inside that context into a single test.

---

11. If your app depends on a lot of static data actually existing in the database, you might want to rethink your design decisions, but that's another story.

This can give you a big speedup.[12] However, it does require that all your single-assertion tests are actually independent and have no side effects. But if you've been following all the advice so far, you're doing that anyway. Single-assertion is very nice during active development. But if you are having a speed issue and want to go back and update parts of the code that aren't under active development to roll the tests together, that's potentially a big speed win for not much cost.

19.5 Using a Faster Test Runner

At some point, you'll reach the end of what you can reasonably do by changing the content of your tests or your application, and it's time to starting changing the context in which those tests run. A number of tools allow you to use your machine resources more efficiently, either by reducing the amount of time spent starting up the Rails environment or by allowing you to run tests in parallel. We'll cover some of the tools here, but this list is not intended to be exhaustive; there are a lot of different tools out there.

Before we dive into various test servers, it's worth mentioning that you may be able to get a speed boost just by changing Ruby versions. Ruby 1.9.2 is significantly faster than Ruby 1.8.7, but 1.9.2 may not be feasible for your production system. The team that created Phusion Passenger also created a Ruby 1.8.7–compatible interpreter called the Ruby Enterprise Edition (REE), which is optimized for server use and uses less memory than the basic Ruby 1.8.7. Converting to REE should be simple for most Ruby 1.8.7, and you could see a big speedup.[13] JRuby is also a possibility for its overall performance, but JRuby's big downside for TDD purposes is that its startup time is pretty slow, which can be an issue if you are starting an interpreter every five minutes to run your new tests.

That brings us to Spork, which allows you to keep a Ruby interpreter open and run RSpec and Cucumber tests in that interpreter without restarting Rails.[14] The name presumably comes from a combination of

---

12. Nick Gauthier, in his Grease Your Suite presentation, http://grease-your-suite.heroku. com, describes a test suite that went from 13:15 to 5:32 using just fast_context.
13. My experience is that you can get about 10–20 percent speedup with little effort. Nick Gauthier's previously mentioned presentation suggests that you can do a lot better if you have the RAM and are willing to tweak some environment variables.
14. There's a plugin that ties Spork to Test::Unit, which we won't be discussing here.

"spec" and the fact that Spork "forks" a new process when you run your tests.

As I write this, Spork is not fully integrated with RSpec 2, but work is in progress, and I expect the Spork installation process not to change substantially. Spork is a gem, so for Rails 3, you need gem 'spork' in the test group of your Gemfile.

With the gem installed, run the following command:

```
spork --bootstrap
```

Bootstrapping Spork puts the following code in your spec/spec_helper.rb file:

`huddle3_rspec2/spec/spec_helper.rb`

```
Spork.prefork do
  # Loading more in this block will cause your tests to run faster. However,
  # if you change any configuration or code from libraries loaded here, you'll
  # need to restart spork for it take effect.

end

Spork.each_run do
  # This code will be run each time you run your specs.

end
```

There are also some commented instructions; let's walk through them. Spork has two kinds of initialization. It runs one block of code exactly once when the Spork server starts and never again, and then a separate block of code gets executed each time Spork spawns a new test process. What Spork wants you to do is split all the items in your spec_helper.rb file (aside from the two require statements needed to load Spork itself) into one of two piles. Any code that you want to run once goes inside the Spork.prefork block. Code you want executed each time goes inside the Spork.each_run block.

I really do mean everything—the other require statements, the RSpec. configure block, any helper methods you are defining—the whole ball of wax goes in either the prefork block or the each_run block. The performance trade-off is simple. For any code that you put in the prefork block, you get the benefit of only needing to run it once for the life of the Spork server, but if anything in that block changes, you'll need to restart the Spork server to see that change.

You don't need to worry about what happens if you've defined the Spork blocks and then run tests without an active Spork server. The blocks just execute on startup, and everything is fine.

Once you have the blocks defined, start a Spork server with the following simple command:

```
$ spork
spork
Using RSpec
Preloading Rails environment
Loading Spork.prefork block...
No server is running
Running specs locally:
Spork is ready and listening on 8989!
```

On the RSpec side, you need to add --drb to the rspec.opts file or add it as a command-line option when you run your specs. RSpec uses the Spork server to get a preloaded process to run, which should start up faster than a normal RSpec session.

Cucumber usage is similar. You can facilitate Spork setup by adding --spork to the command when you generate the initial Cucumber files; the same --drb option causes Cucumber to search for the Spork server.

Spork is handy, but it doesn't actually improve the usage patterns of your CPU during test. If you are using a development machine that has a lot of CPUs or if you are on a network that has a lot of idle processing power at any given time, look at one of several tools that try to run your tests in parallel across multiple cores. We're going to briefly take a look at two representative sample tools, with the understanding that this is a rapidly changing area; no one tool seems to be best for all users (the best tool depends on your situation), and now that you know that tools like this exist, finding the current state of the art should be much easier.

First up is parallel_tests, which you can find at http://github.com/grosser/parallel_tests. The parallel_tests gem supports creating multiple test environments that run parts of your test suite simultaneously. It's a gem, so in Rails 3, you'll need it in your bundler file as gem "parallel_tests". Like RSpec, you'll want it in your development and test group.

With the gem installed, you need to add support for multiple test data-bases. In your database.yml, augment the name of your test database by appending an environment variable like so:

```
test:
  database: huddle_test<%= ENV['TEST_ENV_NUMBER'] %>
```

The database.yml file is evaluated via ERb when loaded, and the test number gets the appropriate value based on parallel_tests managing the various test processes that it creates.

After you change the ERb, create the actual database instances, and load the database schema into them:

```
% rake parallel:create
% rake parallel:prepare
```

Then you can run the test with rake parallel:test for Test::Unit, rake parallel:spec for RSpec, and rake parallel:features for Cucumber. If you have multiple CPUs, multiple parallel test process will be spawned to run all your tests.

Note that the overall processor time needed to run the tests does not go down. Actually, it goes up, because each process needs its own startup time. However, the amount of actual clock time that passes should go down as the test runs simultaneously. One side effect, though, is that your machine will be pretty thoroughly jammed while the tests run, so if you like checking email during test runs, be advised that's going to slow down quite a bit. Also, Spork and parallel_test do not get along at all—don't run them together.

If you are looking for a simple way to distribute tests across your network, Specjour works for networks that have the Bonjour protocol installed. Specjour is a gem, so the usual gem "specjour" goes into the bundler file.

To use specjour, identify the machines on your network that are avail-able to run tests, and set up your application to allow those tests to run. Discovery of available machines is managed automatically by specjour.

Setting up a worker machine is as simple as the command specjour. The worker machine won't necessarily start with your code, so you need to be sure that Ruby is available on that machine, as well as the rsync system command, which is used to move files back and forth.

In your actual Rails project, modify the database.yml in exactly the way specified earlier for parallel_tests. Unlike parallel_tests, specjour will create the parallel database instances for you. Then running rake specjour or rake specjour:cucumber should start the specjour system searching for available workers on the network. You can have specjour running as a manager on the same machine if you just want the parallel tests feature, and not the searching the network feature. You can also limit specjour to a particular number of CPUs or to only accept requests from specific projects.

If you need more complex network behavior, take a look at Hydra, http://github.com/ngauthier/hydra/wiki, which allows for more flexibility.

A slow test suite destroys TDD by making it harder to run the tests with the frequency that good TDD process requires. Although there are no one-size-fits-all solutions to performance issues, in application code or in testing, the options described in this chapter should give you a good start in diagnosing and taking steps to improve the performance of your tests.

19.6 And in the End...

I've tried to present the most current, flexible, and powerful tools and practices for Test-Driven Development. It's been about ten years since I first used JUnit for TDD, and there's no other single tool or innovation I've come upon that has improved the quality of my code and the quality of the time I spend developing.

Tools in this part of the world change fast, and I'm sure that by the time you read this, parts of the books seem out-of-date at best and primitive at worst. If only I could predict which parts...I hope that you'll find some core principles here that will be valuable no matter what kinds of applications you build or what kinds of tools are created. Take small steps, write the code first, and let the code and tests feed back on each other frequently.

Now, go out and test something.

Sample Application Setup

Most of the test examples in this book are based on a simple Rails application called Huddle, which supports Agile teams by allowing them to enter their daily status scrums online. Although the sample code for the Huddle application is contained in the code samples for each chapter, I know that many people like to create the entire example from scratch.

A.1 Basic Rails

This appendix lists the steps I took to create a simple Rails application with Devise for user authentication. The installation instructions for other third-party plugins and gems are contained in the chapter where the extension is used.

You won't need anything for this setup other than Ruby, Rails, and SQLite3. A Rails 3 installation will also need the bundler gem. The Rails 3 installation instructions will take center stage in this chapter, and where Rails 2.x differs, that will be noted separately.

Let's start with the creation of the Huddle app using the rails command. In Rails 2.x, the initial command is rails huddle; in Rails 3.x, the command is rails new huddle. Here is the Rails 3 version:

```
% rails new huddle
«many lines of response»
% cd huddle
% rake db:create:all
(in /Users/noel/Documents/pragprog/nrtest/Book/code/huddle)
```

I'm using the system gem installation of Rails because I expect to have multiple copies of Huddle and don't want to have multiple copies of

Rails in my repository. That doesn't apply to you, though. If you are planning to go back and forth between multiple Rails projects on the same machine, I strongly urge you to check out RVM, the Ruby Version Manager, which allows you to have a custom Ruby version and set of gems for each project. Find it at http://rvm.beginrescueend.com/.

In Rails 3.x, gem management, including that of the Rails gems, is handled by bundler. The Gemfile in your newly created application contains a command starting with gem 'rails', which ties your application to a specific Rails version. There is also a commented-out command to use if you want the cutting-edge version of Rails. We're not going to worry about the finer points of bundler here; see http://gembundler.com for more details.

If you are running a Rails 2.3.x application and if you want to have Rails in your vendor/rails directory, run the following command:

```
% rake rails:freeze:edge RELEASE=2.3.5
```

Alternately, you can download the Rails release from GitHub at http://github.com/rails/rails/tree/master and place it in vendor/rails.

A.2 Devise

Devise is a Rails authentication solution that is distributed as a Rails engine, which, in theory, allows for it to be added to an application with fewer steps. It's also quite modular, allowing you to choose a set of authentication features that you might want. These steps are based on the Readme at http://github.com/plataformatec/devise.

Rails 3 and Rails 2 use different versions of the Devise gem. For Rails 3, install via the following:

```
gem install devise
```

For Rails 2, install via the older version:

```
gem install devise --version=1.0.8
```

In Rails 3.x, gems are managed in bundler. You need to add the following line to your Gemfile to get the Devise gem included:

```
gem "devise"
```

Devise creates its files via a generator. The Rails 3 command is as follows:

```
rails generate devise:install
```

And here is the command for Rails 2:

```
ruby script/generate devise_install
```

In Rails 3, Devise creates an initializer file in config/initializers/devise.rb that has a lot of potential options that we are going to leave untouched for the moment. It also creates a locales file for internationalization purposes. The generator also puts some helpful manual tasks into the console, which require us to do the following:

1. Add the line config.action_mailer.default_url_options = { :host => 'localhost:3000' } to the file config/environments/development.rb. In a real system, we'd need other lines for other environments.

2. Uncomment the line root :to => "welcome#index" in config/routes.rb.

3. Add the following two lines to app/views/layouts/application.html.erb between the body tags:

```
<p class="notice"><%= notice %></p>
<p class="alert"><%= alert %></p>
```

Now we can create our user model with this line. Please note that if you are building the RSpec version of this app, you must have included RSpec in the Gemfile before going any further. See Section 12.3, *RSpec and Rails*, on page 196 for more information.

```
$ rails generate devise User
```

This creates a user model, with tests, a database migration, and a route that references the Devise engine. The fixture file created for a user is invalid; it doesn't have any data, and the tests are going to change. Please edit test/fixtures/users.yml to the following:[1]

```
one:
  email: "one@one.com"

two:
  email: "two@two.com"
```

That should be enough to get us started.

A.3 Huddle's Data Models

With the Devise boilerplate done, we just need to create the basic data structures used for Huddle. We already have a user model generated by

---

1. RSpec users don't need to mess with this.

Devise. We'll need a model for the status reports and one for the project. Right now, a Project is just a string:

```
% rails generate scaffold project name:string
```

A StatusReport has references to Project and User, plus text fields for the "what I did yesterday" and "what I'm going to do today" reports. I've also added an explicit date for the status, separate from the created_at field.

```
% rails generate scaffold status_report project:references \
    user:references yesterday:text today:text status_date:date
```

Projects and users have a many-to-many relationship, so you'll need a join table for that:

```
% rails generate migration project_user_join
```

Edit the migration to look like this:

```
huddle/db/migrate/20090825045451_project_user_join.rb
class ProjectUserJoin < ActiveRecord::Migration
  def self.up
    create_table :projects_users, :force => true, :id => false do |t|
      t.references :project
      t.references :user
      t.timestamps
    end
  end

  def self.down
    drop_table :projects_users
  end
end
```

Then run rake db:migrate one more time.

A.4 First Tests

That's a long way just to get started. Sorry, it's the kind of setup you have to get out of the way to do any kind of example complex enough to be useful.

It's worth pointing out, though, that we already have some tests. Running the default Rake testing task gives output like this (output slightly truncated):

```
% rake
(in /Users/noel/Dropbox/sites/huddle3)
Loaded suite /Library/Ruby/Gems/1.8/gems/rake-0.8.7/lib/rake/rake_test_loader
```

```
Started
...
Finished in 0.059271 seconds.

3 tests, 3 assertions, 0 failures, 0 errors
Loaded suite /Library/Ruby/Gems/1.8/gems/rake-0.8.7/lib/rake/rake_test_loader
Started
.............
Finished in 0.775038 seconds.

14 tests, 20 assertions, 0 failures, 0 errors
```

The first batch is the unit tests; Rails creates a dummy test for each model. The bottom tests are the functional tests. Rails creates a basic suite for each controller scaffold that covers the successful cases of each scaffold method. (The failure cases can easily be covered with mock objects.)

Congratulations, the setup is out of the way; you can now rejoin the rest of the book, already in progress.

Appendix B

Bibliography

[CAD+09]   David Chelimsky, Dave Astels, Zach Dennis, Aslak Hellesøy,
           Bryan Helmkamp, and Dan North. *The RSpec Book*. The
           Pragmatic Programmers, LLC, Raleigh, NC, and Dallas, TX,
           2009.

[Fea04]   Michael Feathers. *Working Effectively with Legacy Code*.
           Prentice Hall, Englewood Cliffs, NJ, 2004.

[Mes07]   Gerard Meszaros. *xUnit Test Patterns: Refactoring Test Code*.
           Addison-Wesley, Reading, MA, 2007.

Index

F

The Pragmatic Bookshelf

Available in paperback and DRM-free eBooks, our titles are here to help you stay on top of your game. The following are in print as of January 2011; be sure to check our website at pragprog.com for newer titles.

Title	Year	ISBN	Pages
Advanced Rails Recipes: 84 New Ways to Build Stunning Rails Apps	2008	9780978739225	464
Agile Coaching	2009	9781934356432	248
Agile Retrospectives: Making Good Teams Great	2006	9780977616640	200
Agile Web Development with Rails	2009	9781934356166	792
Arduino: A Quick-Start Guide	2011	9781934356661	275
Beginning Mac Programming: Develop with Objective-C and Cocoa	2010	9781934356517	300
Behind Closed Doors: Secrets of Great Management	2005	9780976694021	192
Best of Ruby Quiz	2006	9780976694076	304
Cocoa Programming: A Quick-Start Guide for Developers	2010	9781934356302	450
Core Animation for Mac OS X and the iPhone: Creating Compelling Dynamic User Interfaces	2008	9781934356104	200
Core Data: Apple's API for Persisting Data on Mac OS X	2009	9781934356326	256
Data Crunching: Solve Everyday Problems using Java, Python, and More	2005	9780974514079	208
Debug It! Find, Repair, and Prevent Bugs in Your Code	2009	9781934356289	232
Design Accessible Web Sites: 36 Keys to Creating Content for All Audiences and Platforms	2007	9781934356029	336
Desktop GIS: Mapping the Planet with Open Source Tools	2008	9781934356067	368
Domain-Driven Design Using Naked Objects	2009	9781934356449	375
Driving Technical Change: Why People on Your Team Don't Act on Good Ideas, and How to Convince Them They Should	2010	9781934356609	200
Enterprise Integration with Ruby	2006	9780976694069	360
Enterprise Recipes with Ruby and Rails	2008	9781934356234	416
Everyday Scripting with Ruby: for Teams, Testers, and You	2007	9780977616619	320
ExpressionEngine 2: A Quick-Start Guide	2010	9781934356524	250
From Java To Ruby: Things Every Manager Should Know	2006	9780976694090	160
FXRuby: Create Lean and Mean GUIs with Ruby	2008	9781934356074	240

Continued on next page

Title	Year	ISBN	Pages
GIS for Web Developers: Adding Where to Your Web Applications	2007	9780974514093	275
Google Maps API: Adding Where to Your Applications	2006	PDF-Only	83
Grails: A Quick-Start Guide	2009	9781934356463	200
Groovy Recipes: Greasing the Wheels of Java	2008	9780978739294	264
Hello, Android: Introducing Google's Mobile Development Platform	2010	9781934356562	320
HTML5 and CSS3: Develop with Tomorrow's Standards Today	2010	9781934356685	280
Interface Oriented Design	2006	9780976694052	240
iPad Programming: A Quick-Start Guide for iPhone Developers	2010	9781934356579	248
iPhone SDK Development	2009	9781934356258	576
Land the Tech Job You Love	2009	9781934356265	280
Language Implementation Patterns: Create Your Own Domain-Specific and General Programming Languages	2009	9781934356456	350
Learn to Program	2009	9781934356364	240
Manage It! Your Guide to Modern Pragmatic Project Management	2007	9780978739249	360
Manage Your Project Portfolio: Increase Your Capacity and Finish More Projects	2009	9781934356296	200
Mastering Dojo: JavaScript and Ajax Tools for Great Web Experiences	2008	9781934356111	568
Metaprogramming Ruby: Program Like the Ruby Pros	2010	9781934356470	240
Modular Java: Creating Flexible Applications with OSGi and Spring	2009	9781934356401	260
No Fluff Just Stuff 2006 Anthology	2006	9780977616664	240
No Fluff Just Stuff 2007 Anthology	2007	9780978739287	320
Pomodoro Technique Illustrated: The Easy Way to Do More in Less Time	2009	9781934356500	144
Practical Programming: An Introduction to Computer Science Using Python	2009	9781934356272	350
Practices of an Agile Developer	2006	9780974514086	208
Pragmatic Guide to Git	2010	9781934356722	168
Pragmatic Guide to JavaScript	2010	9781934356678	150
Pragmatic Guide to Subversion	2010	9781934356616	150
Pragmatic Project Automation: How to Build, Deploy, and Monitor Java Applications	2004	9780974514031	176
Pragmatic Thinking and Learning: Refactor Your Wetware	2008	9781934356050	288
Pragmatic Unit Testing in C# with NUnit	2007	9780977616671	176

Continued on next page

Title	Year	ISBN	Pages
Pragmatic Unit Testing in Java with JUnit	2003	9780974514017	160
Pragmatic Version Control using CVS	2003	9780974514000	176
Pragmatic Version Control Using Git	2008	9781934356159	200
Pragmatic Version Control using Subversion	2006	9780977616657	248
Programming Clojure	2009	9781934356333	304
Programming Cocoa with Ruby: Create Compelling Mac Apps Using RubyCocoa	2009	9781934356197	300
Programming Erlang: Software for a Concurrent World	2007	9781934356005	536
Programming Groovy: Dynamic Productivity for the Java Developer	2008	9781934356098	320
Programming Ruby: The Pragmatic Programmers' Guide	2004	9780974514055	864
Programming Ruby 1.9: The Pragmatic Programmers' Guide	2009	9781934356081	944
Programming Scala: Tackle Multi-Core Complexity on the Java Virtual Machine	2009	9781934356319	250
Prototype and script.aculo.us: You Never Knew JavaScript Could Do This!	2007	9781934356012	448
Rails for .NET Developers	2008	9781934356203	300
Rails for PHP Developers	2008	9781934356043	432
Rails Recipes	2006	9780977616602	350
Rapid GUI Development with QtRuby	2005	PDF-Only	83
Release It! Design and Deploy Production-Ready Software	2007	9780978739218	368
Scripted GUI Testing with Ruby	2008	9781934356180	192
Seven Languages in Seven Weeks: A Pragmatic Guide to Learning Programming Languages	2010	9781934356593	300
Ship It! A Practical Guide to Successful Software Projects	2005	9780974514048	224
SQL Antipatterns: Avoiding the Pitfalls of Database Programming	2010	9781934356555	352
Stripes ...and Java Web Development Is Fun Again	2008	9781934356210	375
Test-Drive ASP.NET MVC	2010	9781934356531	296
TextMate: Power Editing for the Mac	2007	9780978739232	208
The Agile Samurai: How Agile Masters Deliver Great Software	2010	9781934356586	280
The Definitive ANTLR Reference: Building Domain-Specific Languages	2007	9780978739256	384
The Passionate Programmer: Creating a Remarkable Career in Software Development	2009	9781934356340	232
The RSpec Book: Behaviour-Driven Development with RSpec, Cucumber, and Friends	2010	9781934356371	448

Continued on next page

Title	Year	ISBN	Pages
ThoughtWorks Anthology	2008	9781934356142	240
Ubuntu Kung Fu: Tips, Tricks, Hints, and Hacks	2008	9781934356227	400
Web Design for Developers: A Programmer's Guide to Design Tools and Techniques	2009	9781934356135	300

More Books

Agile in a Flash

The best agile book isn't a book: Agile in a Flash is a unique deck of index cards that fit neatly in your pocket. You can tape them to the wall. Spread them out on your project table. Get stains on them over lunch. These cards are meant to be used, not just read.

Agile in a Flash: Speed-Learning Agile Software Development
Jeff Langr and Tim Ottinger
(110 pages) ISBN: 978-1-93435-671-5. $15.00
http://pragprog.com/titles/olag

The Agile Samurai

Faced with a software project of epic proportions? Tired of over-committing and under-delivering? Enter the dojo of the agile samurai, where agile expert Jonathan Rasmusson shows you how to kick-start, execute, and deliver your agile projects. You'll see how agile software delivery really works and how to help your team get agile fast, while having fun along the way.

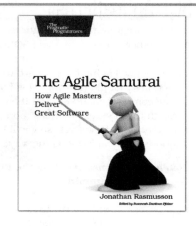

The Agile Samurai: How Agile Masters Deliver Great Software
Jonathan Rasmusson
(275 pages) ISBN: 9781934356586. $34.95
http://pragprog.com/titles/jtrap

More Books

Debug It!

Debug It! will equip you with the tools, techniques, and approaches to help you tackle any bug with confidence. These secrets of professional debugging illuminate every stage of the bug life cycle, from constructing software that makes debugging easy; through bug detection, reproduction, and diagnosis; to rolling out your eventual fix. Learn better debugging whether you're writing Java or assembly language, targeting servers or embedded micro-controllers, or using agile or traditional approaches.

Debug It! Find, Repair, and Prevent Bugs in Your Code
Paul Butcher
(232 pages) ISBN: 978-1-9343562-8-9. $34.95
http://pragprog.com/titles/pbdp

SQL Antipatterns

If you're programming applications that store data, then chances are you're using SQL, either directly or through a mapping layer. But most of the SQL that gets used is inefficient, hard to maintain, and sometimes just plain wrong. This book shows you all the common mistakes, and then leads you through the best fixes. What's more, it shows you what's *behind* these fixes, so you'll learn a lot about relational databases along the way.

SQL Antipatterns: Avoiding the Pitfalls of Database Programming
Bill Karwin
(300 pages) ISBN: 978-19343565-5-5. $34.95
http://pragprog.com/titles/bksqla

More Books

Arduino: A Quick Start Guide

Arduino is an open-source platform that makes DIY electronics projects easier than ever. Readers with no electronics experience can create their first gadgets within a few minutes. This book is up-to-date for the new Arduino Uno board, with step-by-step instructions for building a universal remote, a motion-sensing game controller, and many other fun, useful projects.

Arduino: A Quick Start Guide
Maik Schmidt
(275 pages) ISBN: 9781934356661. $35.00
http://pragprog.com/titles/msard

HTML5 and CSS3

HTML5 and CSS3 are the future of web development, but you don't have to wait to start using them. Even though the specification is still in development, many modern browsers and mobile devices already support HTML5 and CSS3. This book gets you up to speed on the new HTML5 elements and CSS3 features you can use right now, and backwards compatible solutions ensure that you don't leave users of older browsers behind.

HTML5 and CSS3: Develop with Tomorrow's Standards Today
Brian P. Hogan
(280 pages) ISBN: 9781934356685. $33.00
http://pragprog.com/titles/bhh5

The Pragmatic Bookshelf

The Pragmatic Bookshelf features books written by developers for developers. The titles continue the well-known Pragmatic Programmer style and continue to garner awards and rave reviews. As development gets more and more difficult, the Pragmatic Programmers will be there with more titles and products to help you stay on top of your game.

Visit Us Online

Home page for Rails Test Prescriptions
http://pragprog.com/titles/nrtest
Source code from this book, errata, and other resources. Come give us feedback, too!

Register for Updates
http://pragprog.com/updates
Be notified when updates and new books become available.

Join the Community
http://pragprog.com/community
Read our weblogs, join our online discussions, participate in our mailing list, interact with our wiki, and benefit from the experience of other Pragmatic Programmers.

New and Noteworthy
http://pragprog.com/news
Check out the latest pragmatic developments, new titles and other offerings.

Save on the eBook

Save on the eBook versions of this title. Owning the paper version of this book entitles you to purchase the electronic versions at a terrific discount.

PDFs are great for carrying around on your laptop—they are hyperlinked, have color, and are fully searchable. Most titles are also available for the iPhone and iPod touch, Amazon Kindle, and other popular e-book readers.

Buy now at pragprog.com/coupon.

Contact Us

Online Orders:	www.pragprog.com/catalog
Customer Service:	support@pragprog.com
Non-English Versions:	translations@pragprog.com
Pragmatic Teaching:	academic@pragprog.com
Author Proposals:	proposals@pragprog.com
Contact us:	1-800-699-PROG (+1 919 847 3884)